The Zen Impulse and the Psychoanalytic Encounter

The Zen Impulse and the Psychoanalytic Encounter

Paul C. Cooper

Routledge
Taylor & Francis Group
New York   London

Routledge
Taylor & Francis Group
270 Madison Avenue
New York, NY 10016

Routledge
Taylor & Francis Group
27 Church Road
Hove, East Sussex BN3 2FA

© 2010 by Taylor and Francis Group, LLC
Routledge is an imprint of Taylor & Francis Group, an Informa business

Printed in the United States of America on acid-free paper
10 9 8 7 6 5 4 3 2 1

International Standard Book Number: 978-0-415-99764-5 (Hardback) 978-0-415-99765-2 (Paperback)

Library of Congress Cataloging-in-Publication Data

Cooper, Paul C.
     The Zen impulse and the psychoanalytic encounter / Paul C. Cooper.
          p. cm.
     Includes bibliographical references and index.
     ISBN 978-0-415-99764-5 (hbk.) -- ISBN 978-0-415-99765-2 (pbk.) -- ISBN
978-0-203-88346-4 (e-book)
     1. Buddhism and psychoanalysis. 2. Zen Buddhism--Psychology. 3.
Psychotherapy--Religious aspects--Zen Buddhism. 4. Meditation--Zen
Buddhism--Therapeutic use. I. Title.

     BQ4570.P755C66 2010
     294.3'3615--dc22   2009020122

Visit the Taylor & Francis Web site at
http://www.taylorandfrancis.com

and the Routledge Web site at
http://www.routledgementalhealth.com

Contents

Acknowledgments

This collection is truly a dependent-arising with valuable inspiration, suggestions, support, and encouragement deriving from countless individuals throughout the years that the seeds for this project were planted, germinated, sprouted, and blossomed. I am grateful to Alan Roland, who closely guided me through the initial phases of my writing through his generous emotional support, encouragement, and technical suggestions. I am appreciative of my friend and colleague Susan Rudnick, who served as special editor for an issue of the *American Journal of Psychoanalysis* devoted to the integration of Buddhism and psychoanalysis, where my first journal article appeared in 1999. I am deeply grateful to Pat Enkyo O'Hara, Roshi for her influence and teachings and for encouraging my personal expression of the *Zen Impulse* in daily life and in my work as a psychoanalyst and as a psychoanalytic teacher. Many friends and colleagues have provided consistent and generous encouragement, support, and constructive criticism through readings and responses to various versions of this text. They include John Augliera, Jeffrey Eaton, Robert Gunn, Melvin Miller, and Cynthia Stone who read and engaged in many fruitful discussions throughout the development of this project. I am indebted to Maggie Brenner, Michael Eigen, Mark Finn, Amanda George, Merle Molofsky, Ken Porter, Eric Rhode, Arthur Robbins, Tony Stern, and Thomas Wagner for our valuable and encouraging conversations over the years. Marcella Bakur Weiner's initial reading and response to the first drafts of my proposal and sample chapters were extremely encouraging and valuable. I would like to express my heartfelt gratitude to my brothers and sisters in the dharma, to my students, teachers, and colleagues who have all contributed to my thinking and practice, and who continue to deeply inspire me.

I am also deeply grateful to the staff at Routledge. Kristopher Spring, Assistant Editor, provided ongoing encouragement, support, patience, a keen sense of humor, and astute technical assistance. His insightful response to the original proposal contributed to developing a unified text and, ultimately, the publication of this edition. I also would like to thank Kate Hawes, Publisher and Eleanor Reading in Marketing. Susan Horwitz and her staff provided skillful and expedient copyediting and production. Arlene Belzer gave a close and attentive proofreading of the text for which I am grateful. I would also like to thank the anonymous readers for their honest and insightful suggestions and constructive critiques of the original proposal and manuscript.

Last, but not least, I am most grateful to Karen Morris for her unflinching strength, support, and encouragement during every phase of this project. I am especially grateful for her patience and astute comments through seemingly endless readings and re-readings of various chapter revisions.

I gratefully acknowledge permission to reprint the following material:

The translated poem beginning with the line "Playing at writing," reprinted in the Introduction, is from James H. Sanford, *Zen-Man Ikkyū*, p. 154, by permission of the Center for the Study of World Religions, Harvard Divinity School. Copyright 1981 by President and Fellows of Harvard College, translated from *Ikkyu Kyōun-shū (The Crazy Cloud Anthology)*.

The translated poem beginning with the line, "No mind, no Buddha, no being" from *Zen Poetry: Let the Spring Breeze Enter* by L. Stryk and T. Ikemoto, (1995, p. 176). Copyright © 1995 by Lucien Stryk is reprinted in Chapter One and is used by permission of Grove/Atlantic, Inc.

The translated poem beginning with the line, "Magnificent! Magnificent!" from *Zen Poetry: Let the Spring Breeze Enter* by L. Stryk and T. Ikemoto, (1995, p. 26). Copyright © 1995 by Lucien Stryk is reprinted in Chapter Ten and is used by permission of Grove/Atlantic, Inc.

The translated poem beginning with the line, "Who said the sea's concave" from *Zen Poems of China and Japan: The Crane's Bill* by L. Stryk and T. Ikemoto, (1973, p. 54). Copyright © 1973 by Lucien Stryk, Takashi Ikemoto and Taigan Takayama, is reprinted in Chapter One and is used by permission of Grove/Atlantic, Inc.

The translated poem beginning with the line "Not limited," from *The Zen Poetry of Dogen: Verses from the Mountain of Eternal Peace* by S. Heine, Tuttle Publishing (1997, p. 108) is reprinted in Chapter One with the kind permission of Dr. Steven Heine.

The translated poem beginning with the line "Day and night," from *The Zen Poetry of Dogen: Verses from the Mountain of Eternal Peace* by S. Heine, Tuttle Publishing (1997, p. 97, 3-J) is reprinted in Chapter Two with the kind permission of Dr. Steven Heine.

The translated poem beginning with "Attaining the heart," from *The Zen Poetry of Dogen: Verses from the Mountain of Eternal Peace* by S. Heine, Tuttle Publishing (1997, p. 97, 5-J) is reprinted in Chapter Two with the kind permission of Dr. Steven Heine.

The translated poem, "Zazen," from *The Zen Poetry of Dogen: Verses from the Mountain of Eternal Peace* by S. Heine, Tuttle Publishing (1997, p. 117, 57-J) is reprinted in Chapter Two with the kind permission of Dr. Steven Heine.

The translated poem beginning with the line, "Master Joshu and the dog" from *Zen Poetry: Let the Spring Breeze Enter* by L. Stryk and T. Ikemoto, (1995, p. 39). Copyright © 1995 by Lucien Stryk is reprinted in Chapter Four and is used by permission of Grove/Atlantic, Inc.

The original poem beginning with the line "No matter what" Copyright © 2008 by P. Cooper appears in Chapter Four and is used by permission of the author.

The translated poem beginning with the line, "The dog! The Buddha nature!" from *The Gateless Barrier: Zen Comments on the Mumonkan* by Z. Shibayama, reprinted by Shambala Publications, Inc. (2000, p. 20) and originally published by HarperCollins is reprinted in Chapter Four by permission of HarperCollins Publishers.

Chapter 6: "Unconscious & Conscious in Zen and Psychoanalysis," by Paul C. Cooper, was originally published in an earlier version as "Unconscious Process: Zen and Psychoanalytic Versions," in the *Journal of Religion and Health* 39 (1): 57–69. Used by permission of Springer Science and Business Media.

Chapter 8: "Sense and Non-sense," by Paul C. Cooper, was originally published in an earlier version as "Sense and Non-sense: Phenomenology, Buddhist and Psychoanalytic" in the *Journal of Religion and Health*, 37 (4): 357–370. Used by permission of Springer Science and Business Media.

Chapter 9: "The Gap Between Being, Knowing and the Liminal In-between," by Paul C. Cooper, was originally published in an earlier version as "The Gap Between: Being and Knowing in Zen Buddhism and Psychoanalysis," in the *American Journal of Psychoanalysis*, 61 (4): 341-362. Used by permission of Springer Science and Business Media

Chapter 10: "Unitive Experience and the Pervasive Object," by Paul C. Cooper, was originally published in an earlier version as "The Pervasion of the Object: Depression and Unitive Experience," in the *Psychoanalytic Review*. Used by permission of Guilford Press.

Irvington, N.Y.
August 4, 2009

Introduction:
The Zen Impulse and the Psychoanalytic Encounter

PLAYING AT WRITING

> Happiness, sorrow; love, hate; body and shadow.
> Heat and cold; joy and anger; self and other.
> The pleasure of poetry is the road to Hell.
> Yet, stop along the way and see: plum blossoms,
> peach flowers.

—Ikkyu Sojun (Sanford, 1981, p. 154)

In order to speak of the Zen impulse in psychoanalysis and to explore the interaction between Zen and psychoanalysis, we first need to ask: What Zen and what psychoanalysis are we talking about? This is not a question that requires a specific answer. The distinctions are not as clear-cut as some factionalists would have us believe. Rather, the Zen impulse is an idea that needs to be kept in mind as we explore the many possible relationships that exist between various versions of Zen and psychoanalysis. The diverse relationships that evolve in and out of form can be characterized in a manner similar to the way Freud (1933) described psychic structure when he wrote that

> We cannot do justice to the characteristics of the mind by linear outlines like those in a drawing or in primitive painting, but rather by areas of colour melting into one another as they are presented by modern artists. After making the separation we must allow what we have separated to merge together once more. (p. 79)

In the process of defining the territory shared by Zen and psychoanalysis, can we maintain a sense of wonder, spontaneity, and creativity with regard to our work in the consulting room, the meditation hall, or both?

Zen and psychoanalysis are complex, multifaceted, and fluid disciplines, not monolithic structures. For example, Andre Green (2006) speaks of the destruction and fragmentation of psychoanalysis, and he advocates

1

unifying disparate theories along one axis. These issues of perception and definition will be taken up in Chapter 1.

Inside/Outside

One of the gratifying—albeit at times frustrating—challenges of writing this book centered on presenting a balance between internal experience derived through my ongoing Zen and psychoanalytic practice and information garnered through textual study in an orderly, systematic, and cohesive way. Does writing from the inside oppose or conflict with writing from the outside? Ultimately, from the Zen perspective, there is no inside and outside, but relatively speaking there is. There has been an explosion in the literature on psychoanalysis and Buddhism and a recently expanding, seemingly overwhelming body of scholarly work on Zen. In thinking about the outside, one question that emerges is where does this plethora of new material fit in? Does this literature support or obfuscate the articulation of inner experience? In terms of the present work, the challenge has been to maintain a balance between informative and performative aspects of the narrative.

Autobiographical Narrative

I take the position that all psychoanalytic discourse is an autobiographical narrative whether we attempt to conceal or enhance it within a scientific language or not. Language both reveals and conceals as British psychoanalyst Wilfred Bion (1970) writes: "It is too often forgotten that the gift of speech, so centrally employed, has been elaborated as much for the purpose of concealing thought … as for the purpose of elucidating or communicating thought" (third unnumbered page). However, the more concealed the autobiographical narrative becomes, the less impact it exerts as the performative element becomes obliterated. Eric Rhode (1998) observes the operation of the performative function of psychoanalysis in the mystical aspects of being. He argues that without considering the mystical, we are left with a fractured and less than whole psychoanalysis.

If we follow Bion's (1970) line of thinking that "reason is emotion's slave and exists to rationalize emotional experience" (first unnumbered page), questions emerge, such as: What emotions are being defended against by the overly rationalized and reasoned language of the scientific model?

What is the risk that the analyst takes in using an approach to language that integrates both scientific and mystical models without privilege? Without raising these questions, our discussion of the Zen impulse and the psychoanalytic encounter becomes meaningless because the radical salvational potential of legitimate spiritual traditions, such as Zen, becomes removed from the realm of personal experience, completely dismissed, or diminished to a series of ideas and techniques, subsumed into the psychoanalytic "bag of tricks," and forced into the limited parameters of the scientific discourse, a discourse that privileges one set of semiotics at the expense of the other. For example, the idea that Zen is simply a technique that might support psychoanalysis defends against emotions that would normally emerge as the practitioner approaches a radical change. Reliance on old beliefs and a devaluation of Zen can function to resist evolving Truth.* The stages of Zen practice and the psychoanalytic process then become abhorrent rather than attractive because each step brings the participant increasingly closer to the deconstruction of previously unquestioned cherished beliefs and associated internalizations.

The autobiographical narrative always entails a risk because, in a sense, I am talking about religious experience, and such experiences entail belief systems, which are in many ways very personal, have a history, both conscious and unconscious, and awareness of such beliefs often comes retrospectively after the material is committed to writing or to the spoken word.

Beliefs are subject to change; however, I am talking about something more persistent, consistent, and nagging, such as a basic sense of self or "I-sense," if you will.

What are my beliefs? What do I bring to my work as a psychoanalyst? How do these beliefs impact on my I-sense and on the individual who seeks me out for treatment? How do the beliefs that have developed through my immersion in Zen practice and study over the years influence the work that I am actually capable of doing with any patient? And, how do my beliefs, whether consciously or unconsciously expressed, influence the patient? So, we are not simply speaking here of the technical usefulness of isolated practices such as meditation. Rather, within the parameters of a specific definition, I speak of Zen as a religion. In order to take the religion as "whole cloth," I consider its ordinariness, faith, beliefs, and mode of being, to mention a few. The poet and translator Kenneth Rexroth

---

* Uppercase Truth is used throughout this book to refer to the nondualistic experience of ineffable, unknowable, existential reality in contrast to dualistic notions of truth as information or as distinguished from a lie, both of which are aspects of Truth.

described the Zen of Lafcidio Hearn "as a way of life" and as "the effects of its doctrines and common beliefs of ordinary people" (Fields, 1981, pp. 159–160). As psychoanalyst Judith Mitrani (2001) points out, it is the ordinary person who typically comes to psychotherapy.

Upon self-reflection and examination, I repeatedly come to the conclusion that my beliefs are simple, ordinary, and might even seem a bit naive. But, the truth is that they are my beliefs. Again, we don't often see the impact of religious practice except retrospectively over time, and what we often do see is not dramatic. My beliefs center on basic goodness or Buddha nature, the impulse to strive toward wholeness, which, despite radical differences, is one common feature of all legitimate religious traditions and psychologies.*

Despite many years of Zen practice and study that have clearly influenced my beliefs and values, I must consider core beliefs that developed from seeds planted at birth. On this point, with regard to the challenge of bringing Buddhism to America, Anagarika Dharmapada wrote in 1896:

> He was afraid ... that he wouldn't get a serious hearing from people. "They have been taught in their mother's lap the self doctrine of theological Christianity; and the teachings of the Buddha are in direct conflict with the dogmatic thesis of the Bible." He admitted that Buddhism and Christianity seemed to have much in common in terms of ethics and teachings of "divine love." But these were minor points. "In broad principle," he insisted flatly, "we disagree." Christ as a personal savior had to be given up. "Still," he felt, "there is nothing like making an effort to liberate the mind from theological slavery." (Fields, 1981, pp. 133–134)

The important question in understanding the Zen impulse in psychoanalysis centers on what an individual's relationship is to Zen. Broadly stated, the question becomes: What is my relationship to my own religious experience? Ultimately an individual's relationship to Zen, as I see it, despite the importance of study, can only be answered in the realm of practice. Once we understand this question, we can begin to understand the Zen impulse in psychoanalysis. This relationship has evolved differently at different times. For example, the first wave of Zen in America was greeted with an intellectual curiosity by those interested. The following wave of Zen was more practice oriented, and this paralleled a shift from a basically nonreligious sentiment to an increasingly religious/spiritual orientation in the culture and among psychoanalysts. In relation to

---

* See P. Cooper (1997) for elaboration of the relationship of religious practice and psychoanalysis to wholeness.

psychoanalysis, trained psychoanalysts such as Karen Horney and Eric Fromm expressed an interested in Zen. However, it is more common these days that an interest in psychotherapy follows immersion in Zen practice, more often than not, for many years. The Zen impulse has existed in psychoanalysis for quite some time. The close association between Horney and Fromm with D. T. Suzuki has been well documented and will be explored in Chapter 1.

Live Words/Dead Words

Helpful to the balance between the performative and the informative aspects of the narrative in relation to the Zen impulse is the distinction that the ninth-century Chinese Zen teacher Tung-shan made when he admonished his students to pay attention to "live words" not "dead words." For Tung-shan, live words go beyond linear thinking and reasoning processes and express themselves authentically, spontaneously, and creatively. Heine (2008) observes that "living words have usefulness in that they are deployed to expose the futility of and to bring an end the use of dead words" (p. 39). In contrast, he notes that dead words are limited to logical linear thinking and result in "speaking all day long without having said a thing" (p. 39). In a striking parallel to Tung-shan's admonishment to rely on live words, noted above, Thomas Ogden (2005) observes that "when analyst and analysand are able to think and speak for themselves, they do not use 'borrowed language,' e.g., jargon, cliché and technical terms. Their language tends to be alive, their metaphors freshly minted and unassuming" (p. 24).

Similarly, psychoanalysis has been described since its inception as "the talking cure." The psychoanalyst relies heavily on the analysand's narrative. However, for the psychoanalyst, words can serve to both promote insight and obfuscate. Some narratives exert a deadening effect and others engender an enlivening impact.

The implied spontaneity and down-to-earth practicality in Tung-shan's mandate and in Ogden's caution exemplify the Zen impulse both in Zen practice and in psychoanalysis. Similarly, it is this spirit of inquiry—and the accompanying free-associative dialogue initiated by Freud—that defines psychoanalysis as distinctively subjective and experiential and that lives on as a distinct thread in the evolution of psychoanalysis that I hope to bring to the chapters in this volume.

Living the Zen Impulse

The Zen impulse is a universal that is not limited to one culture, time, or place, or a particular language or religious system. It is more a frame of mind and a mode of perceiving, experiencing, being in the world, and relating to others with sensitivity, understanding, and compassion. In short, it is a way of living our lives. For instance, the British scholar R. H. Blyth (1942) identifies and elaborates the Zen impulse in Western literature and oriental classics. He makes the distinction between poetry as "a life in accord with reality; and the writing of poetry" and Zen as "a religious system, that is, a certain way of thinking about life; and living in accord with reality" (p. viii). Similarly, in the ensuing chapters I attempt to demonstrate how the Zen impulse threads through human subjectivity, spontaneity, and creativity as these qualities emerge in the psychoanalytic encounter.

Both Zen and psychoanalysis develop and express an original subjectivity that is inherent in human experience. In my experience, the uniqueness, originality, and spontaneously creative expression of live words are crucial to the efficacy of psychoanalysis and reflect the Zen impulse. For example, British psychoanalyst Donald Winnicott (1964) notes that "when analysis is a going concern their invention is unique" (p. 27).

Subjectivity/Objectivity

I have always been intrigued by this highly subjective and fluid nature of experience. For instance, since childhood I recall feeling a strong sense of a "me" that seemingly remains constant and unchanging. This me seems as strong and present now as when I was a child. Simultaneously, there is another sense of myself that is seemingly in constant flux and has no idea of what goes on. Both experiences engender the possibility for wonder, a crucial aspect of the Zen and the psychoanalytic encounter (Cooper, 2002a). This seemingly paradoxical ongoing oscillation in self-experience finds expression in the Zen notion of the relative and the absolute, which describes the simultaneous fixed and fluid nature of experiences of self and other. From the Zen perspective, the absolute refers to the essential oneness of all phenomena and accounts for what I describe as "unitive experiencing," a topic that I explore clinically in detail in Chapter 10. The relative in Zen refers to the ordinary world of separation, of individual human beings, and of what psychoanalysts describe as the object world.

This lived paradox between relative and absolute translates philosophically from the Zen perspective in the notion of the identity of the "one and the many" and translates clinically in a dynamic balance that is, I believe, crucial to the efficacy of the psychoanalytic encounter and that I describe as the simultaneity of separateness and connectedness, a theme that threads its way throughout the ensuing chapters.

As one grows older, this sense of an original seemingly constant self can become sequestered out of contact by the many fluctuating situational selves that emerge at any given moment, that become reified, and that layer over this nascent sense of original self.

For instance, in the present, I experience a confident, articulate, poetic, at times eloquent, intuitive, knowing, and powerful me who certain patients, at times, experience as analyst. On the other hand, I can experience an equally present fumbling me who can be speechless, clumsy, and helpless as patient in relation to the person whom I call my analyst. I present these extremes to demonstrate the enormous range of oscillation of subjective experience that can occur within the perception of one person. The shifts in perceptual and experiential movement in reality often operate with imperceptible subtlety along the continuum between these extremes. The me who knows maintains the capacity to transcend this movement, paradoxically, by embracing each fluctuating oscillation in the unfolding immanence of the in-the-moment lived present.

Appropriating Territory/Freeing Space

Until recently, psychoanalytic writers have tended to analyze religious and spiritual experiences and related concepts with a reductionist and pathologizing bias. The increasingly positive response among contemporary psychoanalysts to religious experience reflects a radical departure from this early pathologizing stance. However, when operating as an expansion of its own territory that co-opts, misappropriates, and subsumes religious practices and techniques while simultaneously ignoring associated philosophies, ideologies, languages, and beliefs, the psychoanalytic endeavor remains entrenched in the conservative positivist stance of the medical/scientific model that Barnaby Barratt (1993), for instance, notes in his critique of psychoanalytic modernism to be "entrenched in the dominant paradigms and worldviews of the modern era" (p. 6).

In stark contrast, Bion offers the potential for a mystical psychoanalysis through a restoration of the spirit and by a profound regard for the chaotic circularity and ultimate ineffability of human experience. He accomplishes this restoration by relying on Faith, in contrast to knowledge as the primary motivating factor in his unrelenting search for Truth, which in his opus replaces the traditional psychoanalytic search knowledge and meaning. Bion's radical shift away from knowledge and understanding through psychoanalysis entail a potentially infinite expansion of experience and meaning.

His admonition to relinquish memory, desire, and understanding (1967, 1970) has often been compared with the Theravada Buddhist instructions for mindfulness meditation.* I began my own investigation into Bion's work in New York City with Michael Eigen's guidance through course work at the National Psychological Association for Psychoanalysis, where I trained as a psychoanalyst, and through participation in his weekly seminars. This experience and continued dialogue with colleagues has opened both forgotten old worlds and exciting new vistas.

For me, at the time, both Zen and this rarified area of psychoanalysis provided a language for what previously felt unspeakable and for what remained buried, forgotten, and craving for expression. These highly subjective experiential disciplines point ahead in a way that leaves room for what is yet to be discovered and created. This process is crucial for both the psychoanalytic and the religious journey. More importantly, life experiences predating both my Zen and psychoanalytic endeavors began to reemerge during this period of study and practice. This reemergence has allowed me to bring more of my sense of self into the present and to my work as a psychoanalyst, as a Zen practitioner, and as an artist.

From this pivotal position at this juncture between personal history, psychoanalysis, and the spirit, one can trace a path back to a forgotten Freud with a deeper appreciation of his original contributions, although, in a sense, there is never any going back. It's too late for that. One can pull on threads to what is relevant in Zen thought and to what lies beyond awaiting discovery that is neither Zen nor psychoanalysis. Remembering this "forgotten" Freud is not to be misconstrued as a return to origins. As Barratt (1993) notes, "to treat Freud as the progenitive authority—on what psychoanalysis is, or on its philosophical implications—is to accept notions of progeneration and of authority that psychoanalysis invites us to interrogate critically" (p. xiii).

---

* See Chapter 7 for a detailed review of this literature.

Zen makes a similar interrogation performatively through such actions as Te-shan's burning the scriptures.* Despite his critique of religion, Freud's discussion of unconscious processes reveals many parallels to descriptions of mystical experience.†

My initial peregrinations into Eastern meditation and psychoanalysis centered on the remarkable similarity between my experiences with meditation practice coupled with ongoing dialogues with Zen, Vedanta, and Samkya teachers, with instructions for practice in various Theravada Buddhist and Zen texts and with descriptions of Freud's technique of evenly hovering attention. The readily observed parallels created a place to grasp on to. However, during this time experience and intuition kept signaling that something in the obvious parallels seemed flat. This initially exciting potential ground began to feel restricted and narrow. The experiential ground was not accessible simply through examining descriptive parallels. While technically and descriptively correct, this comparative work, for me, lacked a depth of understanding and appreciation for the radical soteriological intention of Buddhism as a comprehensive religion. Similarly, comparative studies lacked an appreciation for the dynamic unconscious and its processes that are central to the psychoanalytic endeavor. Despite the profound and lasting benefits of this exploration, something remained in the background that felt unbridgeable and not workable. The initial spontaneously emerging movements would quickly become forced and contrived. I would find myself during these moments with my back up against the proverbial wall.

Reliance on direct experience accessible through Zen practice coupled with the transformative experiences and associated insights garnered through my own personal analysis opened up the experiential dimension and elicited a freedom of movement and expression. Such openings allow one to move freely between seemingly competing and contradictory theories.

As I sit with an enormous amount of external information, some that resonates, some that doesn't, the question becomes: How does one articulate Zen psychoanalysis or a psychoanalytic Zen? It seems to me increasingly so that the substantial portion of the answer remains an unconscious truth waiting for a consciousness free and unsaturated enough to evolve into awareness and expression. Perhaps the answer can more clearly be

---

* Te-shan, the influential 9th-century Chinese Zen monk who explored the teaching methods, known as shock Ch'an. He initially intended to fight the Zen agenda to downplay scriptural exegesis and doctrinal study, but was abruptly converted to the Zen approach and, upon his enlightenment, he immediately burnt his scriptures and commentaries.

† See Chapter 6.

known in retrospect or through the observations of an impartial third party. This truth, once expressed, becomes the articulation from a subjective and internal source. The external material, in this respect, provides language and validation for this otherwise solitary experience.

In retrospect, it seems that this journey begins with a point that is drawn in a circular direction. The journey encompasses an ever-widening spiral with mutually reinforcing inner and outer dimensions. This movement feels more natural than efforts to make linear, rational, neat, or static comparisons. There are always rough unfinished edges to work on and loose threads to pull on. The flow moves on its own not unlike the rhythm of the breath.

Take a moment to watch. The breath rises, endures, falls, and dissolves into a seemingly silent gap between the completed exhalation and the new inhalation. Each circular movement brings a deepening and more enriched awareness of both the internal environment and the external world. One begins to notice, over time, that internal and external are arbitrary distinctions that eventually dissolve. As S. Suzuki (1970) notes in his now classic *Zen Mind, Beginner's Mind*, "What we call 'I' is just a swinging door which moves when we inhale and when we exhale" (p. 29). Similarly, the distinctions between self and other also crystallize and dissolve in an ongoing series of oscillations, in between the one and many.

One can observe this same natural in-and-out movement in the subject matter at hand. From a theoretical, logical, and intellectual perspective the major players trace their roots to the soil of Freud's classical psychoanalysis. In certain respects their diverging theories might rationally be more true to Freud's original ideas than many of their contemporary critics. Perhaps their unique contributions uncover a forgotten Freud who remained dormant or perhaps lingered silently in the background. Yet they also depart radically. However, experientially, they also move beyond the point of distinction. For instance, Bion's (1967, 1970) reliance on "intuition" parallels Kohut's (1971, 1977) use of "empathic attunement" (Akhtar, 2007; Berger, 1987; Mac Isaac & Rowe, 1991). Despite significant differences in their ideas, theories, and techniques, they share a sense of compassion for the human condition and a sensitivity that comes through in their clinical writings. Both chart previously unexplored realms and thus extend the borders of the psychoanalytic inquiry. Similarly, S. Suzuki's (1970) notion of beginner's mind, which is rooted in Dogen's teachings, parallels Bion's technique of relinquishing memory, desire, and understanding. The farther out one travels along the perimeter, the closer one arrives at the starting point. Connections between diverse points derive from paying attention to the spirit of inquiry living behind what otherwise might become, as noted above, dead words and concepts.

Zen, at least as I know it through study and practice, as a religion with a radically salvational intention, dramatically confronts the self-imposed limits and conditions that mandate human emotional life, cognitive processes, relationships, and being in the world. I take this up in detail in Chapter 1. In this respect, the current explosion of interest in Buddhist teachings and practice within the psychoanalytic community presents itself as one example of a struggle with the reality that the basic assumptions deriving from the medical/scientific model that have governed Western scientific discourse for the past 400 years or so serve unconscious ends in terms of defending against existential anxiety through an over-emphasis on knowing, filling in gaps in knowledge, and defining what ultimately remains ineffable and that provides a shaky and crumbling foundation at best. In this respect, the current appeal of Buddhism among psychotherapists represents a reaction and critique of the modernist ego with its imperialist agenda, and thus complements the growing postmodern "impulse" (Barratt, 1993) among contemporary psychoanalysts. In this sense, Zen promises, at least in the ideal, to provide the possibility for making a different kind of lived sense out of experience, for revealing the transparency and self-deception in what we have imagined to know, and for creatively opening the doors into unknown undiscovered realms. Perhaps psychoanalysis can find its way beyond a need to feel that things must always make sense, an underlying assumption that has guided the initial psychoanalytic endeavor. Zenists understand and articulate this sense-making agenda in the notion of *avidya*, an active not-knowing or ignoring of our fundamental insubstantiality as beings in the world. This active not-knowing becomes a matter of approach. That is, there exists a dual tendency that serves both radical and conservative ends.

Both psychoanalysis and Zen hold the promise for radical change. Both disciplines acknowledge that the processes and practices available can be used or misused to open or occlude experiencing. This issue will be elaborated in Chapter 8 with respect to the functions of sense and non-sense. In this respect, both reveal conservative, conforming, resistive, and dogmatic trends that function in the service of a mythical "stasis."

Alternatively, both disciplines can operate in radical, iconoclastic, idiosyncratic, and creative ways. Both trends operate simultaneously and in oscillation. Every act of creation becomes a revelation and paradoxically an occlusion of what else might have evolved in that moment. Every structuring activity sets the stage for the possibility of new creative permutations and evolutions and for the deconstruction of what was constructed. My impression is that the latter purpose has become embedded in the former. However, in recent years, a strong and growing upsurge that can no longer be contained by conservative impulses has resulted in widening cracks in the more dogmatized, misappropriated, and reified aspects. A newly emerging and distinctively American Zen and contemporary postmodern endeavors among the psychoanalytic community both reflect this transition. For both disciplines, the road can fork in many directions. Multidirectional choices operate as both an advantage and a disadvantage with regard to any potentially creative endeavor.

Individuality and the Question of Technique

When anyone asks me what Zen practice has to offer, I answer "Nothing."

—Charlotte Joko Beck (2005, p. ix)

One question that frequently emerges in the evolving discussion on the integration of Buddhism and psychoanalysis centers on the day-to-day realities of psychotherapeutic technique. This issue emerges at conferences and workshops, with colleagues, students, and supervisees, and with editors of some of my previous articles. Yet, it remains a significant and perennial question. That is, what is it that a Zen psychoanalyst does that is different? No specifically or exclusively pragmatic answer exists that would be true to the original intentions of the versions of Zen or psychoanalysis that have influenced my thinking and practice. The psychoanalytic encounter is unique for each of the participants involved. Creativity can't be predetermined or prescribed. The infinite can't be defined and delimited by general technical statements applicable to all. The danger, if one follows this route, becomes one of overgeneralization, reification, and stifling dogmatism.

I fully agree with Ogden (2005), who confronts the tendency toward dogmatism when he writes: "It is the analyst's responsibility to reinvent psychoanalysis for each patient and continue to reinvent it throughout the course of the analysis" (p. 6). Similarly, to cite another contemporary example, Patrick Casement (2002) provides numerous clinical examples that consistently demonstrate the difference between blind dogmatic adherence to well-practiced procedures and following the subtle communications of each individual patient that might or might not result in the appropriate and well-thought-out use of traditional clinical techniques.

The problem with respect to co-opting Buddhist techniques such as meditation, while ignoring the wider radical salvational intention of genuine and thorough Buddhist practice, reflects in a highly specific way an ongoing problem within psychoanalysis itself. Barratt (1993) summarizes the problem as follows: "Since Freud's beginnings, the revolutionary implications of psychoanalysis have hovered on the brink of extinction brought about by the institutionalization and domestication of doctrine and practice—the subordination of psychoanalysis to the requirements of psychotherapy, and its normalization as a modern science" (p. 17).

With these points in mind, I make no direct attempt to provide any definitive solutions, although I do suggest alternatives based on my own experiences. My suggestions might or might not be useful for any particular individual. This might evoke disappointment in the exclusively pragmatically oriented reader. Perhaps one can take comfort in Bion's (1978) comment that "the way that *I* do analysis is of no importance to anybody excepting myself, but it may give you some idea of how *you* do analysis, and that is important" (p. 206).

It seems that the best we can do for now is to talk about how the Zen impulse influences the conditions in which the analyst and the patient meet and work and how the psychoanalytic encounter might facilitate an individual's religious practice. So, for example, when communicating with a patient, the analyst's language will be influenced by Zen practice if that practice has exerted an impact. I don't mean that the analyst will use a specific Zen religious vocabulary, which might or might not be relevant with a specific individual. Rather, one's outlook as an analyst will be altered as a result of personal religious practice, which will in turn influence one's authentic and personal expression in the direction that Horney (1945) describes as "whole-heartedness and sincerity of spirit" (p. 163).

We might wonder along together by circling the territory. Circumnavigation might be all that can be achieved for now. Wondering along together can be accomplished by remaining open to one's own associations, feelings, and thoughts—whatever emerges while sitting with the ensuing discussion.

In one regard, what is really being asked is "What is Zen and what is psychoanalysis?" On a more personal level, this question might be rephrased as "Who is a Zenist, who is a psychoanalyst, who is a Zen psychoanalyst or vice versa?" Steven Kurtz (1989) asks a perhaps more ambitious question: "Who is an enlightened psychoanalyst?" Both disciplines, at least in the ideal, are highly subjective and egalitarian endeavors. There is no "one size fits all" model. I believe that increasingly, as we continue to question the hegemony of the scientific model, psychoanalysts are realizing the benefits of allowing ourselves to not know. What is crucial is to be mindful of what evolves from a willingness to embrace uncertainty through continued study, practice, and conversation. Perhaps we can be beginners, as S. Suzuki (1970) suggests when he writes that "in the beginner's mind there are many possibilities, in the expert's mind there are few" (p. 21). Suzuki continuously reminds his students to keep practice pure and open—to be a beginner.

In a sense this book represents the sharing of a highly personal continuous struggle. What one can know of Zen and psychoanalysis derives from the uniqueness of personal experiences obtained through serious long-term practice. Our discussion of experience and our capacity for perception and clear articulation of experience are mandated by the larger structures of the sign/symbol systems within which both Buddhists and psychoanalysts live, perceive, think, feel, and communicate. So, the question becomes: Where is this discussion evolving from? Does representation of experience derive from the medical/scientific model, from the spiritual/ mystical model, or from some hybrid language that evolves through the cross-fertilization that might occur through the continuing conversation? What venue does the speaker privilege when choosing to communicate? Are such defining and limiting distinctions necessary? How does one struggle beyond them until what evolves no longer resembles Buddhism or psychoanalysis yet remains decidedly both? This discussion will attempt to respect both models and their associated communication modalities as changing needs arise. The two models complement each other and need not be placed in adversarial roles. My individual expression reflects the influence of involvement in both practices. In their purest forms both Zen and psychoanalysis have the capacity to confront and deconstruct habitual unconscious structuring activities that can lead to a life lived fully and with compassion.

From this perspective, a "what I do response" represents an easy way out and results in facile solutions that plant the seeds for new dogma. The result might be "psychotherapeutic" in a limited or pragmatic sense, but in the larger scheme of things avoids the necessary unrelenting and rigorous personal struggle and ongoing confrontation with spiritual/emotional Truth, however that Truth is articulated or evolves. I become limited to the role of a technician, a purveyor of a bag of tricks, a wise man bearing exotic gifts from the East, which negates the radical salvational intention of Zen practice and, more importantly, the creative potential that lies dormant within each of us.

What seems to be at stake for both Zen and psychoanalysis is not the integration of techniques, beliefs, language structures, or values. Rather, both disciplines in the ideal exert a willingness to question the structures that function as a background that supports and gives rise to our basic assumptions about who we are as beings in the world in relation to others. A failure to assert this willingness is to fall into empty ritual, to avoid Truth, to use dead words to make rote formulaic interpretations, to participate in mindless rituals. As S. Suzuki asks, how do we keep it fresh? How do we maintain a beginner's mind? That is the challenge of an enlivened psychoanalysis and an enlivened Zen and what it is that emerges at their intersection. It is in this spirit of open inquiry that I offer this book and that engenders dual starting points for the ensuing discussion.

Surveying the Territory

First, in Chapter 1, I define Zen as a legitimate religious system with specific practices, such as koan study, meditation, work, and art practice, that support and facilitate its religious goals. I also discuss Zen's unique language in relation to its basic practices. With this foundation in place, in Chapter 2, I examine the history of the discovery of Zen by early Catholic missionaries in China and Japan, which set the tone for the initial negative response to Zen in the West. This historical review serves as a context for an examination of the early negative psychoanalytic response to meditation. In Chapter 3, I examine the Zen koan, its development, use, and structure, as a unique form of religious discourse. This chapter serves to orient the reader to the discussion of specific koans in relation to the psychoanalytic encounter in Chapters 4 and 5. In Chapter 4, I examine the *Mu* koan, "Joshu's Dog," the first koan in the 13th-century koan collection and commentary, *Mumonkan* (Gateless Barrier). This examination serves to exemplify the relationship between being and nonbeing, a primary source of misunderstanding of Zen beliefs and practices among Westerners. In Chapter 5, I use the koan "Joshu Sees Through the Old Lady," also from *Mumonkan*, as a vehicle for discussing the role of language in Zen study and in psychoanalytic practice. Next, in Chapter 6, I examine the unconscious and its processes from structural and functional perspectives as the central organizing principle of the psychoanalytic endeavor. The discussion covers seminal contributions by Freud, Matte-Blanco's radical reformulation through the use of mathematical logical set theory, and D. T. Suzuki's explication of the "Zen unconscious." In Chapter 7, I review the psychoanalytic literature on meditation and psychoanalytic listening. I then explore the relationships among attention, inattention, and unconscious processes and describe a holistic form of listening. Clinical material supports and clarifies the abstract aspects of the discussion. In Chapter 8, I extend Bion's concepts of invariance and transformation to discuss the integration of Zen and psychoanalysis. I argue that observable descriptive similarities between Buddhism and psychoanalysis function as artifacts that can overlay and obscure the primary subjective and experiential nature that the two disciplines have in common. The terms *sense*, *non-sense*, and *no-sense* function as neutral words with which to discuss basic ineffable and unknowable experiences that both systems can access.

Chapter 9 explores and elaborates various relationships derived from the image of gap, precipice, and abyss, with specific emphasis on the interacting dynamics between being and knowing as explicated in the Zen Buddhist teachings of Chinese Zen teacher Hui-neng (638–713 CE) and in Bion's psychoanalytic writings. Chapter 10 details an 18-year psychoanalytic treatment of a neurologically impaired, severely depressed Orthodox Jewish woman and explicates through treatment vignettes and theoretical discussion a working model that demonstrates and operationalizes the various abstract ideas discussed in the previous chapters.

Challenge: Creativity/Destructivity

Creativity and destructivity can only be separated arbitrarily. Every creative movement requires the destruction of something else; otherwise, what might be deemed as creative becomes an add-on or appendage to an existing element, whether that takes the form of a theory or a technique. This add-on approach reflects a conservative creativity that maintains the existing structure intact. The color and design of my necktie become bolder and more radical, but it's still neatly tucked under my collar and in place around my neck. This type of creativity fits well into the psychotherapy modality but avoids the radical potential that psychoanalysis has the capability to evoke. From this perspective, to address the issue clinically, one might engender or impose on a patient a transformation in behavior, thinking, perception, and feeling in socially acceptable and personally useful ways. What this approach usually seems to mean is that the analyst is successful in getting the patient to buy into a new framework, often that of the analyst, who might believe otherwise, and who operates as an agent for the analytic institution, societal frame, culture, and civilization. This approach reflects an implied hierarchical relationship that assumes an exclusive objectivity on the part of the psychoanalyst. In this respect, the therapist becomes society's agent, who becomes an expert in the technique of indoctrination.* The resulting endless spiral co-opts what might have been psychoanalysis to the demands and pressures of the larger society. Spoken and unspoken institutional demands for conformity, current HMO pressures, and the repressive restrictions of licensing laws serve as cautionary tales.

Destructive movements create at least the potential for something new, even if that is not obvious or seemingly not likely. It will take a creative sensibility to fashion something new from the destruction or to adduce through alternate lenses what can be construed as one or the other. It is, in my opinion, the lack of creative sensibility that keeps one attached to present forms, even when the latter become outmoded and no longer useful, or their usefulness is dictated by the demands of larger systems such as psychoanalytic institutes or Buddhist *sanghas*. Zen teachers teach that even the desired enlightenment of the spiritual seeker must be "thrown away" before it becomes another reified encumbrance. However, these same teachers can unconsciously become imprisoned in prescribed meaning systems. This is exemplified, for instance, in the debate as to whether or not Zen koans contain only one or many true solutions.

Can we throw off our neckties, unbutton our collars, roll up our sleeves, and engage in the creative processes accessible through Buddhist and psychoanalytic practice? Can we make room for new modes of being and different intuitive models? For instance, the initial creative intention of the Oedipus myth, the central organizing structure of classical psychoanalysis, has become over time transformed into dogma and thus limits its usefulness as a potentially transmuting and healing force. Do Zen koans function as equally useful intuitive models? Can we tap into unexplored aspects of the Oedipus myth as some contemporary psychoanalysts have (Morris, 2008; Rhode, 1987)? Can we endeavor to find out? Can we take Chi-shan's instruction as we enter this inquiry when he writes: "Thus, turning your light of reflection inwardly, endeavor to enter deeply into

---

* Eric Rhode (1998) discusses the distinction between externally imposed conversions and internal transformations. Barnaby Barratt (1993) makes a slightly different distinction between transformation and transmutation to address similar issues.

a spirit of inquiry.... When this spirit is kept alive without interruption and most sincerely, the time will come to you when you perform, without being aware of it, a somersault in the air" (D. T. Suzuki, 1994, p. 119).

1

Riding the Elusive Ox of Zen:
Problems of Definition

I need to repeat that Zen refuses to be explained, but that it is to be lived.

—D. T. Suzuki (1949, p. 310)

Psychoanalysis is a lived emotional experience. As such it cannot be translated, transcribed, recorded, explained, understood or told in words. It is what it is.

—Thomas Ogden (2005, p. 1)

Introduction

In this chapter, I discuss Zen in an effort to shape a definition that is relevant to understanding the Zen impulse and the psychoanalytic encounter. The shape that unfolds is not static or emblazoned in stone and is subject to an ongoing fluid evolution as Zen develops over time in any given cultural context and in relation to an individual's deepening awareness and understanding, which is an unrelenting, lifelong, and ongoing process. I approach this task from a personal experiential perspective, through the use of definitions of key themes found in the Zen literature and through comparison and contrast with psychoanalytic ideas. My emphasis is geared toward examining and clearing up some confusions and misconceptions that detract from a clear understanding and appreciation of Zen's radical religious intention. For the psychoanalyst who is not familiar with Zen's basic beliefs and practices, the material presented in this chapter will help contribute to understanding the Zen practitioner who seeks treatment. Additionally, I hope to expand further meaningful conversation between Zen and psychoanalysis.

An examination of the Zen literature reveals a complex, multifaceted, and diverse religion with varying sects, often in opposition. The question becomes what Zen is being described. This is further complicated by regional variations and by the experiential emphasis of Zen training, which becomes colored by the personality and interpretation of the particular teacher. For instance, we might ask whether we are speaking of the 11th-century Chinese Zen teacher Tai-hui's tendency to derail dialogue or 13th-century radical Japanese Zen reformist Dogen's efforts to expand dialogue. Another significant question that is germane to this discussion centers on whether one views Zen through the lens of quietist or insight-oriented introspectionist practices or some viable integrated form. Do practitioners of a particular sect believe in quick or gradual enlightenment? Does a particular sect emphasize mysticism, or does it take an iconoclastic position that seemingly negates all positions? Recently, for example, Barry Magid (2005) has written about the differences between what he describes as "top-down" and "bottom-up" Zen practice, which is essentially a critique of the Rinzai emphasis on a rigorous and increasingly intensified practice mediated by its *subitist* orientation. He is supportive of the more relaxed *shikantaza* "just sitting" practice associated with the Soto Zen tradition. This distinction has roots in a complex of cultural and historical factors that require elaboration in order to develop an informed discussion on the relation between Zen and psychoanalysis.*

Much of the early psychoanalytic exposure to Zen was filtered through D. T. Suzuki's teachings, which were Rinzai influenced and which emphasized the irrational, illogical, diachronic aspects in relation to koan study. However, his depiction of Zen shifted over the years. For example, he expresses ambivalence with regard to quietist and insight-oriented approaches over the span of his career. The specific entry point into the stream of his thought becomes crucial. Many of the later influences derived from the *shikantaza* approach that was traditionally associated with Dogen and the Soto tradition. While sectarian extremism exists in all religious systems, when thought of as operating along a continuum of emphasis, as the Zen scholar Steven Heine (1994) notes, the differences are not as extreme as they might initially appear.

I find it to be more fruitful to think of different Zen and psychoanalytic schools and their associated practices and beliefs as constituting what the Chilean psychoanalyst Ignacio Matte-Blanco (1975, 1988) describes as equivalence classes that include both identities and differences. We also need to think in terms of practice within a particular school. For example, within the context of a tradition that emphasizes koan study, new students are typically introduced to a basic concentration form of meditation in

---

* For elaboration see Gregory (1987).

order to strengthen the mind. Such experiences with quietist techniques would then influence how Zen is incorporated into psychotherapy, for instance, exclusively as a relaxation technique. Additionally, within a particular Zen sect, the influence of the teacher's personality and particular slant will exert a strong influence on the student's perception of Zen beliefs and practices. This influence can become quite profound as a result of the student's tendency to idealize and identify with the teacher's personality and particular style.

Etymology

Zen derives from the Japanese translation of the Sanskrit term *dhyana*, which means "concentration meditation" or "meditative absorption." Zen is also known as Ch'an (Chinese), Thien (Vietnamese), and Seon or Son (Korean). This translation places practice and direct experience at the center of the Zen religious endeavor in contrast to other forms of Buddhism that developed in China and which relied on scriptural study and exegesis.

The evolution of Zen meditation, over time, represents a radical departure from its Indian Buddhist roots and associated meditation practices. A primary distinguishing factor is Zen's sudden or direct approach to practice and to enlightenment that developed over time. The distinction between sudden and gradual approaches has been a source of sectarian dispute over the centuries (Gregory, 1987).

Structure

Since Zen is not a monolithic structure, it is important to keep in mind that while there is a historical continuity between Ch'an and Zen, and that the terms are often used interchangeably, there are many fundamental sociocultural and doctrinal differences between these systems, as they developed regionally and as different sects integrated various influences of indigenous religions. For example, Ch'an incorporates elements of Taoism. Zen, as it developed in Japan, was influenced by Shinto. Recently, a rapidly expanding interfaith Zen movement in the United States has integrated many Christian elements (Boykin & May, 2003; Habito, 2004; Johnston, 1976; Kennedy, 1996, 2004; Leong, 2001). Additionally, tremendous variations exist within sects, which have fueled debate and controversy over the centuries. For instance, the use of abbreviated language of the *wato* (shortcut) method of koan practice developed by Ta-hui in China exemplifies a radical emphasis on silence and koan study. In this tradition, koan study is directly connected to zazen in a practice referred to as *kanna-zen* ("koan concentration," "koan meditation," literally: "looking at language"). By contrast, in the Soto sect, koans are traditionally used as part of the teacher's lectures and are kept separate from *shikantaza* practice. Presently in the West, teachers typically integrate the two approaches. This contemporary integration parallels scholarly research that indicates that the purported differences between different Zen sects might be more accurately understood as reflecting sectarian extremism more than serious differences in the day-to-day reality of practice.

Perspectives

Zen has been examined from many perspectives, including religion (Abe, 1985, 1990, 1992; D. T. Suzuki, 1949, 1972a, 1972b, 1994), philosophy (Glass, 1995; Stambaugh, 1999; Watts, 1957), academics (Faure, 1993, 1996; Heine, 1994, 2002, 2008), psychology (Fromm, 1950, 1956; Fromm, Suzuki, & DeMartino, 1960; Rosenbaum, 1998), physics (Soeng, 1996), and the arts (Blyth, 1942). Some authors describe Zen as a religion, but with the qualification that it is a religion that is not a religion. Of course, many writers note that Zen defies description and classification, which has contributed to nihilistic misperceptions of Zen.

With respect to the Zen impulse as a religious endeavor, American Zen master Phillip Kapleau (1966) offers this definition: "Briefly stated, Zen is a religion with a unique method of body-mind training whose aim is satori, that is, Self-realization ... for as a Buddhist Way of liberation Zen is most assuredly a religion" (p. xv).

These diverse investigations, as Heine (2008) notes, "create significant discussion and debate about what constitutes the 'real' Zen" (p. 3). For example, my perspective and understanding derive from the bias of my own Zen and psychoanalytic practice and study.

Soteriological Intention

Zen's radical soteriological intention, that is, its impulse toward salvation, as I see it, places its practices and beliefs in the domain of religion.

However, Zen is not a religion in the sense of the word that religion is typically understood in a Western civilizational context. On this point, Japanese Zen scholar Masao Abe (1985) notes:

> Zen may be said to be one of the most difficult religions to understand, for there is no formulated Zen doctrine or theological system by which one may intellectually approach it. Accordingly, it is not surprising to find various superficial understandings or misunderstandings of Zen among Westerners interested in Zen, whose cultural and religious traditions are entirely different from those in which Zen developed. (p. 3)

Central to the Zen salvational impulse is the development of compassion and wisdom. Abe (1985) draws out distinct and fundamental differences between Zen and Christianity to further develop an appreciation of Zen as a nontheological religion. He writes that "the difference between Christianity and Zen could be formulated in contrasts of God—Nothingness, Faith—Enlightenment, Salvation—Self-Awakening" (p. 187).

Abe (1985) describes the impulse and intention toward salvation as "the genuine meaning of Buddhist life" (p. xxii). Wisdom and compassion are embodied in Zen iconography, rituals, and prayers such as in the Bodhisattva vow to save all sentient beings, which is central to Zen practice:

> Sentient beings are numberless; I vow to save them.
> Desires are inexhaustible; I vow to put an end to them.
> The Dharmas are boundless; I vow to master them.
> The Buddha Way is unattainable; I vow to attain it.

> (Loori, 1998, p. 46)

This salvational intention is also asserted in the Zen impulse toward *satori* (enlightenment, literally: "to understand" or "self-realization") and engendered through personal experience. It is for this latter impulse that Zen emphasizes the wisdom aspect of meditation without which Zen teachers warn that practice becomes an empty and useless endeavor equated, for example, in the traditional notion of "polishing a brick to make a mirror" or "eating painted rice cakes to satisfy hunger."

Regarding Zen's salvational intention, D. T. Suzuki (1949) notes:

> As I have repeatedly illustrated, Buddhism, whether primitive or developed, is a religion of freedom and emancipation, and the ultimate aim of its discipline is to release the spirit from its possible bondage so that it can act freely in accordance with its own principles. (p. 74)

Freedom, Not License

The freedom promised by Zen derives through a series of highly structured and disciplined religious practices. Kapleau (1966), who criticizes the licentious misuse of Zen in the service of self-gratification rather than as a structure for developing responsible and compassionate living, asserts that "the attempt to isolate Zen in a vacuum of intellect, cut off from the very disciplines which are its *raison d'etre*, has nourished a pseudo-Zen, which is little more than a mind-tickling diversion of highbrows and a plaything of beatniks" (p. xv). In his introduction to Yasutani Roshi's explication of Zen, Kapleau writes: "Yasutani Roshi's emphasis on the religious aspect of Zen, that is, on faith as a prerequisite to enlightenment, may come as a surprise to Western readers accustomed to 'intellectual images' of Zen by scholars devoid of Zen insight" (p. 4).

By "Zen insight" Kapleau means the experiential intuitive insight or wisdom that derives through disciplined ongoing practice. The Sanskrit term for this intuited experiential insight or wisdom is *prajna* ("quick knowing," or "intuitive knowing").

In this respect Kapleau points to a dis-ease or discomfort with Zen in the West. We are not able to decide what to call it: religion, philosophy, technique, spiritual path, mysticism, or none of these. The positivistic heritage that formed the foundation for psychoanalysis coupled with the need for things to make sense drive a demand for a definition. Until recently, this demand has not been questioned. We don't question our need to call it a something or a nothing, whatever the case may be. In keeping with this demand, I view Zen as a religion. There is no problem with this view in the East, where most of the scholarship on Zen comfortably describes Zen as a religion, despite problems with definition. However, despite Zen's seemingly enigmatic structure, that emphasizes ineffability, iconoclasm, and illogical linguistic styles, constants can be clearly identified such as the prioritization of personal experience as the nexus of faith and of practice. Clearly definable beliefs such as emptiness, dependent arising, and the relationship between absolute and relative existence drive the Zen enterprise. Zen identifies specific goals, such as self-realization and the development of compassion, and articulates specific practices that support the realization of these beliefs and related goals. The primary religious practices include zazen, koan study, and mindfulness in daily activities.

In contrast, Alan Watts's (1957) antireligious sentiment typifies the Western difficulty with accepting the Zen religious impulse. He writes that Zen is not a religion; rather, it is "a way of life which does not belong to any categories of modern Western thought. It is not a religion or a philosophy; it is not a psychology or a type of science" (p. 3). Watts goes on to assert that Zen is a "way of liberation" (p. 3). Paradoxically, it is this latter salvational intention that Watts identifies "as a way of liberation" that qualifies Zen as a religion.

It is this type of comment that has influenced and distorted the Western perception of Zen. For instance, Canadian psychoanalyst Raphael Lopez-Corvo (2005), who criticizes Symington and Symington's (1996) rendering of Bion's O as "essentially a religious and metaphysical concept" (p. 316), relies on Watts's secular reading of Zen for support. Watts was quite knowledgeable *about* Zen; however, he was clearly not a Zen practitioner, which is problematic given his tremendous popularity and influence.

Historical Overview

Historical accounts attribute the Indian monk Bodhidharma with the introduction of Zen into China during the 6th century. Bodhidharma taught what the Zen literature describes as a mind-to-mind transmission, outside scriptures, and without reliance on words and letters. In the Zen tradition mind-to-mind transmission occurs through various encounters between teacher and student and can include words, silences, or actions. Applied to the psychoanalytic encounter, experientially, this includes whatever evolves in any given session emotionally, relationally, through narrative, silence, and sense perceptions. For the Zen practitioner, mind-to-mind transmission reflects and aims at actualizing Buddha nature in everyday life. Similarly, from a psychoanalytic perspective, Antonino Ferro (2005) notes that "the aim of psychoanalysis is to facilitate the development of potentialities of the patient's mind laid down in the species as pre-conceptions, which, however, appropriate fulfillment through the encounter with the other's mind" (p. 8).

This central Zen theme requires elaboration. The notion of mind-to-mind transmission has often been misconstrued and misused to promote an antiliterary approach to Zen studies resulting in a disregard for its rich, extensive, and diverse literature that often explicates contrasting, contradictory viewpoints. Historical research indicates that Zen teachers were often well educated and typically masters of the Zen literature (Heine, 2008; Hori, 2000, 2003).

Despite sectarian differences with practice at the center of Zen, a new language simultaneously developed that at once supported and reflected this radical departure from Indian Buddhism and distinct from traditions that emphasized scriptural study and conformity to doctrinal teachings. On this point, Robert Buswell (1987) notes:

> Ch'an eventually abandoned the complex descriptive terminology of Sino-Indian Buddhism in favor of a terse rhetoric that it considered to be proleptic and transformative. These new modes of expression were in turn applied to Ch'an teaching as well, resulting in radical pedagogical styles unknown to rival schools of Buddhism. (p. 321)

As a result, statements are concrete rather than abstract, immediate rather than doctrinal, addressed to what is imminent and ordinary rather than what is transcendent and extraordinary. For example, the master's response to a student's abstract question, "Wash your bowl," is immediate and lived, concrete and practical, and in this sense, illocutionary and performative. Yet, it simultaneously expresses a religious stance that is iconoclastic and critical of exclusive reliance on doctrine, scriptural study, and scholasticism. This stance provides a common theme in the koan literature.

This radical departure renders enlightenment accessible to the ordinary individual in the everyday living in the world outside of the monastic system and contributed to the popularity of Ch'an in Sung-era China.*

Bodhidharma's original teachings were transmitted through a series of Chinese patriarchs. Given this emphasis on direct transmission, the role of the teacher is essential and supersedes but does not eliminate the study of the scriptures. This direct teacher to student mind-to-mind transmission follows a lineage that traces its roots through preceding generations to the historical Buddha. In this regard, not unlike psychotherapy, Zen is interpersonal and experiential and relies on direct contact between student and teacher in both individual and group formats. The interpersonal is most evident in the literature, which is comprised predominantly of encounter dialogues that eventually became codified in koan collections and in the recorded sayings of various teachers. In addition to their performative and pedagogical function, the koan and recorded saying collections also provide explicit and implicit guidelines for appropriate interpersonal conduct within the monastic setting. This instructional function gets overlooked

---

* Sung Dynasty: 670–1279 CE.

through the exclusively iconoclastic approach to the Zen literature in the West. Speaking to this point, Heine (2008) writes that "Zen carefully constructs narratives about the role of interpersonal relations and interactions between masters and disciples or rivals in the setting of monastic institutional structures" (p. 41). Both the expressive and the instructional function of the Zen literature require attention for a complete picture. In this context, by "expressive" I mean that language can in and of itself serve as an expression of enlightenment.

Conscious Living

Simply stated, from my own experience, Zen is about being consciously alive and tolerating the resulting impact of alive and conscious living. The Zen notion of "chop wood, carry water" expresses the potential for alive and awake mindful living in the ordinary activities of everyday life. Mindful aliveness finds explicit expression from the psychoanalytic perspective in Donald Winnicott's notion of "going on being" and in Wilfred Bion's experiential concept of "beening." "Can we suffer our aliveness?" serves as the central experiential and existential question for both Zen and psychoanalysis. Zen, as I noted above, identifies three basic experiential practices: zazen (sitting meditation), koan study, and moment-to-moment mindfulness during all daily activities and chores. All contribute to deepening the practitioner's consciousness of being alive. These practices contribute to the development of the capacity to tolerate the ongoing impact of basic authentic aliveness and engender a liberating awareness of reality through an experiential alteration of perception that mobilizes intuited experiential knowing. Zen practice has frequently been characterized as completely derailing cognitive processes. It would be more accurate to describe the process as engendering a balance between intuitive and cognitive processes, an issue that I will elaborate further below in this chapter and in relation to koan study in Chapter 3.

   With regard to developing the capacity to suffer our aliveness and the mutual impacts human beings exert on one another, Michael Eigen (2004a) writes from the psychoanalytic perspective that "any increase in reality or consciousness may stimulate disaster dread" (p. 8). This becomes a problem for both the psychoanalyst and the Zenist since the very idea of practice is to open as fully as possible to our experience of ourselves, of others, and of ourselves in relation to others. The demand of Zen practice in the words of the influential Zen master Taizan Maezumi

(2001) is to be present and intimate with our life and to "refresh it each moment!" (p. 29).

Zen practice magnifies experience. Magnification finds expression in the notions of mindfulness, realization, and enlightenment. Due to the ineffable nature of enlightenment, it is not clear what enlightenment actually means. Further, it is not clear how the highly personal experience of increased mindfulness, realization, and enlightenment come to be experienced by any particular individual. This individualism finds dramatic expression in the enlightenment poems of the Zen masters. The following demonstrate the diverse nature of enlightenment experience and expression:

> No mind, no Buddha, no being.
> Bones of the Void are scattered.
> Why should the golden lion
> Seek out the fox's lair?

—Tekkan (Stryk & Ikemoto, 1995, p. 12)

> Magnificent! Magnificent!
> No one knows the final word.
> The ocean bed's aflame,
> Out of the void leap wooden lambs.

—Fumon (Stryk & Ikemoto, 1995, p. 26)

> Who said the sea's concave,
> Mountains convex?
> Why, I swallow them whole—
> The boneless sky.

—Heishin (Stryk & Ikemoto, 1973, p. 54)

Enlightenment implies the possibility of a new beginning in each moment; for a refreshed life lived productively; for a life lived fully, creatively, compassionately, and wisely; for a life lived with a little more "emotional elbow room"; for a life that balances separateness and connectedness in human relationships; for a life that Freud posits can be lived in which one can work and love well. This understanding defines enlightenment as an ongoing process and points to the fluid, ever-changing nature of experience that cuts through any false notions of enlightenment as an end state, as a reified state of being, as a state of inert complacency.

The Fundamental Anxiety of Being

Ogden (2005) notes that the "psychoanalyst must be able to recognize with sadness and compassion that among the worst and most crippling of human losses is the loss of the capacity to be alive to one's own experience—in which case one has lost a part of one's humanness" (p. 23). If we can benefit ourselves and others by living consciously, compassionately, productively, creatively, and intimately, as implied by Ogden's comment, then what stops us? What is it that separates us from ourselves and from others and engenders alienation, estrangement, aggression, and dread? Zen posits a basic existential or "fundamental anxiety,"* an anxiety of being in the world, engendered by the transience of being and the impermanence of life. This fundamental anxiety in turn engenders ignorance. *Avidya*, the Sanskrit term for ignorance, translates literally as an active, ongoing, and relentless "not-knowing." This active not-knowing operates unconsciously and engenders grasping, aggression, lust, envy, and a host of problems that constitute the human condition. Not-knowing in the misguided process to buffer fundamental anxiety engenders the illusion of a solid, permanent, and separate sense of self. However, this illusion, which requires constant feeding, also engenders self-estrangement and alienation. This fragmentation of self from self and others operates automatically and unconsciously.

The Myth of the Isolated Mind

Writing from the intersubjective psychoanalytic perspective, Robert Stolorow and George Atwood (1992) arrive at a similar conclusion that they describe as "the myth of the isolated mind." They write:

> The myth of the isolated mind ascribes to man a mode of being in which the individual exists separately from the world of physical nature and also from engagement with others. This myth in addition denies the essential immateriality of human experience by portraying subjective life in reified, substantialized terms. (p. 7)

Stolorow and Atwood (1992) share with Zen the view that this myth defends against "anxiety at the prospect of physical annihilation and anguish in the face of the transitoriness of things" (p. 8). They caution

---

* I am grateful to Reggie Pawle for his suggestion of the use of this term.

that the false sense of reassurance that derives from this "differentiation from physical nature may pass over into frank reifications of the self as an immortal essence that literally transcends the cycles of life and death" (p. 8). However, in contrast to Zen thought, they attribute this alienation primarily to societal and economic factors that have emerged alongside the industrial revolution and modernization. They note:

> Viewed as a symbol of cultural experience, the image of the isolated mind represents modern man's alienation from nature, from social life, and from subjectivity itself. This alienation, still so pervasive in our time, has much to do with the culture of technocracy and the associated intellectual heritage of mechanism that has dominated thought about human nature in the 20th century. (p. 8)

Modernization clearly contributes to alienation. However, this romantic understanding implies that everything was fine prior to modernization. Similarly, this stance parallels the dualist "quietist" misunderstanding of zazen practice. The quietist implication centers on the premise that the practitioner can return to an original mental and emotional peace by stilling the mind of thoughts, a romantic notion that implies that we were perfectly fine before we began to think! This false notion has contributed to misunderstanding Zen in both the popular and the academic literature. For instance, Victor Hori (2000), who in a discussion of contemporary Rinzai Zen koan practice and study criticizes this misunderstanding, observes that "in scholarly studies of Zen, again a common view is that first there was an original pure experience and that afterwards thought and language entered and sullied its original purity" (p. 283). Similarly, from the standpoint of practice, the influential Soto Zen teacher S. Suzuki (1970) has observed that true peace functions through the capacity for equipoise in the midst of turbulence. He writes:

> Calmness of mind does not mean that you should stop your activity. Real calmness should be found in activity itself. We say, "It is easy to have calmness in inactivity, it is hard to have calmness in activity, but calmness in activity is true calmness. (p. 46)

While psychoanalytic intersubjectivity theory offers a refreshing, useful, and creative approach to understanding and working with the psychological and relational dynamics of the human condition that coincides with foundational Zen principles in a number of significant ways, this comparison overlooks the issue of the primal or original fundamental anxiety that Zenists address through religious practice. Abe (1985), for example, describes fundamental anxiety and the resulting alienation as part and parcel of being human. He writes:

> Self estrangement and anxiety are *not* something *accidental* to the ego-self, but are inherent to its structure. To be human is to be a problem to oneself, regardless of one's culture, class, sex, nationality, or the era in which one lives. To be human means to be an ego-self; to be an ego-self means to be cut off from both one's self and one's world; to be cut off from one's self and one's world means to be in constant anxiety. This is the human predicament. The ego-self, split at the root into subject and object, is forever dangling over a bottomless abyss, unable to gain any footing. (pp. 6–7)

Abe (1985) attributes this basic anxiety to self-consciousness, which he describes as unique to being human. Our sense of self to varying degrees is dependent on others and contingent on levels of responsiveness or lack of responsiveness, praise or criticism of others. Further, Abe stresses the deep-rooted nature of this basic anxiety by noting that "insofar as one is a human being, he or she cannot escape this basic anxiety. In fact, strictly speaking, it is not that one has this anxiety, but rather one is the anxiety" (p. 224).

The potential for new life, new beginnings, altered perceptions, triggers dread as the Truth of self, other, reality becomes revealed. That is, as one begins to loosen the tightly bound defenses against fundamental anxiety, as spontaneity overtakes rigidity, as we unravel the self-protective cocoon of the illusion of ultimate separateness, as we learn to respond to relative separateness with sensitivity and compassion. In short, Zen practice can provide a strong structure such as Winnicott describes as a "good enough holding environment." This holding permits glimpses and moments of what needs to be experienced to engender deepened consciousness of being alive.*

If we fail to take account of the primacy of the fundamental anxiety of being that Zen posits, we are headed for trouble. For example, with regard to Zen practice, in our search for truth, realization, freedom, enlightenment, peace, heaven—however one may choose to conceptualize it—we are actively ignoring a crucial and central resistance to practice. Zen practice, as Heine (1997) notes, requires "an emotional attunement to impermanence" (p. 22). That is, from the Zen perspective, authentic spiritual awakening derives from embracing and suffering through our emotional,

---

* See Cooper (2007) for elaboration.

psychological, and behavioral reaction to inescapable loss and the ongoing ever-changing flux of life. Heine writes:

> It is the emotional identification with the plight of evanescent things, and the consequent anguish and outrage, that awakens the need for release from suffering. Enlightenment is attained as empathetic grief is transformed into a realization of the nonsubstantive basis of existence. (p. 41)

Without this emotional attunement to impermanence, practice can become appropriated by the "ego-self" that Abe speaks of to maintain *avidya*. Practice then becomes another piece of accumulation as we become "experience collectors," adding practice after practice, technique after technique, belief after belief, analytic hour after analytic hour to the territory of ego-self. However, as this approach is fundamentally flawed, unless confronted with insight practices, aggression, grasping, greed, fear, alienation, and various states of mindlessness continue. The psychoanalytic concept of cathexis serves as an example of how psychoanalysis can facilitate necessary deepened religious insight-oriented practices.

Cathexis

Defining Zen as a religion holds many complex and intertwined implications. Here is one. Psychoanalysis uses the term *cathexis*, first coined by Freud, to refer to an emotional charge of energy that becomes attached to an experience, fantasy, word, thought, or feeling. I don't intend to discuss or "hair-split" this term. For our purposes, it will be helpful to think of cathexis simply as "attachment" or "energy attachment." The false notion that Zen and its associated practices such as *shikantaza* or *kanna-zen* are simply techniques, a view embraced by many mental health practitioners and new age proponents of meditation, defeats the emotional impulse so essential to religious practice. Successful practice necessitates an emotional investment in a belief system that supports practice. This holds practical applications to time spent "on the cushion," especially with regard to the mental habit of what D. T. Suzuki (1949) describes as "pursuing" or "abiding" in thoughts. A failure to recognize and acknowledge Zen's salvational intent supports the misperception of Zen as simply a quietist technique, which has been criticized historically.*

---

* See Chapter 2 for a detailed review of the quietist-introspectionist controversy.

It is important to keep in mind that from both Zen and psychoanalytic perspectives, all experience is neutral and becomes colored in either a negative or a positive way, depending on its use. When the salvational impulse, engendered through insight, is emphasized, zazen takes on a dimension beyond quietism. Zazen as a neutral process has many uses unique to the individual and influenced by both conscious and unconscious processes. Psychoanalysis reveals healthy, adaptive, and growth-promoting as well as unhealthy, maladaptive, and stunting defensive aspects of zazen. As psychoanalysts, it is extremely helpful to respond to the Zen practitioners among our patients on an individual basis to determine progressive/regressive, adaptive/maladaptive uses of beliefs and practices. This requires relinquishing the traditional global pathologizing stance toward religious practices held by many psychoanalysts, which can operate silently and subtly in the background even for the receptive therapist. I refer to this as a "Freudian hangover" that one must be mindful of. I have noticed that for me it will often take the form of a subtle feeling of cynicism that hovers in the background and that paints a negative tinge on my capacity for attentive, nonbiased acceptance of the patient's narrative. Sometimes, these thoughts and feelings provide clues to early object relations. However, they are often the result of the dogmatic pathologizing response to religious experience that I initially encountered during my psychoanalytic training.

Without this religious cathexis, unconsciously cathected mental contents and processes will compete with and, for the most part, defeat Zen practice. For example, we are advised during zazen practice not to get caught up in mental events such as preoccupations with the day's tasks, daydreams, fantasies, worries, concerns, or enlightenment. We simply observe, accept, let go whatever comes to mind and return gently to our practice, such as observing the breath, observing the rising and falling of thoughts and sensations, or concentrating on a koan.

Zen teachings outline two basic strategies. The two methods can be loosely described as active and passive. Both are effective, but can hold an increased efficacious influence with the help of psychoanalysis. There are several problems with both styles that center on the mind's tendency toward dualism. These problems become acerbated when there is a lack of emotional investment in the religious intention of practice stemming from viewing Zen simply as a technique. One aspect of the dualism stems from a subject and object mind-split between what might be perceived as the observer of the meditating mind and a mind observed as object of the meditating mind. Both mental processes are simply aspects of one mind.

Effective and committed religious practice requires cathexis to the practices and beliefs of the religion. The Zen teaching of "no reliance on scriptures, words, and letters, no reliance on others," not to believe anything except what is verifiable through the experience of one's own practice, clearly and cogently articulates the systematization of Zen beliefs. This no-belief/belief system provides the structure of the Zen semiotic and serves as the basis for faith. Cathexis finds expression in the religious language in the Zen literature. For example, in his commentary on the koan "Joshu's Mu," Mumon asserts "practice as if your head were on fire," "practice as if you swallowed a red-hot iron ball and you are trying to spit it out!" Mumon's admonishments clearly and dramatically point to the religious urgency of Zen practice and render absurd any notion of Zen practice as simply a "relaxation technique."

Cathexis to the religion of childhood and various associated internalized objects contributes to the subjectively organized structures of the individual's religious belief system. For instance, internalized Christian images of Jesus, such as Baby Jesus, Crucified Jesus, Risen Jesus, and the Jesus who washed his apostles' feet, function as effective and beautiful iconic representations that can, when used properly, further the salvational goals for Christian practitioners.* However, unconscious attachment to these internalized object images and to identifications with, or relationship to, these objects, along with associated feelings, such as guilt, shame, or humiliation, can engender resistance to new religious forms. As a result, the practitioner can latch on to the life skills aspects of a religion, such as can be found in the calming aspects of meditation available through Zen practice, and safely negate its religious intent. Zen is interested in cutting through such attachments. D. T. Suzuki (1949) speaks to the Zen confrontation with all attachments with regard to satori. He writes:

> Satori is not seeing God as he is, as may be contended by some Christian mystics. Zen from the very beginning made clear its principal thesis, which is to see into the work of creation and not to interview the creator himself. The latter may be found then busy moulding his universe, but Zen can go along with its own work even when he is not found there. It is not depending on his support. [And] with the god of mysticism there is the grasping of the definite object, and when you have God, what is not God is excluded. This is self-limiting. Zen wants absolute freedom, even from God. (p. 263)

---

* I am grateful to Karen Morris for her perspective on these Jesus representations.

One strategy that works synergistically integrates the Zen religious impulse and the psychoanalytic understanding of unconscious processes, entails uncovering the underlying emotional states that drive thought processes and that maintain cathexis to old reified religious attachments, images, and the self states associated with such images. For the Zen practitioner, this approach requires a nonpathologizing response to religious object attachments and associated self states and the willingness to sit face-to-face with fundamental anxiety and the ensuing turmoil. Yasutani (1966) asserts: "When you harbor philosophical concepts or religious beliefs or ideas or theories of one kind or another, you too are a phantom, for inevitably you become bound to them. Only when your mind is empty of such abstractions are you truly free and independent" (p. 78).

In terms of the psychoanalytic encounter, this requires that the therapist be willing to sit through such states, relinquish irrational global or wholesale condemnations of any belief system, question one's own emotional attachment to reified beliefs that operate counter to the patient, and not make premature interpretations limited to genetic constellations that serve a self-protective function. The resulting awareness facilitates a capacity to naturally allow interferences to meditation practice to lose their hold because their defensive function has been reduced or eliminated.

Practice

Simply sitting in zazen, at first glance, seems a weak approach to effectively working through the seemingly complicated and overwhelming task of cutting through the defenses against fundamental anxiety and making the illusion of an apparently permanent, separate, and immortal self transparent. This simple basic practice of sitting can be deceptively difficult, extremely frustrating, and glacially slow. However, sitting provides the opportunity to create a "sacred space," if you will, where one can sit alone or in a group and allow a process to evolve that, for the most part, does not occur in a world plagued by greed, ignorance, aggression, mindlessness, and their ramifications. Over time, as if looking back over one's shoulder, one notices both subtle and dramatic shifts from a self-centered mindless reactivity to a more unselfconscious, compassionate, and mindful response to individuals and situations as they present themselves. Speaking of this process in the language of rebirth, Eigen (2004a) notes:

> The rebirth sequence is not always gone through fully and openly. Often subjects go through it in a pinched, defensive way.... Most rebirths are semi aborted, semi successful combinations of rigidity and openness. One keeps trying to go through it better. (p. 29)

The way through for the Zenist centers on practicing, no matter what! From this vantage point, American Zen teacher Charlotte Joko Beck (2005) notes, "But practice is a lifetime of work and is never done. It is a process of experiencing again and again each thing that enters our life moment by moment" (p. x). As practice deepens and we develop the capacity to sit through both inner and outer distractions and attractions, as Heine (1997) notes, "ordinary emotions are surpassed by means of an impersonal and holistic insight into the nonsubstantive structure of reality" (p. 49). Emotions that drive distracting thought processes are not ignored, dismissed, split off, or negated. Rather, one begins to relate to emotional life differently. Emotional life, not unlike any experience, can function as a fertile ground from which mindful and compassionate living derive. The relation between emotional life and a perspective informed by Zen practice is quite complex. It is from an experiential base that both Zen and psychoanalysis offer different, yet complementary methods for effectively addressing emotional life. The cultivation and coming into being of this attitude informs the psychoanalytic encounter.

Rinzai Zen master Eido Shimano, Roshi, from a perspective that prioritizes experience and practice, would admonish me repeatedly: "Practice, practice, practice, no matter what!" I am reminded here of a children's book that I used to read to my daughter, *The Goat That Went to School* (Sally, 1952). Each page of the book described a challenge that Bucky the goat had to face. After presenting the challenge, each facing page simply said, "But Bucky was plucky, he kept right on going." Continued, ongoing, unrelenting practice engenders the capacity to survive one's own emotional and existential truth, to continue to grow, to open, and to develop true compassion.

It is this actual living everyday practice that defines Zen as an experiential religious system. However, this meaning requires some unpacking because "meditation" in the Zen tradition is not limited to sitting still on a cushion, although such sitting (zazen) is an important aspect of Zen training. Zenists speak more of a frame of mind or an attitude of mindfulness that requires unrelenting total exertion that the practitioner strives to bring to every activity.

Additionally, zazen has been described by many Zen teachers as having a different structure and function than other forms of meditation. For example, Kapleau (1966) makes this distinction:

> Zazen must not be confused with meditation. Meditation, in the beginning at least, involves fixing one's mind on an idea or an object. In some types of Buddhist meditation the meditator envisions or contemplates or analyzes certain elementary shapes, holding them in his mind to the exclusion of everything else. Or he may concentrate in a state of adoration upon his own created image of a Buddha or a Bodhisattva, or meditate on abstract qualities as loving-kindness and compassion. In Tantric Buddhist systems of meditation, mandala containing various seed syllables of the Sanskrit alphabet are visualized and dwelt upon in a prescribed manner. Also employed for meditational purposes are mandala consisting of special arrangements of Buddhas, Bodhisattvas, and other figures. (pp. 12–13)

Kapleau adds that:

> The uniqueness of Zazen lies in this: that the mind is freed from bondage to *all* thought-forms, visions, objects and imaginings, however sacred or elevating, and brought to a state of absolute emptiness, from which alone it may one day perceive its own true nature, or the nature of the universe. (p. 13)

From this perspective, the question for the Zenist who practices psychoanalysis becomes one of intention. That is, how can we bring this religious intention into practice in our daily lives, as psychotherapists and as beings in the world? From a salvational standpoint, the attention engendered through continued practice becomes a means to an end as the humbling power of suffering through one's own experience attunes one to the human condition. As we suffer our humanness, compassion evolves and matures naturally. The need for an external punishment/reward system such as is symbolized in notions of literal heavens and hells diminishes and eventually dissolves. As a result, the need for an external ethical system that might have initially provided support and fostered growth becomes eliminated. Transcendence is not other-worldly; rather, it is deeply rooted in the immanence of everyday ordinary life. This is simple enough, yet remains very difficult to grasp.

In this respect, Zen practice is not, as it has been misunderstood, aimless, meaningless, or purposeless. It includes a highly structured set of practices that support a soteriological aim, which can be asserted, as noted by Kapleau's quote above, as enlightenment or satori. However, enlightenment is not an isolated end in and of itself. Rather, enlightenment engenders wisdom and compassion. Wisdom and compassion derive through an alteration in perception that engenders a unitive experience. Once challenged through disciplined practice, the falsity of a fixed object/subject dichotomy becomes transparent. However, this has often been overstated, misused, and has contributed to a misperception of Zen as exclusively nihilistic. The fundamental paradox and dilemma is that transcendence and immanence are two seemingly contradictory aspects of one reality. This fundamental antinomy holds relational relevance clinically in the notion of the simultaneity of separateness and connectedness, a balance that can be achieved through psychoanalysis. As we will see, sameness and difference coexist.

Zen attempts to accomplish this simultaneous act of growth and survival through practices that continuously, spontaneously, gradually, suddenly facilitate recovering from ourselves by loosening and cutting through the tightly wrapped self-protective bindings and recovering, uncovering, discovering what is real, what is true. In the ideal, the very practice, as noted above, engenders a magnification of experience. In this regard, resistance to Zen practice operates as a resistance to what is real.

Zen Iconoclasm

One source of misunderstanding among Westerners centers on Zen's often enigmatic iconoclastic stance. An overemphasis on this very provocative and challenging aspect of Zen unrelentingly ignores Zen's integration of local religions, mythologies, beliefs, and folk traditions along with the performance of rituals geared toward exorcising or appeasing demons, ghosts, evil spirits, the veneration of local deities, and all aspects of the everyday ordinary reality of indigenous people. With respect to an emphasis on everyday ordinary reality, Rinzai Zen master Zenkai Shibayama (2000) notes that "as repeatedly stressed, Zen is not something to be philosophically thought about or intellectually understood. It has to be the concrete fact personally attained by one's realization experience" (p. 15). In contrast to the concrete, the Zen literature is also full of seemingly irrational, Alice in Wonderland expressions that defy reason, such as: "A bridge flows, whereas water does not flow" [and] "When Lee drinks the wine, Chang gets drunk" (Abe, 1985, p. 3).

Zen's radical iconoclasm has been misunderstood as anti-intellectual and derives, in part, from such slogans noted above, such as nonreliance on words and letters. However, this inaccurate notion has received strong criticism. Abe (1985), who provides a detailed description of the relation between unitive experience and differentiation, addresses this misunderstanding by noting that "although Zen transcends human intellect, it does not exclude it" (p. 23). The issue is not scriptures themselves, but the relationship one forms with them. This admonishment serves as a caution to the student to avoid attachment and to question reification. Further, Abe notes that nonreliance on words and letters "does not, as is often misunderstood even by Zen practitioners, indicate a mere exclusion of words and letters, but rather signifies the necessity of not clinging to them" (p. 23).

Zen teacher and scholar Victor Hori (2003) reports that during his own monastic residency and study in Japan scholarship becomes increasingly important as the aspirant progresses in koan practice. He describes the extensive writing practices undertaken by advanced monks. These detailed and comprehensive writing projects are essential for the completion of the formal koan curriculum in many contemporary Rinzai Zen monasteries in Japan. Two practices merit mention here. They include *kakiwake*, or "written explanation," and *nenro*, or "deft play."

Kakiwake entails a close reading and a detailed componential analysis of the text of a koan. *Nenro* involves writing a poem that expresses the essence of the koan in a traditional Chinese four-line structure. Hori (2003) writes:

> Whereas the *kakiwake* essay is prosaic, detailed, and discursive, the *nenro* verse is supposed to be free and imaginative" [And] "As in the tradition of Asian scholarship, the *kakiwake* essay is written in an anonymous, impersonal voice … the short *nenro* verse, in contrast, is meant to be a performance in which the monk displays his capacity … the monk ritually adopts an attitude bordering on arrogance. (pp. 38–39)

With development and maturity monks become expressive in a wide range of language styles. Through this thorough and comprehensive training the practitioner uses language in novel and creative ways to express Truth. This is exemplified in the following poem:

> Not limited
> By language
> It is ceaselessly expressed;
> So, too, the way of letters
> Can display but not exhaust it.

> —Dogen (Heine, 1997, p. 108)

In his critique of psychoanalytic modernism, Barrett (1993) writes that "rationality involves the structuring of discourse by a system of logical and rhetorical rules, such that statements of pure logic take precedence over statements of pure rhetoric" (p. 58). So-called logical-rational statements are prioritized by the point of view of the scientific model. The predominance and pervasiveness of values associated with the scientific discourse has contributed to the critique of the rhetorical and irrational elements of Zen. Given this bias, it is not surprising then that psychotherapy has integrated techniques such as zazen into its rational/linear semiotic structure, but has not given much attention to the Zen discourse, a discourse that, not unlike the free-associative discourse of psychoanalysis, is unique. This bias runs counter to the free-associative dialogue that is fundamental and distinguishes psychoanalysis as a unique discipline. This linear, sequential, diachronic, rational bias has been questioned implicitly and explicitly, as discussed in Chapter 6, such as in Freud's explication of the laws of the unconscious, Matte-Blanco's articulation of "bi-logic," and Bion's emphasis on Truth over Knowledge.

The Zen Impulse in Psychoanalysis

The influence of Zen has run through psychoanalysis for over a half of a century as a result of D. T. Suzuki's involvement with Eric Fromm and colleagues (1950, 1956, 1960), Karen Horney (1945), Harold Kelman (1960), and others. These psychoanalysts have approached Zen praxis and beliefs with the true spirit of open-minded inquiry distinctive of the psychoanalytic dialogue. A thirst for expanding their vision and looking eastward to do so forms a common thread that ties together this group of psychoanalysts. They questioned the traditional psychoanalytic pathologizing of religious praxes and initiated an open-minded and receptive response by contemporary psychoanalysts, which has expanded to include a wide range of applications from a Zen-influenced short-term crisis intervention (Rosenbaum, 1998) to depth psychoanalysis that integrates basic Zen principles with contemporary intersubjectivity theory and self psychology (Magid, 2005).

Toward the end of her life, Karen Horney developed a close tie with D. T. Suzuki (Morvay, 1999; Quinn, 1987; Westkott, 1998). During the summer of 1952, Horney traveled to Japan to tour Zen monasteries with D. T. Suzuki. Marcia Westkott (1998) reports that "Horney's trip was the culmination of her deepening interest in Buddhism" (p. 287). Horney had increasingly developed a deepening interest in Zen, and as Westkott further notes, "She had cited Suzuki in her last two books and had met with him in the winter of 1950–51 while he was on a lecture tour in New York" (p. 289). She had felt a strong resonance between Zen and her own ideas. For example, Horney (1945) discusses the "impoverishment of the personality" and refers to the Zen notion of "wholeheartedness" or "sincerity of spirit" (p. 163).

Fromm's collaboration with D. T. Suzuki and Richard DeMartino resulted in the classic *Zen Buddhism and Psychoanalysis* (1960). This remarkable book clearly demonstrates a keen and focused Zen sensibility. It is instructive to return to this clear, concise, and cogent gem. Additionally, Fromm included detailed meditation instructions in his popular book, *The Art of Loving* (1956), in which he advises:

> It would be helpful to practice a few very simple exercises, as, for instance, to sit in a relaxed position (neither slouching, nor rigid), to close one's eyes, and to try to see a white screen in front of one's eyes, and to try to remove all interfering pictures and thoughts, then to try to follow one's breathing; not to think about it, nor force it, but to follow it. (p. 102)

Fromm (1956) believed that Zen practice expands the psychoanalytic process through a positive conceptualization of human potential that goes beyond addressing symptoms, and he advised that one should gradually develop a disciplined and regular practice. He recommends that "one should, at least, do such a concentration exercise every morning for twenty minutes (and if possible longer) and every evening before going to bed" (p. 102). In the same essay Fromm also advocated bringing this practice into all of one's daily activities, which, as noted above, is fundamental to Zen practice. In emphasizing moment-to-moment mindfulness, he asserts, "The activity at this very moment must be the only thing that matters, to which one is fully given" (p. 102).

Kapleau (1966), one of the first ordained American Zen masters, in a similar recommendation to practitioners, comments on the mutually reinforcing nature of what he describes as "sitting zazen" and "mobile zazen":

> One who sits devotedly in zazen everyday, his mind free of discriminating thoughts, finds it easier to relate himself wholeheartedly to his daily tasks, and one who performs every act with total attention and clear awareness finds it less difficult to achieve emptiness of mind during sitting periods. (p. 11)

When asked about the benefits of Zen practice in relation to mental health, Fromm responded that "it's [Zen] the only way to enduring mental health" (Kapleau, 1989, p. 14). He viewed both systems as potentially mutually enhancing.

Fromm (1960) viewed this shared experiential agenda in terms of movement from *being about* to directly *being*. He compared psychoanalytic interpretation and Zen koan practice and noted that both engender this movement. He observed:

> The "teaching" method of Zen is to drive the student into a corner, as it were. The koan makes it impossible for the student to seek refuge in intellectual thought; the koan is a barrier which makes further flight impossible. The analyst does—or should do—something similar. He must avoid the error of feeding the patient with interpretations and explanations which only prevent the patient from making the jump from thinking into experiencing. On the contrary, he must take away one rationalization after another, until the patient cannot escape any longer, and instead breaks through the fictions which fill his mind and experiences reality—that is, becomes conscious of something he was not conscious of before. (p. 126)

Similarly, while not speaking from a Zen perspective, Bion (1970) advocates a radical shift away from classical psychoanalysis through a leap of faith from what he describes as "about psychoanalysis" to "being psychoanalysis." He uses the term *beening* to capture the sense of this lived fundamentally ineffable experiential process. The trend away from an exclusively interpretive stance among contemporary psychoanalysts holds significant considerations in terms of the integration of Zen and psychoanalysis. However, there seems to be much more at stake beyond such theoretical and technical considerations that will become clarified through first examining Zen, which has its own set of problems to be dealt with.

For instance, Fromm notes, from a perspective that prioritizes direct being and that values the primacy of experience, that Zen emphasizes the ordinary everyday concrete reality of our day-to-day experience. However, Zen also simultaneously and paradoxically transcends the ordinary in a way that facilitates and reflects a profound alteration in perception, experience, and relationship to the reality of being in the world and in relation to self and other. This becomes most evident in the extraordinarily unique and creative use of language that utilizes puns, word play, paradox, nonsequiter, and conceit that is inherent in the Zen dialogue and through a radical reworking of traditional Indian approaches to meditation, both of which exert a profound impact on the practitioner.

Kelman (1960) argued that psychoanalysis is experientially Eastern. While deriving from fundamentally different theoretical assumptions, he observed that Buddhist thought and technique can deeply enhance psychoanalytic technique, particularly regarding the analyst's attentional stance. On this latter point, Kelman paved the way for a series of articles on attention in psychoanalysis, a subject that will be examined in Chapter 7.

Here, in the opening quotes to this chapter, both D. T. Suzuki and Ogden speak to the potential vitality, spontaneity, individuality, and aliveness that both Zen and psychoanalysis can engender in the committed practitioner. Both observations situate Zen and psychoanalysis in the realm of the experiential. In the Zen literature one encounters a liberal mix of clear, concrete expressions combined with a plethora of seemingly irrational comments. This abundance of nonsensical statements is most typically encountered as a master's response to a student's question. For example, "When Joshu was asked what Zen was, he answered, 'it is cloudy today and I won't answer'" (D. T. Suzuki, 1949, p. 117). Such responses are designed to disrupt logical thought and to engender a moment of lived self-reflection. On this point, Abe (1985) notes, "Zen is something enigmatic, beyond intellectual analysis" (p. 3). However, he also points out that this highly unique and creative use of language has engendered a false perception of Zen practice, and he notes that "Zen is taken to be a form of anti-intellectualism" (p. 3). He observes that this false impression has been further exacerbated by the beat writers. In a series of essays that explicate his understanding of the religious and philosophical significance of Zen, Abe writes: "Firstly, although Zen is often misunderstood to be an anti-intellectualism, a cheap intuitionism, or an encouragement to animal-like spontaneity without consideration of good and evil, it embraces, in fact, a profound philosophy" (p. xxi). As a result, the spontaneity, creativity, and iconoclasm encouraged by Zen and recorded plentifully in the Zen religious literature have often been misunderstood, misused, misappropriated and mangled out of its original form to rationalize selfish and licentious behavior. For example, Kapleau describes Watts's misinterpretation of Zen koans to rationalize his resistance to practice. With respect to disciplined Zen practice, which Watts criticized, Kapleau (1966) writes:

> There can be no doubt that for most Westerners, who seem by nature more active and restless than Asians, sitting perfectly still in zazen, even in a chair, is physically and mentally painful.... Not unsurprisingly, therefore, do we have the attempt on the part of some commentators, obviously unpracticed in Zen,

> to show that sitting is not indispensable to Zen discipline. In *The Way of Zen*
> (pp. 101, 103) Alan Watts even tries to prove, by citing portions of a well-known
> koan, that the Zen masters themselves have impugned sitting. (p. 21)

Watts's (1957) antipractice orientation typifies a fairly common obstacle to serious practice among Westerners. Fromm attributes this resistance to practice to a failure in the development of the capacity to be alone. He writes:

> Anyone who tries to be alone with himself will discover how difficult it is. He
> will begin to feel restless, fidgety, or even to sense anxiety. He will be prone to
> rationalize his unwillingness to go on with this practice by thinking that it has
> no value, is just silly, that it takes too much time, and so on, and so on. (pp.
> 101–102)

Treatment Considerations

The impact of Zen experience on the psychoanalytic encounter can be, at times, subtle and, at other times, quite dramatic. In either case, experience repeatedly demonstrates that Zen practice dovetails with transference and countertransference dynamics (Cooper, 1999). This latter point, depending on one's view of countertransference—whether one takes a contemporary totalistic or classical stance—further complicates matters. For example, the analysand's narrative can both conceal and reveal. It is up to the analyst to discern in the moment whether or not to intervene and how. Will the analyst treat a particular expression as a resistance in the classical sense, or will the analyst continue to encourage the analysand's narrative, take a neutral stance, and observe what evolves? My point is that the analyst's Zen practice will then in turn influence the intervention. For instance, if a patient expresses or otherwise exhibits anxiety directly, indirectly, explicitly, implicitly, consciously, or unconsciously, what will then be the analyst's response? What are the variations of quietist/introspectionist influences that reflect in an individual's psychotherapeutic stance? Will the therapist prescribe meditation as a palliative for anxiety? Will the therapist work with the patient in exploring the underlying factors contributing to the anxiety? Will the therapist use some combination of both? Similarly, we also need to ask, "What psychoanalysis are we talking about?" How do a particular psychoanalytic theory and the associated techniques influence one's perception and relation to Zen? There are many threads to pull on. Dogen's notion of "total exertion" serves as an illustration.

Total Exertion

Gujin, or "total exertion," reflects Zen's emphasis on in-the-moment presence and holds important treatment implications for the psychotherapist who is informed by Zen practice. Philosopher Joan Stambaugh (1999) describes total exertion from the perspective of the moment and writes, "Looked at from the standpoint of the situation itself, the situation is totally manifested or exerted without obstruction or contamination" (p. 6). With regard to the psychoanalytic situation, the notion of goal or a stance of removed passivity contaminates the situation and interferes with presence. Stambaugh asserts, "The person experiencing the situation totally becomes it. He is not thinking *about* it; he *is* it. When he does this, the situation is completely revealed and manifested" (p. 6). From this perspective, the psychotherapist's activity becomes decisive, clean, clear, and precise, not encumbered by guilt, anxiety, convention, or goals.

Total exertion faces being-as-it-is, which demands that neither Zen nor psychoanalysis attempt to engender a replacement or substitution of one set of concepts and beliefs, viewed as erroneous from the standpoint of a dominant worldview, with another set of notions deemed as "more correct." To embrace both Zen and psychoanalysis in the ideal is to relinquish any claim to science or religion in the traditional sense. This can be accomplished, as I noted above, by scrutinizing and questioning the background semiotic systems that influence our thinking and perception. They too become the subject of scrutiny and deconstruction as all fixation points are questioned and challenged.

Zen, for instance, has frequently been misunderstood as a pursuit of silence that destroys language. However, when *prajna* (intuited wisdom) emerges, truth can be expressed and grasped through both language and silence. To favor one side or the other—language or silence—would reflect a dualistic position and an associated reification that engenders polarization and dogmatism. The notion of zazen as exclusively a palliative, a major common misunderstanding, centers on the overemphasis and purpose of meditation. For instance, clinicians frequently ask about how I use meditation with my patients. This emphasis overlooks important relational dynamics that occur through koan study, which not unlike the psychoanalytic endeavor challenge us to think differently about ourselves and others. Meditation is frequently thought of exclusively as a palliative for stress and anxiety and is frequently applied in a prescriptive way. While effective, when used as a stress reducer, this use overlooks its religious function, which is to support the Zen salvational intention. Further, from a psychoanalytic perspective, this use overlooks unconsciously mobilized transference and countertransference dynamics and the underlying roots of the anxiety. Such a prescriptive application can function as a form of counterresistance on the part of the therapist to the deepening impact that can occur in the therapeutic encounter.

Alphabetized: Being and About

It will be instructive here to elaborate the distinction between *being* and *about* made above. Bion's notion of alpha function serves to enter the discussion. He describes alpha function as a process by which the basic raw experience of sensations and affects, which he describes as "beta elements," are worked over and transformed into the precursors or the material of thought. This formulation explains, as Eigen (2004a) writes, "how feelings become real for us, how 'emotional digestion' works" (p. 76). Bion and his followers have spoken extensively about the failure of alpha function in the absence or failure or deficiency of maternal reverie, the lack of, which Lopez-Corvo (2006), for instance, notes, "will hamper the possibility of structuring an alpha function" (p. 99). From this theoretical perspective, Ferro (2005) details the manner in which pathology occurs as a result of deficient or lacking alpha function or in which the alpha function cannot process the intensity and extent of incoming stimuli.

Zen experience informs me that just as such deficiencies, described by the above authors, require attention, one can become over "alpha-betized." This experience finds expression in the human tendency to seek out, discover, uncover, and recover what is the cause, the reason, the why, or the meaning of experience. Becoming alphabetized contributes to what Rhode (1998) describes as viewing the world in a limited and "lexical" manner, imagining that everything must make sense, that we feel comfortable when things make sense, as if all experience can be lined up alphabetically or numerically, as if the crucial existential questions of life can be answered by consulting a master dictionary, as if dream images are devoid of unique meanings for the individual, as if the koan can be "solved" or answered logically and intellectually, as if, as Rhode notes, with regard to the medical vertex, "it has no place in it for a concept of unknowable internalization—a concept of unknowable becoming" (p. 20). Such problems and dilemmas constituted the agenda of the positivists, not the Zenist. These basic existential questions are the type that Zen teachers characteristically and repeatedly scoff at. The Zen literature is filled with stories reflecting this attitude. This sense making operates at the expense of a view of the infinite and creative potential of openings into the unknown. This tendency becomes institutionalized and rationalized through overreliance on theory, logic, linear thinking, and sense making and results in deemphasizing, thus inadvertently buffering, and at the extreme foreclosing the felt, lived impact of experiencing Truth as we find it. Grotstein (2007), for example, takes it a step further. He describes psychoanalytic theories as "veritable psychoanalytic manic defenses against the unknown, unknowable, ineffable, inscrutable, ontological experience of ultimate being, what Bion terms 'Absolute Truth,' 'Ultimate Reality.' It is beyond words, beyond contemplation, beyond knowing, and always remains '*beyond*' in dimensions forever unreachable by man" (p. 121).

Zen practice demands a stripping away of such defenses, which are often characterized in Zen parlance as "dualistic thinking." Practice, in this respect, demands *being*, not simply talking *about*, a koan. Performing, not informing and not speaking, as the Zen master demands, when he says, "Show me!" This demand, however, has often been misunderstood, even by serious Zen practitioners, as an exclusive "showing" at the expense of "telling," at the expense of dialogue, at the expense of intellect, and can result in a radical extremism that devalues dialogue and which has clearly been the subject of criticism among contemporary Zen scholars and practitioners who assert that intellectual and intuitive capacities require integration, and that prioritization of one over the other represents dualistic thinking (Heine, 1994; Hori, 2000, 2003). McRae (2000), for instance, describes the interview between teacher and student as an "encounter dialogue," which he notes involves "a particular type of oral practice in which masters and students interact in certain definable, if unpredictable ways" (p. 47).

This radical disregard for the intellect has clearly not been my experience with several Zen teachers whom I have studied and practiced with over the years, who all, without exception, encouraged discussion, especially during our early meetings. Without exception, these teachers consistently worked through this misconception on my part, which was typically expressed through my own attempts to derail dialogue and that interfered with genuine relatedness. These efforts on my part, while consciously reflecting my intention to demonstrate, in no uncertain terms, my own level of realization, also functioned, at the time, more as expressions of my own unconscious character-driven avoidance tactics than any true expression of any Zen realization, or, as my analyst used to assert it at the time, "You prefer to be a moving target rather than a sitting duck."

The relationship between Zen teacher and student is fluid with specific identifiable phases that traverse the full range between *being* and *about*. For instance, Daido Loori (2009), American Zen master and abbot of Zen Mountain Monastery in Mt. Tremper, New York, outlines this flow as follows:

> The first stage is very much like a child with a parent. The teacher is very direc-
> tive. "This is the way you sit. This is the way you hold your hands. This is the
> way you breathe." It's to get the student started. That quickly dissolves into
> a relationship in which the teacher is more of a spiritual guide, pointing the
> way. The teacher becomes a spiritual mentor. Then that dissolves into spiritual
> equals. The teacher disappears. Finally the teacher and the student exchange
> positions—the teacher becomes the student, the student becomes the teacher.
> That's when transmission takes place. (p. 41)

In this regard, we take in the qualities of our teachers, although teachers will consciously work against such identifications in order to facilitate a process for the student of opening up to who one is, to "true self."
However, just as maternal reverie, according to Bion, facilitates alpha
function and the development of the capacity to digest and use raw experience, the power of unconscious identification and internalization through
cycles of projection and introjection can exert a strong influence in shap-
ing the student's perception, experience, and expression of Zen.

Loori, in describing his experience with his teacher, characterizes the
conversations as sparse. The terseness of language that Loori describes can
be reflective of the evolution of the relationship interacting with both cultural influences and personalities. For instance, during my *sui-zen** training with Japanese teachers, basically nothing was spoken. Teaching was
exclusively through example, playing together, and demonstration. Given
this traditional formalized Japanese teaching style, certain teachers said
more or less than others. By contrast, American teachers who I have studied with tend to speak quite a bit, providing guidance and historical information in between demonstrations and explications on technique. Within
this interactive context, this group of teachers displayed a wide range of
personal variation. For example, one teacher would usually take a break in
between pieces to serve tea during our lessons.

Similarly, the relation between *being* and *about* can be observed in different approaches to psychoanalysis. One approach hinges on the view of

---

* Sui-zen: Literally "blowing meditation," practiced with a shakuhachi, a bamboo flute played
vertically.

psychoanalysis as a collection of theories and related techniques applied to specifically diagnosed pathologies with cure as a goal. The practitioner stands outside looking in and applies the tools. The notion of cure as an exclusive goal can become problematic and, at the extreme, can be intertwined with intolerance, greed, aggression, or fear. Conformity to a system of techniques, at the extreme, reflects an expectation that the analysand conforms. With regard to the role of cure, Barratt (1993) draws a distinction between "psychotherapeutic efficacy" and "psychoanalytic truthfulness and transformation" (p. 41). He further observes that "in short the psychoanalytic method is not the generation of formulas by which lives may be encoded and guided" (p. 42). Joshu's silence and Loori's pronouncement "I am a worthless wretch and have nothing to show you, go see for yourself!" both exemplify this position.

Alternatively, the psychoanalyst facilitates and engages in a free-associative inquiry that constitutes the psychoanalytic dialogue relating to the individual's uniqueness in an accepting and creative way. The ensuing transformative conversation is unique and integrates varying levels of both *being* and *about*. Barrett's observation holds relevance for both disciplines. He notes that "the secret of the psychoanalytic method is the very engagement of a discourse wherein the fixity and certainty of any proffered epistemic configuration are dislodged ... what psychoanalysis offers the subject is thus its discourse as *Otherwise*" (p. 12, emphasis in original).

Dogen's poem, quoted above, points to nonprivileging of silence or dialogue, demonstration, or talking about. In this regard, "experiential being" does not exclude "talking about" direct experience and does not always exclude intellectual discourse. We are thinking and feeling beings. Our relationships are fluid. Such an option and misperception betrays subtle splits and reinforces dualistic thinking. Rather, *being* and *about* become harmonized and exemplify the abstract notion of the identity of the relative and the absolute. *Being* does not exclude *about* or other capacities. Rather, the dialogue evolves and opens an expanded enriched sense of who we are in relation to each other, for instance, as Loori notes in the quotation above, when student and teacher exchange roles.

The Zen master and the student, often through formal ritual, express a commitment to partake in truth evolutions through varying and oscillating combinations of *about* and *being*, discovering moments of balance of simultaneous separateness and oneness. In this way, the ensuing dialogue occurring in the interview reestablishes the basic rhythm of one's personal oscillation, which in this sense becomes restorative and refreshing, albeit at times shocking, disorienting, and terrifying, and often, in my experience, includes a discussion of basic human experiences.

With experience, a sense of trust develops. One begins to experience the breakup of exclusive reliance on the intellect, or dualistic thinking, as Zenists frequently describe it. Breakups in momentary doses exert a beneficial and integrating impact that engenders a psychic balance between *being* and *about*. The transitory and unstable nature of experiences of clarity and insight can be frustratingly fragmentary, occurring in split-second moments. Grasping engenders reification. We grasp at idealized "preferred psychological states."* These states are partial and tantalizing. Zen masters typically dismiss such states and advocate continued practice. Enlightenment experiences in their seductiveness can engender complacency. In such states, we fail to realize that there is no endpoint. We practice. We are plucky goats, and we keep on going. This is the significance of such mandates as "Enlightenment, throw it away!" or "If you see the Buddha, kill the Buddha!" However, as brief as these momentary experiences might be, they can exert a profound influence on our lives in subtle, yet dramatic ways and reverberate outwardly as shifts occur in one's mode of being in the world and affect those individuals with whom we come in contact. This is what I feel in relation to my teacher regardless of whether she is terse or expansive when we meet.

This process takes time and depends on the development of trust in the other and faith in the process. Eigen (2004a), in a discussion of recovery from breakdown, describes a parallel relationship in psychoanalysis. He writes, "One must feel the Other's fidelity in order to risk finding the place of breaking and coming together, in order to establish this psychic pulse-beat" (pp. 23–24). For example, after finishing this manuscript, I commented to Enkyo Pat O'Hara, Roshi, the founder and abbot of Village Zendo in New York City, that I felt like a fraud, that people view me as some kind of expert, which I clearly know I am not. She responded: "How do you think I feel? All of my students expecting me to be enlightened all of the time?" This was followed by shared heartfelt laughter that drove home the point that after all, we are simply human beings seeking the truth together.

This idealized expectation or illusion that the teacher is enlightened or perfect is simultaneously devaluing and dehumanizing because there is a failure to see the teacher in real or human terms. Stefano Baragato, Sensei, would say during interviews, "If we were perfect we would not need the teachings!"

---

* Personal conversation with Sojun Diane Martin, Roshi and Abbott of Udumbara Zen Center.

There is a grandiose expectation of perfection, a perfect mother, father, breast, mirror, anchor. Growth requires seeing through the transparency of this illusion and the accompanying expectations, suffering through the disappointment and realizing that we are simply human beings struggling together. Giving up this idealization of the teacher, giving up this grandiose expectation, requires giving up one's own grandiosity and the idea of the notion that we will find some permanent state of incorruptible perfection.

Nick's Safe Harbor

Similarly, in psychotherapy the patient often entertains the fantasy and holds the desire of some conflict-free endpoint where everything will forever be fine, smooth, and seamless, and he or she will live the fairy tale existence of a "happily ever after." One patient Nick described a "safe harbor" free from waves, turbulence, and chaos. He imagined a move out of the city to a rural environment where he speculated that "I can grow flowers, walk my dog, play music, whatever." I noticed that he would run from relationships when "things would heat up," when the waves appear. He has trouble realizing that the safe harbor is in how an individual or a couple negotiates the waves as they rise and fall. How do they ride them out without drowning in the conflict? Is collaborative and sensitive communication possible, or do defensive aggressive flight/fight patterns emerge? Can we own our humanness in a way that facilitates feeling and surviving the impacts of self and other on self and other? This safe harbor wish might be related to early experiences and might be successfully analyzed. However, analysis can only strengthen the capacity to work with such states, not necessarily make them disappear.

The implication for both Zen and psychoanalysis is the willingness for two individuals to participate in a shared endeavor of becoming real, being human, and living sensitively and compassionately as we become "partners in Truth." From this perspective, the question as I see it becomes not whether to privilege *being* or *about* but how we use or misuse *being* and *about*. Do we exploit their capacities to resist or reveal Truth? Realistically, we operate through variations of blends of both. They are not mutually exclusive. Functions are variable and subject to rising and falling oscillations. The teacher's or the analyst's flexibility to enter both forms of encounter and variations of both engenders growth. Can we transcend such either/or's and ask "How real can we become to ourselves? How real can we become to others?" We will revisit the nondualist understanding of the narrative function of Zen training and psychoanalysis with regard to the rational and nonrational aspects of koan study in Chapter 3.

Concluding Remarks

There is more to definition than I have unpacked. Both Zen and psychoanalysis explore, work with, and endeavor to alter mind, which is fluid, elusive, and intangible. As psychoanalysts, many relevant questions emerge. For instance, how do we nurture and extend these processes to encourage and preserve their potentiality without suffocating and restricting them? How do we keep them growing and evolving? How do we address rigidity, dogmatism, and empty ritualism? How do psychoanalysis and Zen as lived and living disciplines remain open and contribute to creative ways of effectively addressing suffering and human potential? These are questions that have no definite answers; however, they need to be kept in mind in relation to each individual we encounter as psychoanalysts and as human beings in the world.

Do the systems that investigate and work with mind require definitions that strictly adhere to the scientific model? In this respect, the following quote holds relevance to both Zen and psychoanalysis:

> The problem, I think, of great relevance here, is on the one hand the confusion between the phenomena of mind itself, and on the other hand the psychoanalytical methodology used to explore and change the mind. To accuse psychoanalysis of not being an exact science is, in summary, a barbarism, a pleonasm. To be more specific, it is equivalent to stating that surgery is too bloody, car mechanics too greasy, or swimming too wet. In other words, is vagueness the problem in psychoanalytic methodology, or is such vagueness a characteristic of the organ to be explored? (Lopez-Corvo, 2006, p. 22)

As a religion Zen does not particularly strive for definition or nondefinition. D. T. Suzuki (1949) observes that "Zen does not give us any intellectual assistance, nor does it waste time arguing the point with us, but it merely suggests or indicates, not because it wants to be indefinite, but because that is really the only thing it can do for us" (pp. 244–245). It simply just is. The notion that Zen defies definition, as exemplified in this quote, seems to go hand in hand specifically with contemporary Western notions of Zen. This idea might be due in part to the influence of D. T. Suzuki's Rinzai orientation, driven by a sectarian bias and that seemingly promotes the overprivileging of silence over words and illogic over reason.

This reading of the Rinzai Zen tradition has been questioned in the light of contemporary scholarship (Heine, 1997; Hori, 2003). Additionally, Zen's radical iconoclasm articulated through apophatic discourse constantly "speaks away" (Sells, 1994) anything that might be said to define Zen. However, it is this directness of language and its apophatic structure that contributed to Zen's uniqueness and, as Robert Buswell (1987) notes, accounts for its "autonomous sectarian identity" (p. 321). One form that this takes is its refusal, in some quarters, to be defined as a religion. This refusal appears to be multidetermined and contributes to difficulty with any definition.

One explanation centers on the predominant monotheistic religious ethos in the West coupled with modern scientific nihilism among the scientifically oriented psychological community such as psychoanalysts, who have taken their lead from Freud and who tend to pathologize religious experience. The psychoanalytic tendency to psychoanalyze cultural phenomena such as religious systems and experiences engenders a bias that can leave its own basic assumptions unquestioned, such as the classical psychoanalytic belief that everything can be "known" as the unconscious becomes conscious; everything can be defined; everything makes sense when unconscious motivations for seemingly irrational thoughts and behaviors are revealed. This orientation becomes a secular version of the "transcendental privilege" that Ch'an scholar Bernard Faure argues obscured the Christian missionary perception and resulted in a highly critical response to Zen. This bias, whether secular or religious, can interfere with self-reflection and an open-ended cross-fertilization between Zen and psychoanalysis through an open-ended agenda-free dialogue.

Here lies a common thread that paradoxically ties these two otherwise contradictory systems of religion and psychology: the monotheistic notion of essence or soul and its secularized version of the notion of an abiding, cohesive, and independent sense of self. Both of these core aspects of Western religious and scientific ethos are subject to scrutiny and deconstruction through Zen practice. Following Freud, it seems that many Zenists, in order to be taken seriously by their scientifically oriented colleagues, tend to distance themselves from religiosity of the tradition and present Zen exclusively as a science, technique, or philosophy. As a result, Zen has been described in the West, as exemplified above by Watts's definition, as a science, technique, philosophy, mystical tradition, psychology, but not as a religion.

Zen is what it is, no more and no less, whether or not we call it a philosophy, science, religion, or a spiritual path. In this regard, I don't care how Zen comes to be defined. Zen still is what it is—its practices, beliefs (nonbeliefs), experiences, rituals, and prayers. Belief in no-belief is a belief; a no-definition is a definition. Thoughts are a way of making something out of nothing. Practices such as zazen or *Mu* cut through the creation and reification of the many some-things that we create to ease fundamental anxiety. Ultimately, practice requires deconstruction. How does one unsay practice? How does one unsay Zen?

2

First Encounters of a Distant Kind

> If you call this a stick, you affirm; if you call it not a stick, you negate. Beyond affirmation and negation what would you call it?
>
> —Tai-hui (D. T. Suzuki, 1994, p. 287)*

Introduction

This chapter begins with a review of the Jesuit missionary encounters with Zen Buddhism beginning in the 16th century and examines basic misunderstandings promoted by the Jesuits that set the tone for the European response to Zen, which in turn influenced the early pathologizing response among psychoanalysts. The roots of this misunderstanding derive from differing conceptions of being and nonbeing held by the Jesuit missionaries and by the Zenists, which contributed to a negative attitude toward Zen religious practice and monastic life. I conclude with a discussion of implications for psychoanalysis.

As I mentioned in the introduction, Buddhist thought and practice have become increasingly popular among psychoanalysts and psychotherapists. This current trend represents a complete turnaround from Freud's (1927, 1930) critique of religion and Alexander's (1931) negative depiction of Buddhist meditation. A rapidly expanding literature on the integration of the two disciplines reflects this upsurge in interest and serves as a testimony to the positive reception of the various schools of Buddhism

---

* Ta-hui (1089–1163): 12th-century Chinese Zen master best known as a keen advocate of the use of koan practice (kanna-zen) to achieve enlightenment. Although he saw koan practice as the most effective method to enlightenment, he believed that koan practice had degenerated into superficial literary study, and in a radical move, he ordered the suppression of his own teacher's masterly collection of koans, The Blue Cliff Record, burning all copies and the printing plates. The text remained out of circulation for the next two centuries.

among psychoanalysts.* Increasingly, contemporary psychoanalysts and
psychotherapists actively practice some form of Buddhism. In contrast, the
early psychoanalytic response to Zen, whether pathologizing or positive,
was primarily intellectual. Similarly, many longtime Buddhist practitioners are finding their way into psychoanalysis and psychoanalytic training. Despite this recent enthusiasm, the basic limiting misunderstanding
that Buddhist practice is no more than a form of nihilist quietism continues to appear both explicitly and implicitly in the current literature.

Roots: Emptiness and Dependent Arising

The initial negative response to Zen practice and beliefs consisted primarily
of an attack on what at first glance seemed to be an annihilationist philosophy coupled with quietist practices that this group of Jesuits viewed as fos-
tering a total annihilation of the self and a deadening of mental processes.

Jesuit missionaries, who, beginning in the 16th century, traveled
throughout China and Japan, set a tone for the European intellectual
and religious response to Zen, which persisted for centuries. Basically,
the Jesuits failed to appreciate the experiential, salvational, and religious
significance of Buddhist *sunyata* (emptiness, voidness), which, together
with *pratityasamutpada* (dependent arising, dependent origination, interdependent co-origination), constitutes what Buddhist philosopher Gadjin
Nagao (1989), for instance, describes as the foundational cornerstones and
nexus of Buddhist ideology and practice.

From a primarily experiential base Zen has explicated the notion of the
Two Truths. This antinomian teaching expresses the experiential awareness of reality engendered through Zen study and practice. The principles
of *sunyata* and *pratityasamutpada* describe this relationship between what
Zen Buddhists depict as ultimate or absolute and relative or empirical existence. In brief, emptiness or voidness refers to the lack of inherent, absolute,
eternal, separate, or "own" existence of self and phenomena independent
of any causes or conditions. Dependent arising or interdependent origination, the complement to *sunyata*, refers to the notion that all existence
arises contextually subject to causes and conditions. Thus, all phenomena,
and hence all experience, exist relatively or empirically, but not inherently,
absolutely, eternally, or independently. The Zen practitioners encountered

---

* See Cooper (1998, 2007), Epstein (1984, 1988, 1995), Langan (2006), Magid (2005), Molino (1998),
  Rubin (1996), Safran (2003), Suler (1993), and Weber (2006).

by the Jesuits refuted absolute or ultimate existence but accepted relative or empirical existence. The Zen expression "coming down from the mountain cave and going into the marketplace," for instance, exemplifies the importance of relative existence. Additionally, Zen thought describes transcendence in immanence and vice versa. To imagine otherwise, from the Zen perspective, reflects dualistic thinking. This nondualistic perspective finds expression, for example, in the following doctrinal poems written by Dogen, the highly influential 13th-century Japanese Zen monk:

> Day and night
> Night and day,
> The way of Dharma* as everyday
>   life;
> In each act our hearts
> Resonate with the call of the sutra.

(Heine, 1997, p. 97: 3J)

and

> Attaining the heart
> Of the sutra,
> Are not even the sounds
> Of the bustling market place
> The preaching of the Dharma?

(Heine, 1997, p. 97: 5J)

As noted above, Zen practice evokes an experiential intuitive insight into emptiness and dependent arising. When paying close attention to experience through various practices, according to Buddhist phenomenology, the practitioner will discover, as 3rd-century Indian Buddhist sage Nagarjuna asserts: "Arising," "enduring," and "disintegrating"; "existing" and "non-existing"; ... do not have true existence. These terms are used by the Buddha in accordance with worldly conventions"[†] (Komito, 1987, p. 97). Ultimately, phenomena are not as solid as the individual automatically and unconsciously alters perception to have them appear. Buddhist techniques of liberation demonstrate the transparency and insubstantiality of what appears permanent, solid, and eternal.

---

* Dharma: Right living, right conduct, path to higher truth.
† In this context "true existence" means ultimate, permanent, eternal, and independent of causes and conditions.

The Zen notion of the Two Truths frustrated the Jesuits, who relied exclusively on reason and logic in their attempts to convert the Zenists to Christianity. The Jesuit missionaries never considered the Zenist assertion that any notion of an ultimate God/creator is inadequate. On this issue, Abe (1985) writes that "for Buddhists, each and every thing is neither the creation of a transcendent God, nor something immanent … but rather dependently co-arising without an eternal substantial selfhood" (p. 126). From the psychoanalytic perspective, we can say that the Jesuits limited their response to the Zenists to secondary processes, whereas the Zenists utilized both primary and secondary processes, which Zen practice makes accessible.*

Emptiness, as noted above, was not clearly understood by the 16th-century Jesuits and by Europeans who relied on these early missionary accounts for information from which to draw their conclusions about Buddhism. The Jesuits did not understand, to quote D. T. Suzuki (1972a), that "emptiness is not a negative idea, nor does it mean privation, but as it is not in the realm of names and forms, it is called emptiness, or nothingness, or the void" (p. 60).

First Encounters

Basque Jesuit missionary Frances Xavier arrived in Kagoshima, Japan, in 1549. He was followed by Italian Alessandro Valignano in 1579. Italian Jesuit Matteo Ricci arrived in southern China in 1582. This group of Jesuits initiated missionary endeavors and provided the first reports of Zen to Europe through extensive and detailed travel diaries. Ricci's successor, the iconoclastic and aggressive evangelist Nichola Longobardo and his followers, who established the Peking Mission in 1685, most notably Charles LeGobien, Louis LeComte, and Joachim Bouver, exerted a profound influence, as Faure (1993) notes, "on all Western descriptions of Buddhist monasticism" (p. 29). The highly influential 18th-century Jesuit historian and geographer Jean Baptiste-duHalde, for instance, who had never traveled to Asia and who relied exclusively on missionary accounts, described the Zenists as apathetic, monstrously stupid, and amoral. Speaking of so-called quietist practices, he argued "that to aspire to this foolish Inactivity is renouncing the most essential duties … and that if this Doctrine was

---

* See Chapter 6 for a detailed explication of similar limitations in contemporary psychoanalytic scholarship that neglects unconscious processes.

follow'd it would reduce all Members of a State to a Condition much inferior to that of beasts" (Faure, 1993, p. 30).

Similarly, Freud also relied exclusively on secondhand information derived from his correspondence with the French poet and mystic Romaine Rolland, who was a disciple of the Indian guru Sri Ramakrishna, to inform his negative response to Indian meditation (Parsons, 1999).

The Jesuit narratives, fueled by missionary zeal, for the most part, consisted of scathing critiques of Zen beliefs and practices. The highly subjective, obviously biased nature of these reports served colonial expansionist efforts and sectarian ends in both Asia and Europe. For example, the Jesuits endeavored to curry favor with the dominant Confucionists in China, who were critical of the Buddhists. Consider Ricci's depiction of Ch'an practitioners that he encountered:

> This special class of temple servants is considered to be, and in reality is, the lowest and most despised caste in the whole kingdom. They come from the very dregs of the populace.... Not a single one of them could ever have elected of his own will to join this vile class of cenobites* as a means of leading a holy life ... their natural bent to evil becomes worse with the lapse of time.... (Gallagher, 1942, pp. 100–101)

Xavier's response to Zen was complex, ambivalent, and shifted over time. He expressed enthusiasm for the Japanese people in general. Contemporary Jesuit and long-term resident of Japan William Johnston has noted that "within a few months of his arrival, Xavier had fallen in love with the Japanese whom he called the joy of his heart and it seems to me that we shall never find another race to equal the Japanese" (Endo, 1969, pp. vii–viii). It is quite clear that Xavier's comments where meant for Japanese converts to Catholicism. However, he initially described Zen as a "satanic cult" comprised of "men without faith." In a critical review of these early Jesuit encounters with Far East Asian Buddhism, Faure (1993) notes that "the depravity of the Buddhist is a recurring theme in Xavier's descriptions of Japan and he boldly attempted to amend the ways of the monks he met" (p. 17).

The Jesuits confused emptiness for nothingness. Thus the practice of meditation came to be misunderstood by Ricci, Xavier, and their colleagues as a technique for inducing a state of quietism eventuating in the annihilation of the mind. This negative view of Zen practice was further exacerbated by Protestant missionaries who, according to Faure, held

---

* That is, monastics.

Buddhism in "active contempt for what was considered mere atheism and paganism" (p. 36).

The erroneous view, held by the Jesuits, that Buddhism is exclusively a form of annihilationism led to the false notion that Buddhists engaged in meditation practice simply to clear the practitioner's conscience. As a result, the Jesuit missionaries failed to appreciate Zen's religious basis and radical salvational impulse.

Ricci's negative response to Chinese Buddhism was multidetermined and might best be understood in its political-religious context. Politically, on the one hand, Ricci strived to align himself with the dominant Confucionists. On the other hand, religiously, Ricci has been described as an "aggressive Counter-reformation" Catholic "engaged in a spiritual battle to win over Chinese society to Christianity" (Faure, 1993, p. 24). This missionary agenda was further complicated by the strong negative reaction among his fellow Jesuits and European Catholics to his Confucionist leanings. In this regard, Ricci's condemnation of Zen also served to maintain his Catholic Orthodoxy in the eyes of his critics who he had alienated. From a theological perspective, Faure noted that "in a sense the Jesuits had more in common with Buddhist intellectuals than with the Confucionists, and this resemblance may explain the hostility of the former Ricci toward his Ch'an counterparts, and his eagerness to distance himself from them" (p. 27).

Ricci's confusion between Buddhist emptiness and nihilism influenced all subsequent thought and has left an indelible mark on Buddhist studies in the West.* With few notable exceptions, this negative response to Zen continued through the 1920s. For instance, French philosopher Jules Bartolomy Saint-Hillaire, who wrote in 1895 (the same year that Freud published his monumental *Studies in Hysteria*), condemned Buddhism as pure nihilism. Speaking of meditation as practiced by followers of Ch'an Buddhists he wrote: "By this transitory ecstatic state a transitory annihilation is already sought in Nirvana" (p. 144). In 1927, Jesuit Leon Wieger, a Protestant convert to Catholicism, wrote "now such contemplation cannot be sustained as an intellectual act. The only result that it can produce, if it is practiced seriously, is idiocy" (p. 54). Wieger further noted that "at present, the best among them are idle quietists and stupid dreamers" (p. 528). Henri Doré, writing during the same period, described the Zen practice as a preoccupation "to dream idly and do nothing" (1914/1938, p. 23). Scottish theologian James Stewart (1926), also writing during the same

---

* For an extensive review of this negative influence see Almond (1988, pp. 119–123).

period, described the Zenists as "misguided seekers who became half comatose creatures devoid of the glow and splendor of the Divine image within" (p. 254).

Similarly, German psychoanalyst Franz Alexander delivered a paper in Berlin at the Seventh Congress of the International Psychoanalytic Association in 1922 (which was published in *The Psychoanalytic Review* in 1931) with the title "Buddhist Meditation as an Artificial Catatonia." As the title suggests, the paper presents a scathing critique of Buddhist meditation. Alexander sets up Buddhism, which he describes as "the Nihilist theory of Gatama Buddha" (p. 132), as a straw dog through which he promoted his own agenda regarding the perennial mind/body question. Alexander, who comments on the Four Foundations of Mindfulness, writes:

> From our present psychoanalytical knowledge it is clear that Buddhistic self-absorption is a libidinal, narcissistic turning of the urge for knowing inward, a sort of artificial schizophrenia with complete withdrawal of libidinal interest in the outside world. (p. 130)

He adds: "Likewise, in Buddhistic self-absorption the turning of the perceptive consciousness inward is an end in itself, a narcissistic–masochistic affair ... it eliminates reality" (p. 131).

Not unlike his Jesuit contemporaries, Alexander (1931) based his critique on secondhand accounts of Buddhist monastic life. For instance, he quotes Heiler who wrote: "Deep sorrow shakes the meditator, bitter contempt of the world fills him" (p. 133). As a result, Alexander concludes: "It is thus that Heiler describes this phase of absorption, which, in the light of our clinical psychoanalytical knowledge, is exceedingly clear and especially interesting, inasmuch as it presents an experimentally induced melancholia" (p. 133).

For Alexander, nirvana, engendered through meditation, is "a condition which ascribes to the schizophrenic in his catatonic ecstasy" (p. 134). From this pathologizing perspective, nirvana becomes the intensified endpoint of a systematically self-destructive regression. This argument that Buddhism is completely regressive overlooks the Buddhist antinomian perspective. While he correctly asserts that "a distinction between subject and object is truly necessary to an understanding of the libido concept" (p. 137), he incorrectly concludes that Buddhist practice obliterates all object relations in a posited regression. As noted above, Buddhists negate ultimate or absolute reality, not relative or empirical reality. The "one and the many," as Zenists put it, paradoxically coexist. The significance of this identity of the relative and the absolute with respect to clinical experience, transference, and countertransference management will be explicated in subsequent chapters.

Alternatives

In contrast to Alexander, Robert Langan (2006) provides a receptive contemporary reading of the Four Foundations of Mindfulness. Langan compares the goal of psychoanalysis with the fourth foundation of mindfulness, which is mindfulness of mental phenomena, and writes: "Accordingly, its goal, like that of the fourth foundation, is to witness the flow of mental phenomena with discernment. Its goal is an alteration of one's way of being" (p. 50). This witnessing includes the mental phenomena of self and other and in this respect reveals a significant relational dimension and is anything but the narcissistic withdrawal that Alexander suggests. Additionally, whereas Alexander relied on secondhand accounts for his evaluation of Buddhist practice and is in this respect highly speculative, Langan describes his active engagement in Buddhist practice. His descriptions explicate an experiential awareness that derives from serious, committed, ongoing practice.

Fauteux (1995) acknowledges regression in religious experience, but questions the exclusively pathologizing response to religiously engendered regression. He describes stages of religious practice and notes that regression can serve a reparative function, which he compares to the creative process. He concludes:

> The religious individual's disciplined purgation of self can be similar to the artist's disciplined attempt to pierce the superficial self, with both resulting in the recovery of repressed primary processes that lead to illumination in religious experience and to inspiration in art. (p. 33)

The negative evaluation of Buddhist meditation has persisted over the years. For example, Dickes (1965) characterizes Buddhist meditation as a trance phenomenon akin to hypnosis. Relying on secondhand sources, he writes:

> Buddhist monks who devote themselves to meditation deliberately invoke trance states using the typical methods of the hypnotist. The monks' exercises begin with breath control, and then continue with mental concentration, with or without the aid of fixing the gaze on a device such as a patch of color, a spot of earth, a cup of water, the air in an empty bowl, or the flame of a lamp. Then by progressive stages the monk proceeds to abstraction and trance. The

description presented portrays the development of a state indistinguishable from the hypnotic state. (p. 388)

This critical tendency persists, albeit in disguised form in the present. For example, many contemporary psychotherapists and interfaith practitioners view Zen as a practice or a technique rather than as a religion. This view neutralizes Zen of its radical soteriological intention, and in my opinion, this view can function to protect the practitioner from confrontation with cherished beliefs, most notably a belief in an inherently existing permanent immortal soul and the accompanying belief in a supreme being, heaven, hell, or eternal life.

The propensity toward using Zen practices to enhance psychoanalytic technique or to further the goals of Western religious systems serves as a specific example of a general trend in Western scientific, philosophical, and religious discourse that derives from a need to subsume and translate all discourse into the semiotic structures of its own belief systems.

With respect to the psychoanalytic reception of Zen in reductionist terms, one needs to relinquish its preferred mode of discourse, based on a scientific model, and as Faure (1993) notes, to "avoid organizing, stabilizing, and neutralizing multiplicities, according to one's own axes of meaning" (p. 10).

An alternative language that places both traditions on a level playing field demands a fuller, freer, and more spontaneous expression that integrates both performative and informative elements. The notion of fuller and freer expression finds articulation in, for example, Wilfred Bion's (1967) work. He observes that as a result of the therapeutic encounter, the patient will display a fuller and wider range of emotional experience.

Zen's radical iconoclastic stance gears itself toward similar ends. This "positionless position" articulated in the Perfection of Wisdom literature provides a doctrinal foundation for understanding the implications and the context for Zen practice, and most notably for koan study. We will return to this point with respect to various koans in subsequent chapters. This becomes clear, for example, in Zen scholar William Powell's (1986) observation that "the Perfection of Wisdom suggests at least two attitudes relevant to the discourse records. It discredits the language of conceptualization, and it undermines distinctions made between *samsāra*** and

---

* Samsāra: Sanskrit term, literally "continuous movement" or "continuous flowing"; refers in Buddhism to the concept of a cycle of birth and consequent decay and death in which all beings participate.

nirvana,* ignorance and enlightenment, and phenomenal and ultimate reality" (p. 9).

Joshu's (778–897) response, *Mu* or *U* (Chapter 4) or silence (Chapter 5), exemplifies the Zen challenge of all reifications and positions. As apophatic discourse, Zen "speaks away" (Sells, 1994) or deconstructs all assertions, often through the use of questions and responses that are both positive and negative propositions, by challenges, by absurdity, by *non sequitur,* or by actions. The action of turning over the rice bucket and the ensuing dialogue described in the following anecdote from the *Record of Tung-shan* exemplify this point:

> Hsueh-feng was serving as the rice cook. Once, while he was culling pebbles from the rice, the Master asked, "Do you cull out pebbles and set the rice aside, or do you cull out the rice and set the pebbles aside?"
>
> "I set aside the rice and the pebbles at one and the same time," replied Hsueh-feng.
>
> "What will the monks eat?" asked the Master.
>
> Hsueh-feng immediately turned over the rice bucket.
>
> The Master said, "Given your basic affinities, you will be most compatible with Te-shan." (Powell, 1986, p. 37)

What is the Zen motivation to refute both being and nonbeing? We might speculate along with Michael Sells, who notes with regard to Western mystical discourse that "to do anything for God is merely an enslavement to the illusory self-identity of the ego-self" (Webb & Sells, 1997, p. 249).

Historically Zen iconoclasm has often been described as a reaction to mysticism. The literature often depicts exorcisms from visitations by evil spirits and other afflictions conducted by the Zen master. Evil spirits might be understood, as Bion (1970) suggests, as deriving from a lack of understanding of the natural world, such as when internal objects are not understood as such. On the other hand, following this line of thought, we might understand the psychoanalytic formulation of an internal object world as reflecting a lack of understanding of the natural world as well. Gods, demons, and states of grace, for example, are replaced by objects, selves, and the binding affects that psychoanalytic object relations theory posits.

What drives the Zen iconoclastic agenda that cuts through logic and that simultaneously cuts through self and object separation and reification? Bion (1970) argues that "knowledge is in the form of conceptions and image is a similar projection of the ego-self" (p. 249).

---

* Nirvana: Sanskrit term, literally "to cease blowing" (as when a candle flame ceases to flicker); the perfect peace of the mind free from craving, lust, aggression, and other afflictive states.

Here is another example from the *Record of Tung-shan* that exemplifies this point:

> After that Yun-chu constructed a hut on San-feng Mountain, he passed ten days there without coming to the meal hall. The master asked him, "Why haven't you come for meals these past several days?"
>
> "Because regularly, everyday, heavenly spirits bring me food," replied Yun-chu.
>
> The Master said, "Until now I have always said you were an exceptional person, but still you possess such views! Come to my place late tonight."
>
> Later that evening, when Yun-chu went to Tung-shan's room, the master called out, "Hut Master Ying!" When Yun-chu replied, "Don't think of good. Don't think of evil. What is it?"
>
> Yun-chu returned to his hut and peacefully took up meditation. From then on the heavenly spirits were completely unable to find him, and after three days, they ceased appearing. (Powell, 1986, p. 41)

Similarly, Bion (1970) criticizes dogmatic and psychically deadening interpretations. For Bion, interpretation, a cornerstone of psychoanalysis, depends not on such fixed or fixing knowledge but rather on an evolution of O that is common to analyst and analysand. It depends on the analyst "becoming 'O'" (p. 27).

One source of Zen iconoclasm is the doctrine of emptiness as explicated in the Perfection of Wisdom literature. Powell (1986) notes that "emptiness was understood in this tradition, in one sense, as the perception of reality that resulted from the deconstruction of the conceptual and verbal framework by which other Buddhists had sought to rationalize Buddhist teachings" (p. 9). Further, he notes that the "use of language to deconstruct seems to be a use of language that depends on nothing, in the sense of not arising out of an opposing conceptual system" (p. 9).

Bion (1970) captures this shift experientially in terms of his technical recommendations to relinquish memory, desire, and understanding. He writes:

> When the psychoanalyst anticipates some crisis, and especially if he has, or thinks he has, good grounds for anxiety, his tendency is to resort to memory and understanding to satisfy his desire for security (or to resort to "saturation" to avoid "unsaturation"). If he gives in to this tendency he is proceeding in a direction calculated to preclude any possibility of union with O. (p. 51)

Similarly, D. T. Suzuki describes this experience of discontinuity in relation to satori, which, as noted above, parallels Bion's conceptualization of the experience of O. Suzuki (1949) writes: "What a change satori brings in one's idea of things—that is, how it all upsets the former valuation of things generally, making one stand now entirely on a different footing" (p. 260).

Attachment to our religious objects, beliefs, gods, demons, or psychoanalytic theories saturates psychic space and occludes the intuitive experience stimulated by Zen practice. We might speculate that such rationalizations that reduce Zen practice to a useful technique reflect the operation of the pleasure/pain principle. This raises serious questions. With regard to Zen beliefs and practices, for instance, we might ask: What becomes of a foundational cornerstone, such as *sunyata* in relation to a lifelong belief in God, Jesus, or a supreme being? At some point, effective Zen practice will engender the transparency of such reified constructs. Additionally, what becomes of the structure of the practitioner's internal object world, a world that provides familiar reference points? Will the practitioner relinquish old beliefs, objects, self-images, gods, in the light of new and novel firsthand experiences or back away from Zen practice. I have encountered a number of serious Zen practitioners over the years who at some point found themselves "rediscovering the religion of their childhood." I wonder if such rapprochements reflect authentic growth or if they function as well-reasoned resistances to the evolution that Bion speaks of? It seems that the devaluation of Zen becomes a way, to a point, of having one's cake and eating it too. Bion's (1970) awareness of the human tendency to resist Truth is reflected in his comment that "a further source of distortion is the tendency to link Faith with the supernatural because of lack of experience of the 'natural' to which it relates" (p. 48). I wonder if the same statement applies to a highly intellectualized attachment to old theories and habituated techniques, which in turn accounts for the difficulty with an open-minded response to new and novel developments in the field.

Buddhist Critique of Quietism

Zen teachers have actively criticized quietist teachings and practices for centuries prior to the arrival of the Jesuits. They advise that balanced practice requires both mind-pacifying and insight-oriented techniques. Mind-pacifying techniques, according to this point of view, have their usefulness. Nevertheless, they are not adequate. Contemporary Zen teacher Dennis Merzel (1991) emphasizes this point by quoting 12th-century Zen master Kanchi Sosan, who asserts that "when the deep meaning of things is not understood the mind's essential peace is disturbed to no avail" (p. 3).

Sosan's use of the term "deep meaning of things" refers to the experiential realization of the emptiness and dependent arising of all phenomena.

Similarly, 12th-century Zen master Mumon, who authored *Mumonkan* (Gateless Barrier), an influential and important collection of 48 Zen koans, warns that "to sit blankly in quietism is the practice of the dead" (Merzel, 1994, first unnumbered page). This critique of quietism continues to be a consistent standpoint throughout the history of Zen. For example, speaking from a contemporary perspective, Yasutani Haku'un Roshi asserts that "it is probably possible to control the brain so that no thoughts arise, but that would be an inert state in which no creativity is possible" (Aitken, 1991, p. 11). Aitken adds that "such an endeavor only brings despair ... this practice is not intended as a denial of thoughts and feelings" (p. 12).

Kapleau (1966) observes:

> Zazen that leads to Self-realization is neither idle reverie nor vacant inaction but an intense inner struggle to gain control over the mind and then use it, like a silent missile, to penetrate the barrier of the five senses and the discursive intellect (i.e., the sixth sense). It demands determination, courage and energy. (p. 13).

Similarly, D. T. Suzuki (1949) notes:

> To do away with consciousness so that nothing will disturb spiritual serenity was too negative a state of mind to be sought after by those who at all aspired to develop the positive content of the Buddha's own enlightenment mind.... Enlightenment was to be found in life itself, in its fuller and freer expressions, and not in its cessation. (p. 85)

Far from asserting a nihilist stance, the Buddhist position presented the Jesuit missionary with a radical view that, if put to the test of religious praxes, could potentially dislodge the foundational cornerstone of the Jesuit beliefs. That is, all Zen praxes confront the notion of assigning ontological priority to being conceptualized as a distinct God or a supreme being that operates independently of causes and conditions. The Zen confrontation is not incidental. It is central.

In my own experience during sesshin, practice would intensify each day, with earlier risings and later bedtimes for increasingly longer formal sitting periods and encouragement to sit independently and informally during the diminishing free time at night. One could feel the group energy rising and intensifying to a fever pitch. The volume increasingly "pumped up," students being directed into the surrounding forest to shout *Mu* out loud, to scream *Mu* with all one's might. Although a great sense of peace would emerge during the sesshin, as a sort of side benefit, this in no way could be confused as a mind-deadening, quietist practice. Rather, a lucid, magnified, energized, in-the-moment alertness and a sense of decisive determination prevailed and would persist well beyond the retreats.

This anti-quietist stance and accompanying techniques hold practical implications. Merzel (1994) discusses the issue of misguided practices and notes that despite their usefulness, "from a dharma perspective, any teaching that does not cut the root of delusion, however helpful for other purposes, offers only partial truth" (p. 70). Further, he argues that "what gets lost is the importance of realization, genuine compassion and true transmission" (p. 90). The implications clearly extend to the world beyond theory and practice. The notions of compassion and transmission imply involvement with others, not nihilistic withdrawal.

Quietist/Introspectionist Controversy

These critiques of quietism advanced by Zen teachers, prior to contact with the Jesuits, point to the early existence of quietist tendencies among Zen practitioners. In China, during the early part of the 12th century, this quietist movement developed in opposition to the introspectionists. D. T. Suzuki chronicles this sectarian feud. He quotes a letter written by Tai-hui to his student Lü-Chi-I cautioning him against the quietists who question the value of insight leading to realization of emptiness. According to D. T. Suzuki (1994), Tai-hui writes:

> Lately there is an evil tendency growing up among certain followers of Zen who regard disease as cure.... What they aim at is to realize mere emptiness where there is no life, no noetic quality whatever—that is, a blank, nothingness which is regarded by them as something which is eternally beyond the limitations of time.... In order to reach this state of utter blankness and unfathomability, they consume so many bowls of rice each day and spend their time sitting stolidly and quietly. They think that this is what is meant by the attainment of absolute peace.... What a pity that they are altogether ignorant of the occasion when there is a sudden outburst [of intuitive knowledge in our minds]! (pp. 18–19)

The quietists had their rationale for their practice and beliefs that they unquestioningly traced back to the teachings of the historical Buddha and other influential teachers. They rely on a literal reading of scripture to support their position. Yet, their literal interpretation of scripture captures a dogmatic fundamentalism that eschews insight and introspection. For instance, Daiye, an advocate of the quietist position, asserts:

> When Sakyamuni was in Magadha he shut himself up in a room and remained silent for three weeks. Is this not an example given by the Buddha of the practice of silence? ... When Bodhidharma came over to this country he sat for nine years at Shao-lin forgetful of all worldly preachings. Is this not an example of silence shown by a patriarch? (D. T. Suzuki, 1994, p. 19)

Tai-hui counters these quietist arguments by asserting that "mere quiet sitting avails nothing, for it leads nowhere, as no turning-up takes place in one's mind" (p. 20). D. T. Suzuki concludes that "those quietists, whose mental horizon does not rise above the level of the so-called absolute silence of unfathomability, grope in the cave of darkness. They fail to open the eye of wisdom. This is where they need the guiding hand of a genuine Zen master" (p. 20).*

In his summary of the historical development of the Zen koan, D. T. Suzuki notes "the rampant growth of Zen quietism since the beginning of Zen history most dangerously threatened the living experience of Zen" (p. 95). It is from this historical perspective that Suzuki came to view the Zen koan as necessary "to save Zen from being buried alive in the darkness of quietism" (p. 95).

The assertion that supports the primacy of still mind, the introspectionists argued, stems from dualistic thought. That is, that stasis and movement are perceived as separate. Further, a high value is placed on utter stillness while movement is criticized. However, the same critique can be applied to the above critics of quietism. That is, the value of stasis can easily be overlooked. Extreme views from both camps in this sense reflect sectarian agendas and lose sight of the intention of either school's founding fathers (Heine, 1994). True realization knows the transitory nature of both stasis and turbulence. The enlightened individual experiences the emptiness of both conditions.

Dogen captures the nondualistic nature of truth in both stasis and movement in his poem "Zazen":

> The moon reflected
> In a mind clear as still water:

---

* Tai-hui's argument is relevant to contemporary psychotherapy in terms of the misguided use of meditation as a palliative without regard to unconscious meanings and transference/countertransference issues and without engendering insight. (See Chapters 6 and 10 for a detailed discussion of these issues.)

Even the waves breaking
Are reflecting its light.

(Heine, 1997, p. 117: 57-J)

Being and Nonbeing

The problem with the misperception of Zen practice as a nihilist quietism becomes clarified by examining the radically different perspectives between the Buddhist and Christian understandings of the relation between being and nonbeing. These differences explain the Jesuit negative response to Buddhism, which extended to both philosophy and practice.

From the philosophical perspective, Christian theology advocates the primacy of being over nonbeing. That is, the Christian conceptualization of Being, which precedes and supersedes nonbeing, sets up a dualistic theology articulated through the positing of a supreme being, the antithesis of light and dark, good and evil, sin and grace, devils and angels, heaven and hell. This stance is necessitated by a theology that posits an immortal soul and a supreme being. God and being are equated. Thus, being becomes *Being*. The Christian notion of Being/nonbeing, unlike the identity of the relative and the absolute, derives from these dualistic assumptions "by virtue of its being ontologically prior to non-being" (Abe, 1985, p. 130). Similarly, Western intellectual traditions tend to attribute ontological priority to positive principles. Buddhist philosophy calls this Western assumption into question. For example, Abe, writing on the relation between being and nonbeing from the Zen perspective, asserts that "it is natural that 'Being' as the quintessence of this ontological priority should be regarded as the ultimate and as the symbol for liberation" (p. 130). Abe further argues: "An objection must be made to this understanding of being; however, for in reality there is no ontological ground on which being has priority over non-being" (p. 121).

The Jesuit missionaries, operating, understandably, on the basis of their own religious assumptions, became the self-appointed bearers of grace (positive principle), light, and Truth. Their task, however politically and economically motivated, clearly became to enlighten the "evil, inferior Zenists." Thus, it seems obvious that the Jesuits would make a misguided effort to overthrow the encountered negativity, dispel darkness, misperceived as nihilism, with what they earnestly believed to be a positive force.

The Zenist does not endeavor, nor has a need to overcome, nonbeing. Rather, ignorance, understood as a misperception of reality, that engenders and maintains a false dualism requires resolution. Further, the Buddhist acknowledges the need to realize that emptiness is also fundamentally empty to come to final liberation. That is, there is no essence, soul, substance, spirit; no relationship with God; nothing to hold on to. Life in its suchness is being just as it is. Yamada, Roshi (1979) articulates this point succinctly and tersely in his expression "Just this, just this!" The Zenist privileges no side: being/nonbeing, negative/positive, language/silence, assertion/denial, light/dark. On this point Loori (1994) quotes *The Book of Equanimity*: "A jewel in the sunlight ... it has no definite shape. It cannot be attained by mindlessness nor known by mindfulness" (p. 77).

Further, the Zenist privileges no center point. Abe (1985) asserts: "Here the symbol of liberation is not Being as the quintessence of the ontological priority of being over non-being, but the dynamism of 'Emptiness,' which is simultaneously Fullness" (p. 131). Or stated differently, as Merzel (1991) notes: "When you truly lose everything, you gain everything, which is absolutely nothing" (p. 39). Kanji Sosan asserts that "those who do not live in the single way fail in both activity and passivity, assertion and denial" (Merzel, 1991, p. 36).

From the Zen perspective, the Jesuit stance that prioritizes Being over being and nonbeing, in terms of a belief in an immortal soul and a divine being, functions as a resistance to the truth of the ultimate insubstantiality of our own being, which engenders existential anxiety. Zen practice demands that the individual comes to terms emotionally with impermanence and insubstantiality. This relative duality demands resolution through experiential "intuitive" wisdom (*prajna* or quick knowing). Prajna grasps the Truth that is both beyond and intrinsic to being and nonbeing.

By positing an ultimate Being that is equated with God, then nonbeing implies that God is lacking. By prioritizing the positive principle, the foundational cornerstone of Buddhist belief system, emptiness is conceptualized exclusively in negative terms and given nihilist connotations. Hence, Zen emptiness is equated with the devil, godlessness, and annihilationism. This misconception of Zen practice as solely nihilist led to the erroneous view of meditation, a major experiential vehicle, exclusively as a form of quietism. The missionary comes to view the Zenist, as noted in the above, as lacking. Thus, the missionary's task becomes clear-cut.

Subjectivity, in the form of the theological assumptions of the Jesuit missionaries, who held a belief in a supreme being, was never subjected to self-reflection or called into question through religious practice. Further, the Jesuits never seriously considered the possible validity of basic Buddhist assumptions. Thus, the lens of the 16th-century Jesuit observations and explorations into Buddhism was initially colored by a belief system that posits a positive principle (Being), which is assigned ontological priority, and conceptualized as "essence." The Buddhist notion of *sunyata* refutes the notion of essence. For the Jesuits and the European philosophers who relied on their reports for secondhand information concerning Buddhist soteriology, as Abe (1985) notes, "it is assumed that being embraces *both* being *and* non-being" (p. 121).* However, for the Buddhist, to quote Abe, "the very basis on which *both* being and non-being are embraced must not be 'being' but 'that which is neither being nor non-being'" (p. 121).

This point is exemplified in the following anecdote:

> If a man has insight into the nature of his own being, said the master, he will understand the truth in whatever way it is presented either affirmatively or negatively. He knows how not to get attached to either side since he has grasped the principle of things as they move on. (D. T. Suzuki, 1994, p. 73)

Elsewhere, D. T. Suzuki (1949) writes: "When the mind is trained enough it sees that neither negation (*niratta*) nor affirmation (*atta*) applies to reality, but that the truth lies in knowing things as they are, or rather as they become" (p. 143).

"Tokusan's Thirty Blows"

This ideological notion finds expression in the koan "Tokusan's Thirty Blows." Whether a student negates or affirms the reality of things, Tokusan would respond by hitting the bewildered student with his stick. If the student simply remained silent, Tokusan would still strike. It is from this orientation that Loori (1994) notes in his commentary on Mumon "do not attempt nihilistic or dualistic interpretations" (p. 54). This intention moves the student past conceptual knowledge into the realm of experiencing Truth. The point, to reiterate, is that no state, whether positive or negative, being or nonbeing, enlightenment or delusion, immanence or transcendence, should be reified or privileged.

---

* Ontological priority of being over nonbeing seeps into Freud's discussion of the "rules" of the unconscious. He argues that at the deepest levels of unconscious negation does not exist.

This perspective points to a relationship and to an attitude of nonattachment and not so much the actual state itself. In this respect, Mumon releases the student from the tension of being and nonbeing. He says, "Don't consider it to be nothingness. Don't think in terms of 'has' or 'has not'" (Aitken, 1991, p. 17). Aitken argues that such reified thinking will ultimately result in a loss of connectedness and a feeling of oneness with the world.

It is clear from this discussion that Zen articulates a denial of opposites in the ultimate or absolute sense but not in the relative or empirical sense. From the Zen standpoint, both negation and assertion engender dualistic thinking. On this point, D. T. Suzuki (1949) observes that "so long as the intellect is to move among the ordinary dualistic groove, this is unavoidable" (p. 275). Truth, from the Zen perspective, finds expression when there is neither assertion nor negation.

We can examine this question both technically and philosophically. Technically, as noted above, meditation, confused with quietism, is misunderstood as a form of annihilationism. Philosophically, to quote Aitken (1991):

> Although the realization of Emptiness is essential, one should not cling to Emptiness as Emptiness. This is why Mahayana Buddhism, which is based on the idea of Emptiness, has throughout its long history rigorously rejected the attachment to Emptiness as "a confused understanding of Emptiness," a rigid view of nothingness," or a "view of annihilatory nothingness." (p. 128)

The above representative comments from both philosophical and technical perspectives unequivocally articulate strong and clear critiques of nihilist misinterpretations of Buddhist theory and practice. Yet, descriptions of the first European encounters with Buddhism resulted in an ongoing attribution of nihilist extremism to Buddhism.

Relative and Absolute Reality as Identical

From the Zen standpoint relative and absolute reality are ultimately identical. Absolute reality, activity/passivity, positive/negative, being/nonbeing are not distinct. This aspect of the discussion addresses a misperception of Zen reality that derives from reified dualist distinctions. Thus, active and passive come to be viewed as coexisting antagonistically in a relative world. Psychoanalysts have made similar observations. For example, Freud described psychic energies and the various forms that they take as basically neutral. Their positive or negative coloration, he argued, derives from whether such mental events are deemed acceptable or forbidden. Variations on this theme find expression throughout the history of psychoanalysis. For instance, from a contemporary perspective, Eigen (2001) writes: "In the mad unconscious, these differences wash out. Active/passive meld, become equivalent. Energy is more primary than evanescent forms it takes" (p. 14). From a contemporary perspective that integrates Buddhism and psychoanalysis, Langan (2006), with respect to mindfulness to emotional experience, writes that "feeling ranges from positive to neutral to negative, and like everything else, changes moment by moment, arising and passing away. The positive feelings come, I want to cling; the negative, to avoid; the neutral, perhaps to sleep" (p. 48).

Being and nonbeing both arise codependently, subject to causes and conditions with both relative and absolute aspects. Thus, nonbeing is not subsumed under being. Not unlike primary psychic energies, negative and positive manifestations hold equal status. This philosophical point holds clinical relevance. In clinical work one can observe a tendency to overvalue or overprivilege seemingly positive emotional states and to eschew what are perceived as negative states. Meditation is frequently used in the service of engendering seemingly positive states. Such a stance, however, while well intentioned, can cover over certain emotional states with short-term, superficial treatment results. Additionally, this stance can inadvertently exacerbate conditions such as, for example, helplessness and entrenchment in depressed or self-destructive states, to name a few. Not unlike the child's Chinese handcuff, a woven tube that traps the fingers, the analyst and patient can get more deeply stuck. The more one attempts to pull the fingers out, the tighter the woven tube becomes. The key is to lean in a bit so that the tube loosens, thus freeing the fingers. Similarly, the analyst can loosen the grip of impasses related to what appear as negative states by leaning in, which is accomplished by paying attention and by complete acceptance. Clinically, this observation speaks to the need for the analyst to attend to the moment without privileging sides. Consider the following vignette.

Bena

Bena was feeling vulnerable about what she described as "crossing boundaries." That is, she could not expect or ask for anything from me, such as rescheduling our sessions to accommodate a change in her work schedule related to a promotion that she had successfully competed for and had just been awarded. Her increased responsibilities as a manager required additional hours. As we sat together she began to feel a sense of calmness and peace. She arrived to her next session the following day 20 minutes early (she usually arrives right on time, if not a few minutes late). I asked her about it. She said that she had wanted to recapture the feeling of well-being that sitting with me engendered the previous week. She further explained her view of the transference ramifications. That is, to summarize, she said that any movement on my part—either toward or away—such as through making an interpretation, would have felt like an abandonment to her. Whether the interpretation was accurate or not, I would have been experienced by her as abandoning the experiential space of the lived moment.* In this situation, I believe that an interpretation would have functioned as a counterresistance to the evolution of the Truth of the session and to the unitive nature of the experiential moment. We pursued this further in the following session. Bena's self-hatred, which she experienced as her greed and aggression, with her wish for making a request felt to her like a violation of our boundaries. She was afraid that I would view her negatively and that I would act out my negativity by withdrawal of attention and harsh criticism. She experienced her promotion and her increase in salary as manifestations of her greed and aggression and imagined that I would be judgmental of her achievement. We both understood the early object relations that perpetuated her fears. These self-perceptions and imagined expectations of my reactions, we discovered, despite their harshness, felt safer than the deeper, more vulnerable feelings of hunger, longing, and the wish to be loved unconditionally via my undivided attention no matter what. Bena imagined that she would be aggressive if she asserted these needs. As noted above, she also considered her wish to express her needs as a violation of our boundaries. She was welling over with feelings and feared that she would "flood the room and wash me away." Not unlike her early objects, I simply could not and would not handle them. She wondered if I would be strong enough, compassionate enough, and present enough to willingly respond to and hold her feelings, and acknowledge her needs, hunger, and longings, unconditionally. In short, would I love her unconditionally no matter what? My capacity for acceptance, to love

---

* This is a problem with what one might consider a "good interpretation," as the reaction of the patient, in this case feeling abandoned, would be treated technically as a "resistance," as if to preserve the authority of the analyst.

unconditionally, meant sitting still, staying right where I was—in the present moment, attending the moment, embracing the moment, in full acceptance of what S. Suzuki often describes as "being-as-it-is." Together could we, as the old Zen teaching story asserts, "taste the strawberries"? At this point, she said that she felt anxious but that it was a "good kind of anxiety," that there was something fundamentally anxious about feeling fully alive, present, and loved.

This identity, interpenetration, relationship is represented in the Taoist Yin/Yang symbol. The terms *Mu* (no, negativity, nonbeing) and *U* (yes, positive, being) detail this fundamental Buddhist stance and give poetic expression to this relationship/identity/interpenetration. This identity will be further clarified by examining the *Mu* koan, "Joshu's Dog," in Chapter 4.

Impacts

It is clear from this historical review that Freud's critique of religion and Eastern mysticism parallels his contemporaries and thus reflects prevailing enlightenment trends. Despite Freud's development of the theory of a dynamic unconscious, which is central to psychoanalytic thought, his response to Eastern spirituality reveals a complexity of diverging roots and developments. One influence that has received extensive treatment derives, as I noted above, from his conversations with the French poet and mystic Romaine Rolland (Parsons, 1999). Further, within this context, his understanding was filtered through his psychoanalytic lens and colored by his agenda to find a unique place for psychoanalysis on the European Enlightenment positivist map. However, despite the explanatory power engendered by psychoanalytic thought, his vision was also defined and shaped, as Faure (1993) asserts, "by the circumstances of the Western reception of Buddhism" (p. 3). Thus, Freud's critique of meditation as regressive represents and reflects the European religious and philosophical critique of quietism.

The misperception of Zen as an exclusively quietist practice and related issues spill over into contemporary psychoanalysis and psychotherapy. For example, the prescription of meditation as a palliative for symptomatic relief for anxiety reflects a widespread devaluation of Buddhist soteriology. This view has been promulgated by Benson and his collaborators, who have conducted extensive research into the effects of meditation but who completely miss the soteriological intention of Buddhist praxes by subsuming all meditation traditions under the general rubric of "relaxation response" (Benson & Klipper, 1976; Benson & Procter, 1985). Their mass-market publications reinforce this view and have clearly influenced a large segment of the professional and lay readership. While there is no question as to the beneficial impact of Benson's work, Buddhism's potential for radical change is completely ignored.

Zen soteriology, not unlike psychoanalysis, seeks much more than symptom relief. In the ideal, both Zen and psychoanalysis hold the potential to engender radical transformations that are reflected in one's mode of being in the world, which in turn reflects often profound internal psychic changes morally, ethically, relationally, and spiritually, and which finds lived expression in an increased capacity for compassionate living.

On the other side of this controversy one finds an overidealization of Asian religions. This view promulgates a belief that Asian wisdom traditions can fill in deficits that would otherwise impede the psychotherapeutic encounter. This wider Western trend of oscillation between pathologizing and idealizing Eastern philosophy and religion asserts itself in the evolution of psychoanalytic thinking about Buddhism.

Despite the clear and cogent admonishments of Buddhist teachers throughout the ages, a quietist misunderstanding continues to pervade clinical thinking with few exceptions. Misinformed clinicians dichotomize emotional states into categories of "good" and "bad" and prescribe meditation as a palliative. This response overlooks transference and countertransference implications.* The explanatory power of what we have learned about unconscious processes is rarely exploited. Not unlike our Jesuit predecessors, such interventions turn the well-intentioned clinician into a "missionary" with a focus on "saving" the patient from horrific mental states. This stance results in a failure to find the peace at the center of chaos that S. Suzuki refers to. We fail to negotiate the states of catastrophic turbulence that Bion, Eigen, Rhode, Grotstein, and others describe as necessary to the pursuit of lived emotional Truth.

Overattachment to a still mind rather than experiencing the normal oscillations between experiences of being and nonbeing and the accompanying emotional states can be likened to being attached to what Sojun Diane Martin describes as "preferred psychological states," or to so-called "enlightened states of mind." From this perspective, the influential ninth-century Zen master Rinzai compared enlightenment to a donkey chained to a hitching post. He noted that "one peep into essential nature is a great

---

* For a detailed discussion see Cooper (1999).

release and a great encouragement, but if you take it as be-all and end-all, you'll drop straight into hell" (Aitken, 1991, p. 15).

3

The Zen Koan:
Speaking the Unspeakable

Introduction

The seemingly enigmatic koan has generated a vast literature from both the scholarly and practice perspectives. Additionally, multiple translations of various koan collections are currently available. They typically include commentaries written by historical and contemporary Zen masters layered over one another.* This overwhelming plethora of literature generated by a tradition that claims "no reliance on words and letters," not unlike the koan itself, can simultaneously provoke clarity and confusion in the reader and the practitioner alike. The best source of koan understanding derives through personal experience and remains to be elaborated within the context of the ongoing relationship and encounter dialogues with a Zen teacher, for which there is no substitute. The reader interested in seriously pursuing koan study should seek out an authentic and qualified Zen teacher. The definition that I provide in this chapter is limited and geared toward understanding the role of the koan in religious practice and how the koan can be understood and influence the psychoanalytic encounter in terms of its narrative function.

Definition

Simply stated, the koan is Truth, or the place where Truth resides. The uppercase spelling references religious, fundamental, or existential Truth.

---

* Full and partial translations and contemporary commentaries of *Mumonkan* [Gateless Barrier] include Aitken (1991), Chayat (2008), Loori (1994), Shibayama (2000), Sogen (2005), and Yamada (1979).

Fundamental Truth is not a fixed, static, or stable entity. Rather, Truth emerges and fades in oscillation in relation to resistance to Truth. This resistance serves to protect the individual from fundamental or basic anxiety.* The tension between Truth awareness and resistance accounts for the need for a lifetime of practice.

As a literary form and as a functional tool, the koan captures, exemplifies, and facilitates a narrative that at once engenders and expresses spiritual realization. Unfortunately, the term *koan* has become co-opted into the English language to mean any enigmatic and unsolvable riddle or nonsense statement. This general definition renders any life puzzle fair game to be defined as a koan, for instance, the psychoanalytic koan "Tell me what brings you here." The scholarly literature seriously questions this popularized usage of the term and brings its religious function into clear focus.

The koan is typically described in the contemporary Zen literature as terse, succinct, cogent, indefinable sayings and vignettes characterized by their "peculiar use of language" (McRae, 2000, p. 47). Heine and Wright (2000) elaborate on the unique use of language in terms of the koan's religious function and note:

> Koans are generally appreciated today as pithy, epigrammatic, elusive utterances that seem to have a psychotherapeutic effect in liberating practitioners from bondage to ignorance, as well as for the way they are contained in the complex, multileveled literary form of koan collection commentaries. (p. 3)

The actual term *koan* derives from the Chinese term *kung-an* and literally translates as "public case" or "public record."† Zenists borrowed the term from the Chinese legal system, in which a public case implies a standard of judgment, which serves to maintain the integrity of Zen, and in the context of the teacher and student relationship, it functions as a determinant of the student's level of spiritual understanding. On this point Wright (2000) notes:

> In the same way that "public records" limit both the waywardness of the law and its arbitrariness, the "public records" of Ch'an "awakening" were thought to preserve the identity of enlightenment over time and to render refutable the assertions of imposters....

---

* See Chapter 1.
† Kung: public; an: case or record.

Its intention is to publically establish the kung-an as a set of standards—weights and measures—in juxtaposition to which all claims to religious attainment could be discernfully judged. (p. 200)

Case Study: Zen and Psychoanalysis

Dialogue occupies a central position in both koan practice and psychoanalysis. In this respect, the koan as public case parallels the psychoanalytic case study, which captures the dialogue between the psychoanalyst and analysand. As a central form of both verbal and written communication among psychoanalysts, case studies serve as the public record of psychoanalysis. For the most part, the case study connects, exemplifies, and integrates hypothesis, speculative writing, theory, and technique. The case study communicates the effectiveness of psychoanalytic ideas and techniques in a lived and pragmatic way. It, thus, exemplifies the writer's thinking in terms of specific interventions through documentation of the psychoanalytic encounter. The case study bridges the gap between general theory and specific application. They render the abstract into concrete form just as the Zen notion of the identity of the relative and the absolute finds expression through concrete anecdotes and expressions such as "when hungry eat, when tired sleep," or "chop wood, carry water."

The formalized final case that psychoanalytic candidates are typically required to present and the ensuing spontaneous question-and-answer dialogue that occurs among the participants create the opportunity for senior analysts to judge the level of attainment, understanding, and expertise of the candidate. As an entry into the community of psychoanalysts, similar to the koan as public case, the final case guards against false claims to authority or expertise and functions as a form of legitimization that safeguards the integrity of the psychoanalytic community and of psychoanalysis as a discipline.

Psychoanalytic theory and technique become operationalized and exemplified through the case study, which articulates and serves as a model that facilitates effective treatment. The koan operationalizes Zen enlightenment didactically and experientially and serves to actualize religious realization. Simultaneously, the koan functions as a dialogical tool designed to facilitate and support spiritual development. In this manner it serves as a highly charged, enigmatic, and often seemingly outrageous functional tool and, at the same time, as an expression of enlightened being. With respect to the koan's religious function Wright (2000) notes that "if the language of the koan is not considered to be linked to the enlightenment of the great masters, no grounds for their use in contemplative practice remains" (pp. 202–203). As we will explore below, with few exceptions, references to koans in the psychoanalytic literature overlook this religious intention and typically refer to the koan as any riddle or enigmatic nonsense expression.

Centrality of the Koan

Koan practice distinguishes Zen from other forms of Buddhism, and as Heine (2002) notes, the koan "defines the heart of Zen Buddhism and is the single most distinctive feature in the thought and practice of the Zen sect" (p. 1). Why do Zenists ascribe such a central place to the koan? As I noted in Chapter 1, from the religious perspective, Zen holds a salvational function, which finds expression in the notion of satori. The koan and the associated dialogue function to both facilitate and express satori as a lived experience. It is from this salvational standpoint that D. T. Suzuki (1994) observes that "the koan exercise came to be recognized as the necessary step towards realization of satori in Zen Buddhism" (p. 31).

Koan Variations

Zen commentaries describe three basic koan forms. They include the story, the "catchphrase koan" (Schlütter, 2000, p. 171), and confrontation with an unanswerable question. The first type takes the form of a story, anecdote, or dialogue and typically documents an incident, situation, or conversation between a revered historical Zen figure and a student. "Joshu's Mu" or "Does a Dog Have Buddha Nature or Not?" which will be discussed in Chapter 4, is typical of this form. The second type, the catchphrase koan, is not referenced to a particular Zen master. Popular catchphrase koans include "What was your original face before you were born?" and "What is the sound of one hand clapping?" The third type of koan confronts the student with a logically unanswerable question or impossible challenge, such as "How do you step off a 50-foot pole?"

Regardless of the form, all koans contain loose threads that can be pulled on from multiple directions with the aim of working through resistances to Truth and engendering a here-and-now presence that facilitates living life as we find it. From this perspective the question becomes "Can we live life as we find it with all its terrors and delights?" Failure to successfully face the challenges posed by such a question typically creates the problems that drive many individuals toward religious practice or into psychotherapy. An idea often persists that life is something that will happen in the future when "things are better," "when the problem is solved," "when we figure out what's wrong with me," "when I become enlightened." Sadly, such individuals miss the life that is happening now. In this sense, the most challenging koan is often said to be life itself.

Historical Development

The koan exercise developed in 10th- and 11th-century China as a reaction and corrective to elitism, intellectualism, and quietism, which had eroded authentic Zen experience and threatened the demise of Zen as an effective religious system. D. T. Suzuki describes the development of koan practice as crucial to the revitalization of Zen, which had, over time, become lifeless and calcified. During the 13th century, Dogen revitalized koan study, which had once again, to a large extent, become lifeless. He accomplished this by offering novel and contradictory interpretations of traditional koans in an effort to expand dialogue (Heine, 1994).

A pattern of question-and-answer dialogues emerged, in which a question is turned back on the student or is given a seemingly illogical response by the master. This dialogical encounter evolved into the koan system. Recorded koan exercises were eventually organized into collections, such as *Blue Cliff Record* (12th century), *The Book of Equanimity* (12th century), *Shobogenzo* (13th century), and *Mumonkan* (13th century), mentioned above. These collections served to systematize and formalize the spontaneous dialogues and enlightenment experiences of the early Zen masters. As these stories became compiled into anthologies, formal courses of study developed that were intended to express the enlightenment experiences of the masters and engender such experiences in Zen students. These collections, along with the compiler's attached commentaries, were referred to as *nien-ku* (picking up the old cases). When poems were attached, which succinctly summarized the old cases, they were referred to as *sung-ku* (eulogizing the old cases). The Japanese monk Hakuin (1686–1769) further formalized koan practice into a systematic and structured course of study. Miura and Sasaki (1965) describe Hakuin as "the organizer and revivifier of Japanese Rinzai Zen" (p. x). Koan practice thus simultaneously popularized and preserved the authenticity of Zen experience.

The Koan and Narrative Function

Zen characterizes itself, for the most part, as a "special transmission out-side of the scriptures." This places the teacher and student relationship at the center of the Zen religious endeavor. Koan study and practice provides a fundamental and vital structure for the teacher/student dialogue. The relationship that developed out of this dialogue was central to the devel-opment of Zen in China, beginning historically with Bodhidharma, an Indian Buddhist monk who was said to introduce Zen to China during the 6th century. Albert Welter (2000) observes that "history rewritten from the Ch'an perspective posits Bodhidharma as champion of 'mind-to-mind' transmission, focusing on the enlightenment experience occurring in the context of the master–disciple relationship, as an alternative to the exegetical teachings of the scholastic tradition" (p. 78).

The koan and the associated student/teacher dialogue together func-tion to engender an alteration in perception that cuts through dualistic thinking and derails reasoning processes.

The koan functions as a facilitator of experience and evolving discourse. It serves as a vehicle that renders the ineffable unspeakable into the speak-able knowable through the evolving narrative. Through successful koan practice, over time, a notable shift occurs in the quality, style, and impact of the narrative as intuitive and rational processes become more fully inte-grated. Zen poetry, for example, serves as a most condensed, rarified, and radical expression of this shift. In this way the koan functions as a point of departure for the ever-evolving narrative that engenders insight, whether expressed through silence, action, or an expanded narrative characterized by its freshness, aliveness, openness, and creativity. The posited dichotomy between silence and language fades. Both become interwoven into the fab-ric of the discourse—a discourse that reflects a deepening, expanding, and magnified awareness of reality.

Both the Zen master and the psychoanalyst are ever on the alert for dialogue that deteriorates into emotionally flat intellectualism or logi-cal philosophical discourse. While not totally disregarding the intellect, with different goals in mind, both endeavor to go beyond its limitations and break through to a directly lived and felt awareness. The Zen master and student strive toward enlightenment and compassionate living. The psychoanalyst, depending on a particular orientation, strives with the analysand to resolve unconscious conflicts, reduce symptoms, increase the patient's capacity for self-reflection, and extend the range of personal expression. When these experiences generalize beyond the confines of the zendo or the consultation room, both practices contribute to a life lived more fully, openly, honestly, and compassionately. In this sense both Zen koan practice and psychoanalysis free up interferences with and expand the individual's capacity for basic aliveness.

Koan Practice

After a preliminary period of practice of some form of zazen, such as breath concentration or breath counting, the Zen student will receive a koan to focus on during periods of zazen and as the subject of discussion during face-to-face interviews with the Zen teacher.

In practice, as noted above, koan study engenders a spontaneous, intuitive knowledge beyond teachings and scriptures. In this regard, Miura and Sasaki (1965) note that "koan study is a unique method of religious practice, which has as its aim the bringing of the student to direct intuitive realization of reality without recourse to the mediation of words or concepts" (p. x). This spontaneous direct knowing that Miura and Sasaki points to finds succinct expression in the contemporary American Zen master John Daido Loori's (1994) comment that "we *do* koans, we don't talk about them" (p. xvii). Koans are designed to defeat rational, linear cause-and-effect thinking, and for this reason, they frequently appear irrational to nonpractitioners. On this point, D. T. Suzuki (1994) observes, "for the koan is not a logical proposition but an expression of a certain mental state resulting from Zen discipline" (p. 83).

The initially nonsensical nature of any specific koan becomes meaningful with the practitioner's deepening awareness within the context of the teacher/student relationship. This sense of meaningfulness, however, is not exclusively or necessarily didactic. The teacher's response to the student is not meant to be simply informational. Not unlike an analytic interpretation, which might or might not make sense outside of the dyad in which it is asserted, can be considered, depending on the patient's response, successful or unsuccessful, effective or ineffective. The student's response to any koan reflects deepening or penetrating levels of awareness of reality as a result of cutting through or temporarily short-circuiting logical, linear thinking. However, as Taizan Maezumi notes, the koan

> is much more than a paradoxical riddle designed to prod the mind into intuitive insight. The koan is literally a touchstone of reality. It records an instance

in which a key issue of practice and realization is presented and examined by experience rather than by discursive or linear logic. (Yamada, 1979, p. vii)

Accordingly, as I noted above, the Zen master can only witness or judge the student's level of mastery through the interview process. The Zen master can point toward realization, but does not actually teach the student anything since realization derives through internal processes and personal experience. At the same time, the master's function as witness engenders that capacity in the student to more fully live, trust, and express one's own experience with compassion. This witnessing and pointing serves as an essential aspect of the student's training and demonstrates in a lived way Ferro's (2005) psychoanalytic observation "that every mind, at birth, needs another mind in order to develop" (p. 1).

Rational and Nonrational

This typical and terse assertion in the Zen literature, such as Sasaki's comment quoted above, that koan practice demands the complete exclusion and utter annihilation of reasoning processes requires elaboration. Such statements have resulted in a misunderstanding that engenders a false dichotomy in terms of the practitioner's relationship to rational and nonrational modes of processing experience. In Chapter 1 we discussed this issue in terms of *being* and *about*. We will revisit this misunderstanding here in terms of the conceptual and nonconceptual modes of mental processing. The negation of conceptual processes erroneously implied in such terse statements sets up a false dichotomy. This dualistic approach assumes that conceptual and nonconceptual perspectives and mental processes are mutually exclusive rather than simply differing aspects of any individual's capacity to experience, whether developed, underdeveloped, or hyperdeveloped. The intuitive and cognitive modes are not mutually exclusive, as is suggested in the literature that advocates the total negation and obliteration of cognitive functioning. Rational and nonrational perceptual capacities coexist and are intertwined. They oscillate between foreground and background over time. Some individuals need to develop thoughtfulness and learn to deal more compassionately with their impulses. Others need to relinquish an overreliance on thinking processes and develop spontaneity. The key is balance. The notion of mutual exclusivity that implies a total negation of the rational aspect constitutes a dualistic misperception commonly attributed to koan study and can engender a destructive imbalance.

Abe (1985), who advocates for the integration of both processes, notes that "although intellectual understanding cannot be a substitute for Zen's awakening, practice without a proper and legitimate form of intellectual understanding is often misleading. An intellectual understanding without practice is certainly powerless, but practice without learning is apt to be blind" (p. 4).

This misperception that reasoning processes function exclusively as obstacles to Zen realization, and therefore require complete abandonment, has contributed to a misinformed negative response to koan study among psychoanalytic writers. This inappropriate critique of koan practice parallels the early psychoanalytic critique of meditation as exclusively nihilistic that I reviewed in Chapter 2. Ross (1975), for example, in a discussion of mystical experience from a psychoanalytic perspective, describes the koan as "a statement containing the most extreme absurdities and contradictions which one must ruminate upon" (p. 90). Ross echoes Alexander's (1931) conclusion that Buddhist meditation practice serves exclusively pathological and regressive ends. Koan practice, according to Ross, engenders "a persistent erosion of the secondary process which induces a regression to a state in which 'affect as cognition' takes over the psychic apparatus" (p. 90). He draws a negative conclusion and notes: "But I wonder whether the world today can afford such irrationalisms in the face of the ominous threats to human freedom issuing from the cold-blooded protagonists of *1984*" (p. 90).

The effort to write off the koan simply as illogical nonsense keeps the critic safely tied to exclusively cognitive and linear modes, or to what psychoanalysts describe as secondary processes. Rejecting what does not make sense runs counter to the free-associative inquiry that informs the psychoanalytic narrative function. The rejection of what appears on the surface to not make sense forecloses the seeming incoherence and non-rationality of what can be potentially known through intuitive processes. On this point, from a contemporary psychoanalytic perspective, Donnel Stern (1983), who addresses this split in terms of what he describes as "me" and "not me," observes:

> The self-system includes all those experiences and ways of relating to others which have been found through experience to be safe and secure. Or from the other direction: The self-system rejects all experiences and modes of relating which are associated with anxiety. (p. 74)

Stern concludes that "anxiety leads us to search for the familiar and comfortable in experience and throw out the rest" (p. 75). In this respect, koan practice invites a narrative that more fully engages the psychic potential of both primary and secondary processes. However, this requires that the individual address and resolve the anxiety entailed in the task of temporarily relinquishing what from the perspective of secondary processes does not make sense and by allowing the space for and sitting with the uncertainty of not knowing. Overreliance of the sensible and the known can stifle the wonder necessary for sitting with the unsettling feelings such as anxiety that might arise when facing the potential for new experience (Cooper, 2002a).

Initially, as I described in Chapter 1, ignorance, as a reaction to the fundamental anxiety of being, functions to actively maintain subject and object separations. Practice engenders a deconstruction of this sense of separateness and a deepening awareness of unitive experiencing. The practitioner realizes that ultimately there is no separation of subject and object, or between a sense of self as the object of attention and the sense of self as subject. Similarly, the practitioner begins to realize that there is ultimately no differentiation of self as permanent and separate. However, unitive experiencing and this negation of self must be integrated with an affirmation of the truth of relative self and other separation. As Rhode (1994) notes, from the psychoanalytic perspective, "intimacy is not oneness: it sets in motion separation as well as closeness" (p. 88). Similarly, oneness is not intimacy and does not constitute a relationship. This requires a simultaneous awareness of the identity of oneness and twoness. Abe (1985), who clearly elaborates this crucial and frequently overlooked point, notes that "this negative realization is important and necessary for ultimate Reality to be disclosed, but to remain solely within the confines of this negative realization would be nihilistic" (p. 8).

The practitioner must work through a subtle dualism between unitive and dualistic experiencing. Resolution is required to create a foundation for life, activity, and relationships. This is the meaning of the Zen expression "You must come down from the mountain cave and go into the marketplace." Unitive experiencing functions as a corrective to anxious grasping, greed, aggression, and violence associated with our ignorant exclusively dualistic perception and experience of the world. However, unitive experience in and of itself is not the final solution to the problem of ignorance. We need to put awareness into action, which requires a lifetime of mindful, moment-to-moment practice and a compassionate acknowledgment of other.

The psychoanalyst's capacity to become emerged in unitive experience engenders a lived and intuitive awareness of aspects of the patient's experience that he or she might not be able to communicate in language. The ability to then make a separation enables the psychoanalyst to formulate the experience into language and respond to the patient. In this respect, both intuitive and cognitive processes operate together. The clinical ramifications of the relationship between unitive and separate experience will be explicated in detail in the context of an extended case study in Chapter 10.

Buddhist practitioners who I have consulted with can get stuck in this nihilistic extreme of negation of self and other. Eric, a long-term analysand, for example, who maintained a strong and consistent long-term practice with periods of residency at the monastery where he studied, presented himself in treatment in a state that can best be described as a reified sense of no-self. He conveyed a strong narcissistic indifference toward himself and others. His world appeared to be unpopulated by other human beings, as if he lived in the midst of a vast and barren landscape. Eric imagined that there were no consequences for his inappropriate behavior, and he typically rationalized the legitimate complaints of others as an expression of the other's ignorance and attachment to the "illusion of self." For individuals such as Eric, Zen practices and teachings become co-opted into a false self system and exploited to rationalize inappropriate behaviors.

From the Zen perspective false notions of both self and no-self require scrutiny and deconstruction; however, these individuals miss this crucial point. The negation of self with the resulting reification of no-self requires working through. Ultimately, the negation of no-self becomes an affirmation of relative self and a simultaneous negation of ultimate self.

An alternative understanding of the Zen emphasis on the nonrational aspect of koan practice in relation to psychoanalysis centers on the view that the process of breaking up rational processes serves as an initial step. This enables the practitioner to exercise and develop intuitive and empathic capacities that might or might not be nonrational. That is, different modes of processing experience are accessed and utilized during koan practice that might have been underused, not developed, or suffocated and stifled by the tendency to rely exclusively on rational linear thinking processes.*

This understanding holds implications for the psychoanalytic encounter. For instance, we can consider pathology as the result of the splitting off of intuitive processes that can potentially render unitive experience

---

* See Cooper (2007) for a discussion of the overuse of linear thought processes in communications between psychoanalysts.

accessible or realizable. This splitting, in turn, maintains subject/object separations. Healing requires the integration of both cognitive and intuitive functions that render unitive experiencing accessible and communicable. This notion of cure requires qualification because from this perspective there is no fixed endpoint, no final outcome, nothing to be predetermined, as if, for instance, we know in advance what we are looking for. From the creative perspective that informs this view, Truth evolution is an ongoing process and is either promoted or disrupted. The dialogue between the Zen teacher and the student and the dialogue between the analyst and analysand both engender *and* express truth or they don't.

Initially, during the phases of koan practice, there might appear to be a radical disregard for cognitive processes. However, ultimately, integration occurs. We can track a similar evolution over time during the psychoanalytic encounter. For instance, during a case examination that was required as part of my psychoanalytic training, one of the committee members said, "You seem to demonstrate an unrelenting disregard for the cognitive self of your patient." Initially, I thought of responding by speaking to my countertransference vulnerability for colluding with this young man's highly intellectualized and emotionally flat narrative. Additionally, he was enrolled in a graduate theology program. He could easily engage me in conversations regarding his fascinating studies and ideas, which at times served as a good point of making contact with him. However, the risk of the neglect of his emotional life would be too much of a sacrifice and a disservice to my patient. He had experienced a lifetime of emotional neglect and didn't need more of the same from me. Despite the truth of this aspect of the treatment, I found myself responding by commenting: "I am primarily concerned with him being born right now. We'll clean up the afterbirth afterwards." This troubled young man had virtually no access to his emotional life. He experienced his life as if living on the outside looking in. Over time, he began to integrate his emotional and intellectual experiences. At the conclusion of our work together he said, "I now know and can say what I am feeling and I know that this is a good thing." As we negotiated a difficult and lengthy psychic birth, he slowly and increasingly became more expressive, more related, and he began to develop deeper and more consistent friendships. He developed the capacity to use his intellect in a nondefensive, emotionally connected, and thoughtful way. In time, he began to date and eventually became involved in his first intimate relationship.

The Koan and Psychoanalysis

Despite the centrality of the koan in Zen practice coupled with the recent surge of interest in the relation between Buddhism and psychoanalysis, it is surprising that, with few notable exceptions (Gunn, 1999; Magid, 2000; Stone, 2007), there are no comprehensive discussions of koan study in relation to psychoanalysis in the rapidly expanding psychoanalytic literature. Psychoanalytic studies related to Buddhism typically focus on meditation practice and core Buddhist principles, such as emptiness and the relationship between self and no-self.

D. T. Suzuki's *Essays in Zen Buddhism* (1949) provides a comprehensive and detailed account of the koan from a Rinzai perspective, which, as discussed in Chapter 1, exerted a strong influence on Karen Horney, Erich Fromm, and others. Yet, the koan remains marginalized and misunderstood in the psychoanalytic literature, with rare exceptions.

Buddhist practices, such as meditation, are frequently characterized as solitary one-person endeavors. However, koan practice involves meditation that is coupled together with an absolutely necessary dialogue that occurs between the teacher and the student. The student, during such interviews, communicates an understanding of the koan that derives through meditation and mindful work practice. The teacher keeps this dialogue fresh, moving, alive, and dynamic through responses and further questions. In this way the teacher facilitates a lived and emotionally alive experiential awareness in the student that fosters integration between intuitive knowing and cognitive understanding. The student might ask specific questions about practice, which the master will respond to in a straightforward didactic and informative way. These types of responses serve to structure and strengthen the student's practice. Within this structure, a transformative impact occurs through the in-the-moment immediacy of the dialogue. This emphasis on the relationship and the ensuing dialogue between teacher and student take account of the teacher's role and commitment in facilitating spiritual development and can include variations between words, silences, and actions.

This relational dynamic between teacher and student continuously evolves and engenders shifts that parallel psychotherapeutic aims in certain fundamental ways. Kapleau (1966) describes the following shift. "Dryness, rigidity and self-centeredness give way to flowing warmth, resiliency, and compassion, while self-indulgence and fear are transmuted into self-mastery and courage" (p. 14).

Some of the noted evolutions that I am aware of through my own practice, through the reports of fellow Zen practitioners and through the narratives of patients I have worked with include movements from contrivance to spontaneity; shifts from rigid, unquestioned, and dogmatically held beliefs to a more flexible iconoclastic orientation; increases in an authenticity of true self-expression and a fading of false self-expression. The tendency toward intellectualization gives way to increasing emotional expressivity. Rinzai characterizes true self-experiencing and expression with the image of the "man of no rank."

The evolving dialogue between teacher and student reveals a movement away from exclusively objective observation and toward subjective experiencing that closes the gap between objective and subjective self and other. Betty Joseph (1975) traces a similar movement in psychoanalysis that she describes in terms of the split between a needy self that has become sequestered out of awareness and a resistant self who appears to be involved in the treatment, but who actually restricts the needy self from making contact. This defensive split results in a pseudoanalysis if the analyst goes along with this dynamic. Such individuals relate to the analyst and to themselves as if watching a third party from the distance, as if they are analyzing someone else. As a result, they deprive themselves of the benefits of the lived experience of the analysis. When the anxieties and associated splits are worked through during analysis, such patients begin to give up the high level of self-protection that they bring with them to analysis. As a result, lived experienced truth begins to replace the accumulation of information, intuitive knowing replaces conceptual understanding, and unitive experiencing becomes accessible and provides a counterpart and balance to exclusively conceptual understanding.

Both Zen and psychoanalysis viewed from this perspective prioritize Truth experiencing over knowledge accumulation. In expressing the truths of Zen, we become more truthful because we are basically expressing the lived truth of who we authentically are. As this expression becomes fresher, more alive, spontaneous, and authentic, we expand our capacity for creative and compassionate living. D. T. Suzuki (1994) describes this as a feeling of exaltation "due to the fact that it is a breaking up of the restriction imposed on one as an individual being … an infinite expansion of the individual" (p. 29). Similarly, with respect to psychoanalysis practiced free from memory, desire, and understanding, Bion (1967) notes that "the pattern of analysis will change … 'Progress' will be measured by the increased number and variety of moods, ideas and attitudes in any given session" (p. 18).

The Koan and Psychoanalytic Writing

Despite the shifts in experience and awareness that reflect increased intuitive awareness, it is noteworthy that psychoanalytic papers on Zen, with few exceptions, are highly intellectual, speculative, and privilege an academic style of communication at the expense of the possibility for a more expressive style that is consistent with Zen practice and that more accurately reflects the dialogue the occurs during the psychoanalytic encounter.

The koan is typically mentioned as an aside meant to amplify a point with regard to other topics (Adams, 1995; Galatzer-Levy, 2002; Ringstrom, 1998; Ross, 1975; Weber, 2006). For example, in a touching reflection on her analyst, who had recently died, Adams (1995) writes: "How much time I wasted before I yielded to his Zen-like teachings. 'How do you want your suit, too large or too small?' A koan from his vast store of Jewish humor" (p. 735).

Other psychoanalytic writers view the koan simply as any riddle or existential question that they might devise (Harrison, 1994; Taketomo, 1989). For instance, Harrison (1994), speaking from the context of his efforts to cope with contemporary life, concludes: "I locate myself freely when I have the courage to ask myself a koan I devised, 'Who dies?' What does this man look like to himself when he is away from the mirror?" (p. 14).

A small group of psychoanalysts comment insightfully on how the koan facilitates the freeing up of intuitive processes that engender experiential knowing. Fauteux (1995), for instance, in a discussion of the adaptive role of regression in relation to religious practice and creativity, writes, "So too, the Zen student's struggle with the koan 'What is the sound of one hand clapping?' dismantles the neatly ordered rational through processes that inhibit more intuitive ways of thinking" (p. 43). In contrast to Ross's work, referred to above, Fauteux articulates a nonpathologizing evaluation of the emergence of primary process as a result of koan practice and further notes that this same koan "similarly helps dismantle ineffective logical reasoning and restore intuitive primary process" (p. 45). While Fauteux provides an accurate depiction of the koan's function, he does not consider its performative function. With regard to religious praxes, the koan operates to simultaneously evoke and express religious insight. As a catchphrase koan, it is intended to, as Schlütter (2000) notes, "evoke a state that is before and beyond any existence, which is the true state of Buddha-nature in which all sentient beings already dwell, although most are unaware" (p. 175). Hori (2000) provides an example of the performative function of language:

> A sentence like "I do," uttered at the appropriate moment in a wedding cer-
> emony, does not describe or denote an action, object or state of affairs; given
> the appropriate social, legal and ritual context, the utterance itself performs an
> action with real consequences, just as surely as does any physical act. (p. 285)

In this regard, the master's response is not necessarily informational, descriptive, or a statement of fact. Rather, in terms of its performative function, it either works or it does not work. In this respect, Rosemont (1970) refers to the "shock value" (p. 118) of the Zen teacher's response. The Zen literature is full of performative responses reflected by the actions of masters who raise fingers, hit with sticks, cut cats in two, walk away, sit silently, place a sandal on the head, or assert *non sequiturs*, all with the intention of evoking religious realization in the student.

Detailed and comprehensive discussions of koans in direct relation to psychoanalysis are typically written by psychoanalysts who are deeply committed to formal Zen training (Gunn, 1999; Magid, 2005; Stone, 2007). For example, Robert Gunn (1999) addresses notions of dualism, splitting, and culturally reified gender roles through a close reading of the 35th koan from *Mumonkan*, "Seijo's Soul Is Separated." He writes that "an analysis of the story from Buddhist, feminist and psychodynamic perspectives sheds light on the ways in which gendering and deconstructing of gender, leading to transformation might take place" (p. 413).

Cynthia Stone (2007) examines the 31st koan in the same collection, "Joshu Sees Through the Old Woman."* She uses the koan as a model for understanding alternative approaches to the psychoanalytic encounter. With respect to empathic attunement and attention to the said and the unsaid, she concludes:

> The story of Joshu and the Old Woman points to the need for both analyst and
> patient to immerse themselves directly in the patient's experience. They need to
> know together, with one mind, as one does when one recalls an experience with
> someone who has shared it. Words may evoke the experience, but the experi-
> ence is more than the words. It is a pooling of affects and images. For a moment
> the two people become one experience. (p. 16)

Stone (2007) clearly points toward unitive experiencing in a nonpathologizing way and draws a parallel to the psychoanalytic encounter. She observes that "when this happens there are no longer two separate people, only one awareness. In the best moments of psychotherapy, the same thing happens" (p. 16).

---

* See Chapter 5 for a detailed explication of this koan in relation to psychoanalysis.

Erich Fromm alludes briefly to the koan as a means to access the dynamic unconscious. While the dynamic unconscious appears to be an aspect of what evolves through koan practice, there are limitations with this point of view. Fromm's observations are influenced by the semiotics of an exclusively knowledge-based orientation deriving from his roots in classical psychoanalysis. Despite the creativity that he brings to his thinking, there seems to be no getting around this. Despite Fromm's receptivity to Zen, he fails to consider the underlying assumptions of the Zen position. When we consider the foundational Zen principles of emptiness and dependent arising in relation to contemporary psychoanalytic ideas regarding the relationship that constitutes the psychoanalytic encounter, our range of understanding expands and is not restricted or limited to simply making the unconscious conscious or to an endless accumulation of knowledge.

Application to Psychoanalysis

During teacher/student interviews the interpersonal field is mediated by a particular koan and by the various ways in which the two individuals interact. The teacher and the student engage in an ongoing and continually changing narrative. The language of the narrative can be considered as derivative of ineffable experience. Applied to the psychoanalytic encounter, this dynamic creates a shift in how the patient's narrative within the dyad evolves. There tends to be less emphasis on meaning, content, and the accumulation of knowledge, such as through genetic interpretations. The ongoing evolution of experiencing and awareness can include genetic interpretations, but they are not prioritized. In this regard, the intention of the interpretation shifts from filling in information about the past to an increased emphasis on the here and now, with the purpose of keeping the narrative fresh, alive, dynamic, and moving. D. T. Suzuki (1994) notes that "what is required of Zen devotees is to see into the phrase that liveth and not into one that is dead" (p. 92). Similarly, what is required of the psychoanalyst are responses that are enlivening, not deadening.

This approach continuously opens up meaning and maintains the active participation of the analysand as facilitated by the analyst. In this regard, as I noted above, interpretations can be said to be successful or unsuccessful. Either they have impact or they don't. This orientation provides an alternative to thinking of interpretations as accurate or not. In both koan practice and psychoanalysis viewed from this perspective, the patient's narrative arises in the immediacy of the present relational moment.*

This model, as noted above, does not exclude the consideration of transference and countertransference or their role in interpretation. Rather, they are included as currents in the wider stream of the patient's narrative, which broadens the experiential field in relation to the here and now. From this vantage point, both the past and the present occur in the present moment. They are encapsulated in the transference and countertransference dynamic. Here-and-now interpretations simultaneously address the present situation as it is lived and the past as an active aspect of the dynamic present.

In the next two chapters we will explore two koans in depth with an eye toward their relevance to issues raised in this chapter as they emerge during the psychoanalytic encounter.

---

* See Chapter 8 for a discussion of interpretations that keep evolution open and interpretations that shut down evolution as a resistance function of the analyst.

4

"Does a Dog Have a Buddha Nature or Not?" Nihilism, Absolutism, and "Joshu's Mu"

> Master Joshu and the dog—
> Truly exorbitant, their foolishness.
> Being and non-being at last
> Annihilated, speak the final word!
>
> —Soen, 1859–1919 (Stryk & Ikemoto, 1995, p. 39)

Introduction

In Chapter 2, I described how differing conceptions of being and nonbeing held by the Jesuit missionaries and the Zenists resulted in a misunderstanding of Zen practice and beliefs. This chapter takes up the Zen koan "Joshu's Mu" in relation to the psychoanalytic encounter.* This koan is one of many that address dualism/nondualism and serves as a specific example of the Zen discourse characterized by the use of apophasis and cuts through absolutist and nihilist extremism. The duality/nonduality antinomy is a fairly common theme throughout the various koan collections. For instance, the *Mumonkan*, the 13th-century Zen master Mumon's (Wu-men) collection of koans and commentaries, which is introduced by "Joshu's Mu," addresses this theme in 10 of the 48 cases in the collection. They include Case 5, "Kyogen Up a Tree"; Case 11, "Joshu and the Hermits"; Case 14, "Nansen Cuts a Cat"; Case 23, "Think Neither Good Nor Evil"; Case 24, "Separate From Words and Language"; Case 26, "Two Monks Roll Up Blinds"; Case 35, "Senjo Separated From Her Soul";† Case

---

* Alternatively: "Joshu's Dog" (Yamada, 1979); "Chao Chou's Dog" (Aitken, 1991; Magid 2005); "Joshu [on the Inherent Nature of a] Dog" (Kapleau, 1966). I refer to the koan as "Joshu's Mu" throughout for consistency.

† For an explication of this koan from a psychoanalytic perspective, see Gunn (1999).

36, "On the Road Meet an Adept of the Way"; Case 43, "Shuzan's Bamboo Rod"; and Case 44, "Basho's Staff."

The terse and cogent text of "Joshu's Mu" is as follows:

> A monk once asked Joshu, "Has a dog the Buddha Nature or not?" Joshu said, "Mu!" (Shibayama, 2000, p. 19)

It is noteworthy that some translations miss both aspects of the duality presented by omitting the final phrase "or not." This omission inadvertently and unconsciously privileges being. *Not* holds both conceptual and practical significance. This becomes clear with respect to practice and the salvational goals of Zen practice, which we will discuss below along with implications for psychoanalytic theory.

Joshu's assertion, "Mu," operates as a highly charged condensation and expression of *sunyata* (emptiness, voidness), a nonobjectifiable reality that is neither being nor nonbeing but that simultaneously includes and transcends both. Translations that omit "or not" reinforce one-sidedness in both the question and the resulting answer. On this point in his critique of scientism and nihilism, Abe (1990) observes that "Sunyata not only is not Being or God, but also *not* emptiness as distinguished from somethingness or fullness" (p. 27).

Although Mumon asserts that there is no significance to the order of the koans in this collection, commentators note that the importance of "Joshu's Mu" can be ascertained by its placement as the first in the *Mumonkan* (Aitken, 1991; Shibayama, 2000; Yamada, 1979). Additionally, variations of "Joshu's Mu" appear with considerable frequency in numerous koan collections and recorded saying texts.

In his introduction to Yasutani Roshi's *teisho* (talk) given during a *sesshin* (retreat) in 1961, which incidentally was the first English commentary to be given on "Joshu's Mu," Kapleau (1966) notes that "even to this day no koan is assigned to novices more often. It is commonly agreed among Japanese masters that it is unsurpassed for breaking asunder the mind of ignorance and opening the eye of Truth" (p. 63). In practice, many Zen teachers rely exclusively on "Joshu's Mu" with which to train their students. For instance, Aitken (1991) describes *Mu* as "the foundation of our koan study" (p. 9).

In my own experience, the opening *teisho* given at the start of a *sesshin* is typically on *Mu*. I have also attended retreats that were devoted entirely and exclusively to "Joshu's Mu" both in group practice and as the subject of *dokusan* (private one-on-one interviews). During *dokusan* with Enkyo

O'Hara, Roshi, responding to my expressed frustration and embarrassment with my seemingly endless struggle with *Mu*, she said "If *Mu* were my final utterance, I will be satisfied with my life."

Mumonkan, the collection's title, translates to "Gateless Gate" or "Gateless Barrier." "Gateless Barrier" graphically captures Zen's antinomianism and the paradoxical relationship of being and nonbeing that Zenists posit as inclusive rather than as reducible to a positivist set of mutually exclusive and known elements expressed dualistically as "either/or." In this context, *barrier* or *gate* refers to the discriminating mind, which functions as an obstacle to liberation. Shibayama (2000) notes in his commentary on this collection that "the barrier of the ancient masters is the barrier to Zen, and an obstacle to transcend is the dualism of yes and no, subject and object" (pp. 25–26).

Taken as discrete units, the monk's Buddha nature and "Joshu's Mu" represent polarized extremes of affirmation and negation; however, taken holistically and inclusively, the koan in its totality cuts through dualities. "Joshu's Mu" cuts through reification of both "Buddha nature" and "not" as objects, things, fixation, or endpoints. As a whole, the text of the koan represents a relationally engendered examination eventuating in a process of experiential self-realization that the individual becomes solely responsible for. For instance, Abe (1985) notes that "in Zen the absolute is grasped as 'Mu' or absolute Nothingness which is completely nonsubstantial, thus the individual is paradoxically identical with the absolute, and as such is thoroughly realized as an individual" (p. 20). This self-realization places complete responsibility for action on the individual. Nothing exists behind the individual—no soul, god, demon, and no spirit. In this respect, Zen parallels the psychoanalytic agenda of engendering personal responsibility, by, for example, as relinquishing infantile wishes. Such relinquishment requires making such wishes and claims conscious and establishing developmentally more adaptive and age-appropriate forms of human relatedness.

Mu Practice

> No matter what,
> sitting with eyes opened or closed;
> Just "Mu"!
> nothing more, nothing less;
> nothing more, nothing less.

(Cooper, 2008)

From the point of view of practice, the koan presents the student with the opportunity to experientially and intuitively confront the dualistic, discriminating mind that makes distinctions between being and nonbeing. In this context "discriminating mind" refers to our ordinary consciousness, which is dualistic, moves in a linear manner from cause to effect, and maintains relative subject and object separations and discriminations. Discriminating mind, according to Zen thought, results in the perpetuation of suffering, ignorance, alienation, and aggression. Therefore, according to Shibayama (2000), "the dualism of being and non-being is the barrier that requires breaking through" (p. 26). The full translation of the koan is crucial in this endeavor.

Mumon's commentary following this koan highlights the intense degree of activity and engagement demanded of the practitioner. He writes, following Aitken's (1991) translation: "So then, make your whole body a mass of doubt, and with your three hundred and sixty bones and joints and your eighty-four thousand hair follicles concentrate on this one word 'Mu.' Day and night keep digging into it" (p. 8).

Mumon then admonishes the student to "exhaust all of your life energy on this one word 'Mu.' If you do not falter, then it's done! A single spark lights your dharma candle" (p. 9). He conveys the strong sense of urgency and the intense level of energy applied to this task of concentration by comparing the process of internalizing *Mu* to "swallowing a red-hot iron ball." He adds that "you try to vomit it out but you can't" (p. 9).

The 12th-century Zen master Tai-hui asserts:

> This matter (i.e. Zen) is like a great mass of fire; when you approach it your face is sure to be scorched. It is again like a sword about to be drawn; when it is once out of the scabbard, someone is sure to lose his life. But if you neither fling away the scabbard nor approach the fire, you are no better off than a piece of rock or wood. Coming to this pass, one has to be quite resolute of character and full of spirit. (D. T. Suzuki, 1994, p. 25)

This level of highly charged and focused concentration depicted in various commentaries on *Mu* is highly purposeful and is intended to engender movement between cognitive and intuitive processes. On this point, D. T. Suzuki (1994) speaks to this intense active energy in his discussion of what he describes as a transitional phase between study and experience. He writes:

> It is to be distinctly understood that this period of incubation, which intervenes between the metaphysical quest and the Zen experience proper, is not one of

passive quietness but of intense strenuousness, in which the entire consciousness is concentrated at one point. Until the entire consciousness really gains this point, it keeps up an arduous fight against all intruding ideas. It may not be conscious of the fighting, but an intense seeking, or a steady looking down into the abysmal darkness is no less than that. (p. 53)

"Joshu's Mu" clearly and tersely reflects one-pointed practice geared toward cutting through dualistic thinking. In response to the student's question, Joshu simply says *Mu*. Joshu might have easily said *U* (yes). According to some commentaries, he sometimes would! For example, the following dialogue is recorded in the *Joshu Zenji Goroku* [Sayings of Master Joshu]:

Another monk asked Joshu, "Has a dog the Buddha Nature or not?" The master said "U" (yes). The monk asked, "Having the Buddha Nature, why is he in such a dog-body?" Master: "Knowingly, he dared so." (Shibayama, 2000, p. 23)

From the Zen perspective, yes or no does not matter because Truth manifests in infinite form, but is not limited to any particular form, object, and word. Ultimately there is no difference. Truth is Truth as myriad forms emerge, crystallize, solidify, dissolve, and fade in constant oscillation. If we leave it with *Mu*, if we leave it with Joshu's silence, or the kicked over rice bucket,* or with the sting of Tokusan's stick, we are left with what can be described as a "fundamental error" (Sells, 1994), that is, as a fixed and reified endpoint to a fluid nonsubstantial endless process of lived ongoing being. Such an error engenders a split, which in turn, if not addressed, creates conflict. This conflict holds internal psychic, relational, and global implications and from the Zen perspective is the source of all conflict. Zen describes this conflict as "dualistic fixation," which, as Zenists point out, stems from an attachment to the reified fixation point and keeps one caught in relative reality and maintains an illusion of the individual as an isolated, separate, and distinct human being. Zenists understand the illusion of distinct independent being through the operation of *avidya* (ignorance, not knowing). For the Zenist, the resolution of avidya through perceptual alteration becomes a matter of life and death and can only be resolved experientially. The *Mu* koan serves to facilitate this process. Loori (1994) notes, "This Mu gets to the heart of our very existence" (p. 64).

Joshu's response (*Mu*, *U*, or silence) exemplifies Zen's direct iconoclastic challenge of all reifications and positions. As apophatic discourse, Zen

---

* See Chapter 5.

"speaks away" (Sells, 1994) or deconstructs all assertions and negations, often through the use of questions and responses that are positive or negative propositions, or by challenges and by actions. From a synchronic perspective such challenges might be considered to be linear responses to student questions because dualistic consciousness automatically organizes Joshu's *Mu* into an answer. From a synchronic perspective, cause-and-effect linear sequencing comes into view: question → answer, yes or no, *U* or *Mu*. It is the habit of the conditioned mind to think of language as exclusively linear, logical, and didactic. The issue here is not whether Joshu answers in the affirmative or the negative or that *Mu* can even be considered as an answer.

Considered exclusively from a linear sequential perspective, yes or no would reify one side or the other. Reification engenders and maintains a split sense of reality. "Joshu's Mu" thus becomes, not unlike Tokusan's action to beat his student regardless of the latter's negative or positive response, or even silence, an example of what D. T. Suzuki (1949) describes "as merely utterances of the supreme moment" (p. 249). Rather than an answer or an informative response, "Joshu's Mu" becomes a performative presentation of Buddha nature. That is, as Shibayama (2000) notes, *Mu* becomes "the experience of Buddha Nature itself creatively expressed here by 'Mu'" (p. 21). *Mu* demonstrates the truth that transcends yes and no, being and nonbeing. Considering its performative function, "Joshu's Mu" is not a statement of fact. It is not meant to be descriptive or informational and therefore has no "truth value" (Hori, 2000, p. 285). As I noted in Chapter 3, "Joshu's Mu" exemplifies what I referred to as a "shock value" (Rosemont, 1970, p. 118).

Alternatively, when considered from a diachronic perspective, linear sequential relationships dissolve. In this regard, Joshu's response is neither an answer nor a response, as if Joshu's response depends on the question, as if the answer is actually an answer, as if either question or response can be privileged or ignored. "Joshu's Mu" does not depend on a preceding question. Rather, *Mu* naturally and spontaneously arises as an integral aspect of a cocreated contextually emerging situation; *Mu* simultaneously affirms and deconstructs being (Buddha nature) and nonbeing ("or not"). As an integral aspect of the total situation *Mu* operates as a free expression of Joshu's enlightened mind. As an expression, it is meant to cut through delusion and dualistic thinking. One might speculate that Joshu might be saying "No, don't ask." "No, how could you ask such a question?" "No, look at what you are asking!" Such questions split reality into yes's and no's. Speculation, as creative as it might be, functions as a conditioned habit of mind that engages conceptual processes and derails the potential for lived experiential intuited and performed Truth. Similarly, effective psychoanalytic interpretations will both inform and perform and can be quite terse, condensing long periods of the patient's narrative into what might appear to anyone outside of the dyad as enigmatic and meaningless statements. For instance, in one case, which I won't elaborate at present, after an extended period of sessions and a seemingly endless patient narrative, I simply said, "Rejection begets rejection." Similarly, in another case, I simply said, "Like Uncle Joe." Both patients knew and felt exactly what I meant both emotionally and cognitively. Just as the Zen master can evaluate the student's awareness during the interview, so too the responses to both of these comments indicated a level of understanding and development.

In this regard experiential actualization of emptiness unlocks the gate to what D. T. Suzuki describes as "Wondrous Being." Further, as gateless barrier, *Mu* does not simply function as a vehicle or key to emptiness/ultimate reality. *Mu is* being ultimate reality, suchness, or as S. Suzuki (1970) describes, "being-as-it-is" or "as-it-isness," and as Abe (1990) describes as "things as they are," "so of itself" (p. 31). As Abe (1985) notes, emphasizing the "here and nowness" implicit in Zen's experiential focus: "Without existential actualization of absolute Mu, there is no awakening to ultimate reality" (p. 130).

What is at stake is a freeing up of the intellect, conception, and discourse. There is no need for the intrusion of conceptual thought through speculation, abstraction, epistemological interpretation, or scriptural exegesis. The focus is exclusively on *Mu* or *U*, plain and simple. The meditator sits with *Mu*, becomes *Mu*. When we face *Mu*, we face the ego. We face the transparency of the need for things to be complex, profound, and deep. *Mu* is simple and simple is too easy. There is no ego in the simple, the easy, the concrete, or a sip of tea. So in searching for the profound we escape the moment. *Mu* is the moment. On this point, Albert Welter (2000) describes what "amounts to a categorical renunciation of the possibility of meaningful statements" (p. 76).

Zen practice supersedes, transcends, and cuts through this conditioning and the dialectic tension in the question. This one-pointed practice is clearly reflected in the *Mu* koan. Similarly, as we will explore below, the implications of "Joshu's Mu" as a Zen practice can cut through the dialectic tensions of seemingly contradictory psychoanalytic concepts and theories.

From a holistic perspective, the student's affirmation and Joshu's response function together as what Sells (1994) describes "as a discourse of double propositions, in which meaning is generated through the tension between the saying and the unsaying" (p. 12). In other words, as apophatic discourse, *Mu* speaks away both "Buddha nature" and "not Buddha nature." From the Zen perspective, transcendence and immanence are one. In this regard Joshu's response is both informative and performative. *Mu* and *U* become what Sells refers to as a "meaning event," which he describes as the moment when expression and meaning are fused in the moment. The meaning event is the moment that occurs during the psychoanalytic encounter when the analyst's interpretation and the patient's response are no longer exclusively hypothetical, speculative, informative, and based solely on discovered "evidence" and words, but are spontaneously emerging expressions of lived-in-the-moment deeply felt emotional truth that can be transformative for both analyst and analysand alike.

D. T. Suzuki (1949) emphasizes this unity of the transcendence and immanence and notes:

> Salvation must be sought in the finite itself, there is nothing infinite apart from finite things; if you seek something transcendental, that will cut you off from this world of relativity, which is the same thing as the annihilation of yourself. You do not want salvation at the cost of your own existence. (p. 25)

He ties this together with a critique of nihilism and writes:

> To do away with consciousness so that nothing will disturb spiritual serenity was too negative a state of mind to be sought after by those who at all aspired to develop the positive content of the Buddha's own enlightenment mind.... Enlightenment was to be found in life itself, in its fuller and freer expressions, and not in its cessation. (p. 85)

Mu as Gate: Openings and Closings

Gate functions as both an entry and a block. From the religious perspective gate can function as an entryway, for instance, as Wilkenson (1994) asserts: "O gateway to the abyss, I come to you" (p. 139). Block, from the point of view of the medical model, fills in a space, such as an element that is first hypothesized, then discovered and added to a preassigned block on the periodic table of elements. The basic function of "Joshu's Mu," whether construed as an opening or a closing, is fundamentally neutral. The context in actual practice determines its positive or negative function.

For example, with respect to beginning practice, *Mu* fills in psychic space and dispels intruding thoughts and feelings. This initial practice prepares the student for facing openings. However, at some point, the practitioner realizes the emptiness of *Mu* along with the innate tendency to reify any experience. *Mu* is no exception and must be dropped so that the opening aspect of the gate functions to transform into an entry, which from the mystical perspective has to do with openings. In this regard, *Mu* can both activate and impede.

Continuing with *Mu* at this point might be perceived as a resistance to evolving Truth. This message is implicit in the story of Bodhidharma, the first patriarch of Zen in China, who sees no value in prayer, offerings, building monuments, and so forth. In answer to the emperor, he describes these activities as "nothing sacred" and holding "no merit."

Similarly, to cite another example, in preparation for practice I can recite the Heart Sutra to open and define a practice space. Alternatively, recitation can oversaturate the psychic space and suffocate me out of the practice space. This oversaturation of the practice space can defend against the anxiety associated with the evolving unknown and can function similarly to an accurate but poorly timed interpretation that is more a reaction to the analyst's anxiety than a response to the patient's material. In both situations, prayer and interpretation can operate as impingements into practice space and analytic space.

Mandates such as "Kill the Buddha" or "Enlightenment, throw it away" reflect how openings are also subject to reification and can become barriers. Both functions exist. Typically, openings and fillings oscillate during the course of any psychoanalytic session. Rhode (1998), for example, describes how the medical model has derailed the natural oscillation that occurs during the psychoanalytic encounter by splitting off devaluing and negating the presence of the mystical model. One variation is the tendency to devalue mystical techniques by subsuming religious practices such as meditation into the domain of technique. They are condemned to the shadow land of psychoanalytic technique, and their radical religious potential becomes safely neutralized and defused.

A psychoanalytic interpretation can become subjected to the same process until the life is drained out of it. Once it is given, analysand, analyst, or both might co-opt it and add it to their "territory." It then becomes a reference point that might or might not facilitate continued movement, growth, creativity, and discovery. One question that emerges centers on the various uses of interpretations. They can point toward conceptual realities and understandings, or they can facilitate entry into nonconceptual intuitive realities. In this respect, *Mu* functions as a live word beyond intellectual conceptualization. Ideally, when not weighted down by dogmatism and conceptual reification, *Mu*, as Heine (1994) notes, "functions as both a hindrance to illumination and sword cutting through all obstacles [and] ... if even a thought of discrimination comes, the truth of 'Mu' is altogether gone" (p. 31). Similarly, Shibayama (2000) writes that "when one is really 'Mu' through and through, to call it 'Mu' is already incorrect, for that belongs to the dualistic world of letters. 'Mu' here is just temporarily used in order to transcend U (yes) and Mu (no)" (p. 31). This is the reality that Bion speaks of when he writes that no analysis can be considered complete without the experience of what he describes as "at-one-ment" (1970).

Implications for Psychoanalysis

"Joshu's Mu" tersely represents Zen's radicalism, which if put to the test of religious praxes could potentially dislodge the practitioner's foundational beliefs. That is, as noted in Chapter 2, all Zen praxes confront the notion of assigning ontological priority to being conceptualized as a distinct God, a supreme being or self that operates independently of causes and conditions. Similarly, psychoanalysis confronts previously unquestioned beliefs regarding one's perception and experience of self and other. Such relations often operate out of conscious awareness and repeat early relational dynamics and associated affect states.

For the Zen practitioner, "Joshu's Mu" serves an analyzing, integrating, and synthesizing function. As noted above, the koan expresses in a terse and condensed form the totality of the Zen teaching of the identity of the relative and the absolute both performatively and informatively. "Joshu's Mu," as an alternative intuitive model, can also serve as a basis for unifying seemingly incongruent psychoanalytic theories that capture these different aspects of experience. In this respect, this koan can contribute to enriching our understanding, use, and further development of psychoanalytic theory and technique by creating a focal point for weaving together seemingly contradictory theoretical models while simultaneously respecting their differences.

For instance, contemporary intersubjectivity theorists have offered cogent and convincing critiques of the tendency in the literature on self psychology and object relations toward reification, agentification, and personification of the metapsychological concepts of self and object (Atwood & Stolorow, 1984; Stolorow & Atwood, 1992; Stolorow, Brandchaft, & Atwood, 1987). As a result, intersubjectivity theorists completely dismiss basic concepts that are central to object relations theory, such as projective identification, which they describe as implying a "unidirectional influence system" (Stolorow & Atwood, 1992, p. 22). This critique requires some unpacking. The idea of unidirectional system suggests a view of projective identification as exclusively a metapsychological construct that functions as an experience-distant, intrapsychic, unconscious defense mechanism that object relations theorists view as serving exclusively pathological evacuative, manipulative, and control functions. Such a view is consistent with Klein's original description of the process and reflects an accurate depiction of Klein's conception. Spillius (2007), in a review of Klein's unpublished notes, clarifies Klein's use of the term:

> Throughout these notes, and indeed throughout her work in general, it is clear that Klein thinks of projective identification as an unconscious phantasy. For her it was an intrapersonal not an interpersonal concept and she did not discuss the possibility that an individual's phantasies about projective identification might affect his behavior in a way that would have an effect on his actual relationship with another person. (pp. 108–109)

However, this limited view of projective identification depicted by the intersubjectivists fails to take account of the normal communicative function described by Bion (1962a, 1962b), Ferro (2005), Grotstein (2007), Meltzer (1992), Rosenfeld (1965), Spillius (1988), and others. For example, Grotstein (2007) describes projective identification as a "realistic, intersubjective extension" (p. 168), which he views as "foundational" (p. 169).

Bion extended Klein's concept of projective identification beyond the limitations of metapsychological speculation and as exclusively a one-person unidirectional unconscious phantasy to a two-person experientially based bimodal intersubjective system. Without negating the potential for pathological aspects of projective identification, he emphasized the normal preverbal communicative function and described oscillations through a mutual projective/introjective cycle, and that includes the reciprocal process of the analyst's reverie, containing, and interpretive function. During his São Paulo lectures in Brazil during 1973 he noted: "I am not sure, from the practice of analysis, that it is only an *omnipotent* phantasy" (1990, p. 68). He then makes a distinction between the correctness of theory and the experience that takes place in the consulting room, thus shifting from metapsychology to experience. He writes: "But I do not think that the correct theory and the correct formulation happen in the consulting room" (p. 68). He adds that "I have felt, and some of my colleagues likewise, that when the patient appears to be engaged on a projective identification it *can* make me feel persecuted, as if the patient can in fact split off certain nasty feelings and shove them into me so that I actually have feelings of persecution or anxiety" (p. 68).

As a defense, projective identification serves, albeit ineffectively, to expel reified self and object images and associated intolerable affect states. In this respect this process is geared toward altering one's perceived state of being, with often disastrous consequences for interpersonal relationships. This is in part due to the escalation of persecutory anxieties and the further exacerbation of reification processes and a resulting vicious cycle. Zen practice, as exemplified in "Joshu's Mu," cuts through the transparency of seemingly reified states of being, which in my experience diminishes the intensity of persecutory anxiety and the need for evacuation, which in turn can restore the communicative function and engender more beneficial relationships.

The process of analysis results in the healing of the split and the integration of good/bad/self/object images and associated affects leading to an integrated self depicted in Kleinian theory as a movement from the paranoid schizoid position to the depressive position. In this respect, the intersubjectivists rightly critique the reification of selves, objects, fragments, and so forth. In terms of the Zen notion of the relative and the absolute, we can argue that intersubjectivity reflects the nihilist extreme and the object relations theorists reflect an absolutist extreme. That is, the Kleinians, as I see it, generally do not question reification, and the intersubjectivists do not seem to make room for the actuality of false perceptions of self and other that result from reification processes. Rather, they attempt to address the reifications theoretically.

From the Zen perspective, as noted above, all reifications are ultimately false, and in this respect, the intersubjectivity theorists rightfully question the misuse of these important concepts. For example, Stolorow et al. (1987) cite "the central emphasis on the primacy of self experience" as one of the "essential contributions" of self psychology (p. 15). However, they are critical of what they describe as a typical confusion between "the self-as-structure and the person-as-agent" (p. 18), which they exemplify in the statement "the fragmented self strives to restore its cohesion" (p. 18). They argue that such a use of the concept of self "as an existential entity transforms the personal agentic 'I' into a reified 'it,' not unlike the id, ego, and superego of classical theory" (p. 18). They offer a linguistic/theoretical solution to this problem and write:

This problem can be minimized if we restrict the concept of self to describe organizations of experience and use the term person (an irreducible ontological construct that falls outside the domain of empathic-introspective inquiry) to refer to the existential agent who initiates actions. (pp. 18–19)

However, this proposed theoretical/linguistic solution does not address the fundamental human process of unconscious reification, which Zenists attribute to fundamental anxiety. Zenists further argue that effectively addressing reification and the consequent object/subject separation requires an experiential solution. The identity of the relative and the absolute points to the simultaneity of the fluidity and the reification of human experience that engenders, in turn, the experience of ultimate oneness of reality as well as the experience of relative subject/object separation.

A total dismissal of reification and the important concepts that are articulated through object relations theory reflects an underlying nihilism, which is also subject to reification and objectification. One danger becomes assigning subjective experiences, which are intrinsically fluid and ultimately nonsubstantial, the reified role of the "real objectivity." Relatively speaking, as Zenists point out, reification is an active process that functions to defend against fundamental anxiety, and this deeply rooted emotional response to our ultimate insubstantiality can't be worked out simply through new theoretical constructs. The necessity of experiential insight finds acknowledgment in such expressions as "You can't slay the tiger on the road by imagining that it is an elephant." The illusion of solidity and separateness holds very real earth-shattering consequences and must be addressed experientially and intuitively. One constructive way to speak to these processes theoretically is to view "Joshu's Mu" and the monks' "Buddha nature or not" as symbolic of this human tendency toward reification, and we can also think of the intersubjective point of view and object relations theory as highly rarified and well-thought-out theoretical manifestations of these basic human tendencies condensed in the terse "Buddha nature or not."

The dialogue between Joshu and the monk reflects different aspects of internal psychic processes and variations of experiencing that range between primary and secondary processes, dualistic and unitive experiencing, intuitive and cognitive perceptions, and the shifting relational experiences of self and other that extend across the range between separation and complete alienation, merger and a loss of a sense of an autonomous self, and the potential for a balance of simultaneous separation and connection. There is an infinite range of variation, expression, and response. For example, from a holistic perspective, the dialogue serves as a nonpolarized model of unitive experiencing, that is, an experience that is the basis for understanding in Zen practice and that holds implications for the psychoanalytic encounter. Zenists, as noted above, describe this balance as "the identity of one and the two." This identity speaks to the simultaneous separateness and connectedness that occurs during the psychoanalytic encounter. That is, unitive experiencing implies merger and dissolution of boundaries between self and other, while simultaneously maintaining an experience of individual separateness. The clinical implications of this simultaneity will be explored in depth through an extended case study in Chapter 10.

When considered holistically as differing aspects of one reality, they point to different characteristics of human experience. When one side is privileged, such as when one assumes a noninclusive approach to psychoanalytic theory, suggests parallels to the dropping off the "or not" phrase in "Joshu's Mu" by certain translators. Similarly, psychoanalytic notions such as theoretical constructs, diagnosis, and cure can also become reified as things and endpoints. The notion of cure, for example, in psychotherapy often implies a fixation point, an endpoint, and at the extreme denies and alienates the individual from the truth of constant change. As I noted above, there are no reified endpoints, only a series of ongoing meaning events with varying degrees of depth, contingent on a particular context and emotional intensity at a specific moment in time—one moment in an ongoing series of ever-evolving moments. This specificity shifts from moment to moment with different patients. In this regard, the claims of Truth are not compatible with the notions of diagnosis and cure. Rhode (1998) summarizes this perspective by noting:

> As the variable, "O" activates a state of *becoming* unrelated to any claim to therapeutic progress or cure. In the religious vertex nothing progresses or is cured. There is either an evasion or a recognition of "O" by way of a *becoming*. (p. 118)

For example, a young man ended our work together by noting: "Now I know what I am feeling and I know that's a good thing." As a result he had become more tolerant and compassionate toward others. This point that neither aspect be privileged is clear in the Shibayama (2000) rendering of

Mumon's poem that accompanies the koan and serves as an appropriate conclusion to this chapter:

> The dog! The Buddha nature!
> The Truth is manifested in full.
> A moment of yes-and-no:
> Lost are your body and soul. (p. 20)

5

Sand in Rice:
One Koan, Infinite Possibilities

> Hsueh-feng was serving as the rice cook. Once ... the Master asked, "Do you cull out pebbles and set the rice aside, or do you cull out the rice and set the pebbles aside?"
> "I set aside the rice and the pebbles at one and the same time," replied Hsueh-feng.
> "What will the monks eat?" asked the Master.
> Hsueh-feng immediately turned over the rice bucket. (Powell, 1986, p. 37)

Introduction

This vignette* exemplifies the apophatic nature of the Zen discourse in terms of action. That is, whatever statement is made about ultimate reality or the ineffable also needs to be "spoken away" or "unsaid" (Sells, 1994). Koan dialogues typically oscillate between reified reference points and the ongoing deconstruction of such references. Hsueh-feng turns over the rice bucket and walks away, thus privileging neither side—rice nor pebbles.

The following koan from the *Mumonkan* provides an opportunity to examine this language structure more closely in terms of both the informative and performative functions of the Zen koan with respect to the salvational intention of koan study and with regard to implications for the psychoanalytic encounter.

---

* From the Record of Tung-shan.

"Joshu Saw Through the Old Woman"

> A monk asked an old woman, "Which way should I take to Mount Gotai?"* The old woman said, "Go straight on!" When the monk had taken a few steps, she remarked, "He may look like a fine monk, but he too goes off like that!" Later, a monk told Joshu about it. Joshu said, "Wait a while. I will go and see through that old woman for you." The next day off Joshu went. He asked her the same question. The old woman, too, gave him the same reply. When he returned, Joshu announced to the monks, "I have seen through that old woman of Mount Gotai for you." (Shibayama, 2000, p. 223)

Joshu's enigmatic response to his students regarding his encounter with the old woman also serves a performative function. That is, as Michael Sells (1994) notes, with respect to mystical languages (and certain psychoanalytic languages), "unnameability is not only asserted, it is performed" (p. 3).

Issues of koan interpretation center on variations in a relationship that fuses action, language, and symbolism in terms of their religious function and structure. The relation between language and dialogue exemplifies this issue with equal relevance to both psychoanalysis and Zen. One might ask: "What is the intention of a statement? Does an interpretation, for instance, promote or derail dialogue?" In either case, the basic question for the iconoclastic Zenist is whether or not the interaction deconstructs reified conceptions, cuts through linear discursive thinking, and dissolves dogmatic preconceptions that occlude the practitioner's direct experience.

Similarly, the psychoanalyst might ask if an interpretation, regardless of whether or not it facilitates dialogue or engenders silence, deconstructs old object relations, self-object dyads, and transferences, and synthesizes disparate aspects of the person? For instance, an obsessive narrative that leaves the analyst feeling excluded, closed out, or erased might result in an intervention intended to disrupt the analysand's monologue, short-circuit a tendency toward intellectualization, engender an in-the-moment, lived emotional experience, and create an opportunity for relatedness and self-reflection.

Heine (1994) notes, with equal relevance to psychoanalysis:

> The main factor that contributes to the effectiveness of the koan as a means of spiritual training is not a matter of setting up a contrast between words and wordlessness, speech and silence, or prolixity and brevity. Rather ... that the interpretation ... resists being turned into a formula, conceptual crutch, or object of dependence, that is, ritualized so that mere repetition diminishes spontaneity. (p. 61)

---

* Mount Gotai is also known as Mt. Taizan and Mt. Wu tai shen.

For the psychoanalyst who practices Zen any response to a patient will depend on how one's theoretical orientation and religious experiences are internalized. For example, the psychoanalytic notion of pure neutrality, "blank screen," or the Zen notion of "no-belief" are also subject to unconscious reification, dogmatic skewing, and require scrutiny. Both neutrality and no-belief reflect a particular bias on the part of the individual who holds such views.

Both Zen and psychoanalysis exploit the polysemous nature of words, phrases, and silences. The capacity for a word to hold several meanings contributed to Freud's conceptualization of unconscious processes and to his technique of unpacking condensations in dreams and uncovering the latent meaning of manifest content. With this point in mind, koan study holds the potential to provide an entry into the examination of the multidetermined meanings and functions of the said and the unsaid in the psychoanalytic encounter without dualistic polarizations. In this regard, we can think of Zen and psychoanalysis as members of what Matte-Blanco (1988) describes as equivalence sets that include similarities, differences, and identities. For Dogen, koans simultaneously function both as a means and as an expression of realization. He used what Heine (1994) describes as the "scenic route" because Dogen endeavored to promote dialogue. Although recently subjected to the critique and questioning of modern scholarship, traditionally Dogen has been contrasted with Ta-hui, who utilized the *wato* or cutting-word (shortcut) method to disrupt intellectualized dialogue and provoke a self-reflective silence. In different ways, both Dogen and Ta-hui criticized traditional koan study, which, they argued, shut down creative dialogue because the koan became subjected to the same pervasive reifying forces they were designed to cut through, and thus became institutionalized, codified, brittle, stagnant, and oppressive.

The koan's disruption of logical, sequential thinking engenders a gap. The iconic function of the gap, to use Eric Rhode's meaning, facilitated by Zen praxis engenders an intuitive experiential awareness of emptiness and of the truth of "unity of self and reality, humans and nature, subject and object" (Heine, 1994, p. 44) and parallels what Bion (1970) describes as experienced through the intuition of O. Through O Bion keeps the ineffable open. He writes, "I shall use the sign O to denote that which is the ultimate reality, absolute truth, the godhead, the infinite, the thing-in-itself" (p. 26). Rhode (1998) adds: "It explores and defines the existence of the gap, as though to exorcise the gap of meaning" (p. 35). In this regard, the identified and experienced gap is stripped of meaning. Meaning, from this perspective, can occlude experience and thus requires deconstruction or unsaying.

D. T. Suzuki (1949) notes that "Zen in its essence is the art of seeing into the nature of one's own being, and it points the way from bondage to freedom" (p. 13). With this Zen salvational intention in mind, we might ask: How does the koan "Joshu Saw Through the Old Woman" facilitate experiential knowing of one's own mind as the old woman suggests by asserting "Go straight on!"? Enigmatically, she directs the seeker inwardly.

Commenting on this koan, Yamada (1979) notes that "old woman" in the Zen tradition is a title of respect that connotes a spiritually advanced being. However, women are often depicted as simultaneously wise and dangerous in the Zen literature. Not unlike the psychoanalyst, their identity is typically intentionally left ambiguous (Heine, 2002; Powell, 1986).

The text's performative function provides access to another dimension of experiencing. What movement does the old woman exert on the student who reads, studies, and practices this koan? Does the student look outwardly or inwardly for an answer? Does the patient repeatedly get to the same old bad place and then proceed to blame the other, the boss, the lover, the therapist, or the circumstance and, in this manner, resists looking inwardly, resists taking any responsibility for the dilemma, resists any possibility for inner change?

The old woman's response and Joshu's silence operate to open the gap between being and knowing and stimulate the potential to alter perception, which is the key to Buddhism's salvational function (Klein, 1986). In this regard, "the way to Mt. Gotai" is the actual practice. One climbs the mountain sitting still. Mt. Gotai was believed to be the dwelling place of Manjushri, who in Buddhist cosmology represents wisdom and, as Aitken (1991) notes, "is our archetype of insight into the void" (p. 196).

The answer to the question "straight ahead, keep practicing" parallels the New York City koan: Tourist: "How do you get to Carnegie Hall?" Taxi driver: "Practice!" The woman instructs the student to go straight into his practice. Yamada (1979) notes that "if the practitioner searches for Manjushri somewhere outside of himself, he is going the wrong way" (p. 164). Ninth-century Zen master Rinzai notes: "There is something at this moment at work in you, never doubting, never faltering—this is your living Manjushri" (p. 196). As icon, Manjushri becomes an entry point into internal self-insight, into O evolution. As idol, he is worshiped and sought after externally.

Eigen (1985) writes: "Bion notes that the human race is ill-equipped to tolerate its own experiential capacity. It naturally orients itself toward external objects and the tasks of survival" (p. 224). For the Buddhist, ignorance, as noted previously, reifies fluid experience and phenomena into solid fact, engenders a separation of self and other, and perpetuates grasping for externals such as Manjushri and Mt. Gotai. Joshu's silence, the student's mindless walking, and the woman's ambiguous directive reflect different aspects of this fundamental human tendency and become simultaneously a diagnosis and a prescription.

Eigen (1985) also notes that "it is more natural to be related to objects in sensuous terms and avoid the uncanny intuition of alternate psychic realities" (pp. 220–221). Koan practice and the psychoanalytic encounter, similarly, are *not* natural psychic realities. They both press through and beyond old established patterns of individual and mass hallucination that have become habituated and seemingly natural. Both disciplines confront the individual with a disruption of such patterns. This koan functions as a tool that reflects this basic movement and the difficulties encountered in the process involved in cutting through established patterns of reasoning and intellect, with its dualistic baggage, hardened through time and experience. Bion describes this process of movement as emotionally turbulent and catastrophic, ultimately engendering the experience of at-one-ment. Similarly, Heine (1994) characterizes this process as a "constructive conflict resulting in a spiritual release from fixation and delusion" (p. 51). A koan does propel the practitioner to a basic ground of being, which Lopez-Corvo (2005) identifies by defining Bion's O alternatively as "origin" (p. 315). He elaborates this point by quoting German philosopher Eugen Herrigel's classic, *Zen and the Art of Archery* (1953). Herrigel writes, "He must dare to leap into the Origin so as to live by Truth, like one who has become one with it" (pp. 80–81). However, it is important to note here a significant point of divergence between Bion and the Zen experience related to this ground of being. Bion struggles with the original catastrophe of psychic birth. Zen posits an original fundamental anxiety that reifies experience that is then maintained by this active "not knowing" and that supports splitting and reification.

Reification processes contribute to a patient's transferences and object relations. Anxiety forces the individual's search into the external world. For example, consider the following situation.

Glenn

Glenn presents to me as helpless and wants to move forward. He pressures me for direction and answers. His path to Mt. Gotai is his development, which he describes as "delayed." He sees himself as "lagging behind, immature, a Peter Pan." Unable to tolerate internal states, he compares himself to a rudderless boat that does fine on a calm sea, but not in an emotional storm. His need to present himself to me as helpless and child-like resides in the unconscious dimensions of the transference. Without experiencing the transparency of this reified transference dynamic, Glenn's aggression, capacity for assertion, and self-motivation remain split off and his life remains stalled.

Language is also subject to reification processes and results in the activation of the idolic function of the koan. As idol, Manjushri and the way to Mt. Gotai are both taken as a linear, sequential, logical external literal path "straight ahead!" The monk who continues on this literal path simply accumulates in a manner that Bion describes as K (knowledge) accumulations, which saturate psychic space, cloud the gap, and foreclose potential O evolutions. Rhode (1998) describes the destructive function of K accumulations related to a pervasive overidealization of the scientific model and the complementary devaluation of the mystical model. He points to the pervasiveness of unconscious reification processes, which he identifies as a "specificity and configuration." Human beings crave structure, predictability, and the illusion of an ordered reality. It *feels* better when things make sense. Freud's dictum "Where id was shall ego be" echoes this basic need. The old woman's rote response represents this craving for structure, answers, and predictability. However, her noted ambiguity also simultaneously points to infinite possibilities presented by the potential gap. She points to a disconnection from internal awareness and responds to the question in terms of its religious or salvational significance. However, the student hears her answer from a linear perspective. In order to hear from the mystical perspective, all expectations need to be dropped. Such expectations, when not dropped, as noted above, saturate psychic space and obscure the capacity for experiential wisdom from which Zenists argue ultimate truth can be intuited.

This position holds practical implications. For example, Zen and psychoanalysis can function as palliatives or as radically salvational. Joshu remains silent. He offers no solution, no palliative. Can Glenn steer his own boat or does he need a palliative reassuring tow? Both functions exist in the practice. As palliative, the gap becomes sealed along with the anxiety engendered by awareness of the gap and the overwhelming infinite possibilities that it presents. As radically salvational, the gap opens and the void is experienced as it is. In Zen parlance: "Just this, just this!"

Similarly, a psychoanalytic interpretation can function in both ways. An interpretation that Bion would describe as well practiced, rote, and oversaturated with meaning closes off the gap. Such an interpretation might be viewed as the "last word." If the patient disagrees, he or she is believed to be resistant. We are all familiar with the extensive psychoanalytic literature on resistance, which I am not interested in devaluing or negating. I simply point out its vulnerability to reification processes and the potential for oppression when viewed and misused dogmatically or rigidly in an endeavor to foreclose the gap. The iconic function of the interpretation facilitates openings; it becomes a creative entry point and an invitation—just as the old woman invites the student to open up to an alternative way of experiencing that is not necessarily linear and logical. The call is to break out of the tyranny of oppression of preconception and dogma. From the point of view of logical thinking, question and answer imply cause and effect in linear progression and are part of what Rhode (1998) describes as "an idealization of continuity" (p. 20). The intuited meaning becomes occluded by an oversaturation of continuity. He notes that "in the religious vertex, on the other hand, discontinuity may be a source of meaning" (p. 20). Similarly, none of our concepts and intellect-driven ideas can facilitate contact with the experienced wisdom that the koan holds. None of our well-reasoned hypotheses about Glenn's unconscious dynamics can replace his lived experience of the moment-to-moment fluctuations of lived Truth as he begins to risk rowing and steering his own boat as I watch from the psychic shoreline without impinging into his ocean.

The koan engenders access to the infinite, which is its iconic function. This is the iconic function of a good interpretation: opening, expanding, creating more emotional elbow room.

For Glenn, this means taking personal responsibility and discovering that he can row his own boat in both calm and turbulent waters. He appears delighted with his "newfound skill" and notes that he "probably could have done this all along, but didn't know it!" Joshu "gets" the iconic function of the old woman's directive. Do we get it? Can the Zenist climb Mt. Gotai sitting still on the cushion breath by breath? Can we as psychoanalysts get it sitting still with our patients hour by hour?

In his commentary to this koan, Mumon says, "Tell me now what insight did Joshu have into the old woman?" (Shibayama, 2000, p. 164). Do we really need to know? Joshu's insight is his own. Hence, silence. My insight is my own. Glenn's is his own. Can insight be embraced and then relinquished before it becomes another source of saturation and foreclosure? What insight will facilitate an awareness of our rote, habitual repetitions, our transferences and our countertransferences, our capacity for and our failures in attention and intuition of evolving truth?

Concluding Remarks

Joshu's silence typifies the apophatic approach, which Sells (1994) summarizes by noting that "at the heart of that unsaying is a radical dialectic of transcendence and immanence. That which is utterly 'beyond' is revealed or reveals itself as most intimately 'within'" (p. 7). At-one-ment evolves experientially. In his commentary, Mumon notes, "for the first time her heart and soul were penetrated by a true acquaintance" (Shibayama, 2000, p. 166).

In a striking parallel, Herbert Rosenfeld (1987) writes:

> I have found that patients respond to our interpretations not only as tools which make them aware of the meaning of the unconscious and conscious processes, but also as a reflection of the analyst's state of mind … particularly his capacity to retain quietness and peacefulness and to focus on the central aspects of the patient's conscious and preconscious anxieties…. It is very reassuring for the patient if the analyst can succeed both in functioning well in his interpretive role and in retaining his quiet thoughtful state of mind. (pp. 31, 40)

Mumon concluded his commentaries on each koan in *Mumonkan* with a poem. The following poem concludes "Joshu Saw Through the Old Woman":

> The question is the same each time
> The answer, too, is the same.
> In the rice there is sand,
> In the mud there are thorns.

(Shibayama, 2000, p. 224)

Mumon also notes in his commentary that "upon close examination, they are both at fault" (p. 223). What is Joshu's fault? Did he fail to sit still as Rosenfeld suggests? Can Joshu see through for others? The student must see for himself. Joshu can't do this for him. But, Joshu does, in fact, have his own insight. He "saw for himself." If he shared his insight, he would only be creating more "sand in rice." Can I sit still with Glenn or do I need to help him in reaction to my own anxiety? How can the analyst abstain from creating sand in rice while simultaneously sharing observations? Depending on how it is used, language can create or destroy true insight. Joshu does not judge or evaluate. He witnesses and just sits with the experience, "Just this!" He makes no diagnosis.

As analysts we are continuously faced with the fork in the road between conscious and unconscious, primary and secondary processes, knowledge and truth. These are not necessarily mutually exclusive states that one must choose. There is no privilege. Both forms of experience are necessary for an integrated and whole psychoanalysis. Relationship implies a dialogue of what is said or not said. This dialogue is an important aspect of Zen training. Heine (1994) observes:

> Genuine awareness must come through an active engagement with another person who helps illuminate the self. Ideally, this encounter becomes equalized without a sense of priority or hierarchy in the relationship ... "killing the Buddha" requires eliminating the gap between superiority and inferiority, or objective instruction and inner realization. (p. 47)

Hence, Joshu's visit and his resulting silence. In this manner, Joshu shifts responsibility for inner realization from external objects to a dialogically engendered self-realization and experientially realized personal discovery. We see this trend in contemporary psychoanalytic theories. Without attention to the dyad in Zen practice and in the consulting room and in the Zen/psychoanalytic conversation, we are left with "sand in rice," "thorns in mud," and the potential for stagnation.

The dialogue between the old woman and the monk is no ordinary conversation. It is a teaching directed toward the *kanna-zen* practitioner. It contains both primary and secondary processes in that it is performative and exerts an emotional impact, and simultaneously the conversation is didactic or informational. The monk locked into secondary process is listening and simultaneously unable to listen.

In another koan, also in *Mumonkan*, Joshu tells a monk who is full of philosophical questions to "wash your bowl!" In pointing to the sand in rice, the psychotherapist is being asked to wash one's bowls to see clearly what is. Without the obfuscation of theory or preconception, seeing clearly what is, no more, no less, in the said and unsaid moments of a psychoanalytic session. It is from this vantage point that Cynthia Stone (2007) observes, from the combined perspective of Zen and psychoanalytic practice, the inclusive nature of the relative and absolute in terms of the intertwined nature of primary and secondary processes. She writes: "Both Zen and psychoanalysis aim at opening the channels to genuine experiences of the sensory, affective, undifferentiated primary process in the context of secondary process, adaptive functioning." This koan shows how the intrusion and overprivileging of secondary process can obscure our capacity for intuitive knowing. As such, the koan might serve to explore subtle nuances of relationships in the psychoanalytic encounter. The relevance of nonprivilege finds cogent expression, for instance, in Stephan Mitchell's comments on Hans Loewald in a discussion of Paul Russell's work. Mitchell (1998) writes that "Loewald stresses that primary process and secondary process are two alternative terms of organizing experience. Both equally real, there is no illusion involved" (p. 56).

The Zen/psychoanalytic conversation is a dialogue in and of itself that uses two very different languages and that holds the capacity to transform into a mutually enriched language. Often, the scientific language becomes privileged while mystical languages become subsumed, although their presence and influence can be traced. Various permutations represent what Matte-Blanco describes as occurring along a continuum of "symmetrization," oscillating between foreground and background. I feel invited by my patients to listen to the said and unsaid of both. I feel challenged by Joshu and the Joshu in my patient to discover, create, co-create, re-create what Truths might emerge in each lived moment.

6

Unconscious and Conscious in Zen and Psychoanalysis

The concept of there being unconscious mental processes is of course one that is fundamental to psycho-analytic theory.

—Freud (1915, pp. 161–162)

When we are enlightened as to the selflessness of all beings, what difference is there between my face and Buddha's face?

—D. T. Suzuki (1972a, p. 29)

Introduction

Attention to unconscious processes and their influence on conscious mental life forms the nexus of Freud's psychoanalysis both theoretically and technically. His work, despite frequent contradictory developments, begins and ends with the unconscious and unconscious processes. From the psychoanalytic perspective, unconscious processes are fundamental to psychic life, and understanding their operation is critical to psychoanalysis. Despite the limitations imposed by Enlightenment secular philosophy and an associated dualistic scientific objectivism that Freud (1938a) felt compelled to conform to, his delineation of this "Realm of the Illogical" (p. 169) provides a creative, radical, and monumental point of entry for understanding and transforming the psyche.

Despite the significance Freud attributes to unconscious factors in the development of psychoanalysis, at present, no comprehensive discussion of the unconscious and unconscious processes exists in the expanding literature on Zen and psychoanalysis. As a result, a full and constructive conversation between Zen and psychoanalysis remains incomplete. With this point in mind, this chapter serves to discuss the role of unconscious processes in Zen practice. I will first trace Freud's placement of the unconscious at the center of the psychoanalytic endeavor. I will then review Matte-Blanco's radical reformulation and expansion of the Freudian unconscious, discuss D. T. Suzuki's explication of what he describes as the Zen unconscious through his discussion of the Chinese Zen monk Huineng's "no-mind" doctrine, and elaborate on implications for the psychoanalytic encounter.

Freud: The Impact of Discovery

Freud's discovery of the unconscious through his experiences of self-analysis and dream analysis, his understanding of the uses of hypnosis, and his collaboration with Breuer (Breuer & Freud, 1895) into the workings of hysterical processes marks the advent of a revolutionary new psychology. Freud developed and clarified his thinking regarding the unconscious in a series of writings that spanned his career (1900, 1912a, 1914, 1923, 1938a, 1938b). For example, with regard to hypnosis Freud (1938b) observed that "it is possible in the case of persons in a state of hypnosis to prove experimentally that there are such things as unconscious psychical acts and that consciousness is not an indispensable condition of (psychical) activity" (p. 285).

Conflicts: Psychoanalysis, Academic Psychology, Philosophy

Freud's insights and descriptions regarding the active unconscious aspects of mental life distinguished psychoanalysis from academic psychology and speculative philosophy. In this regard he (1938a) noted that "the majority of philosophies … declare that the idea of something psychical being unconscious is self contradictory…. But that is precisely what psychoanalysis is obliged to assert" (p. 158).

Freud's (1900) position engendered controversy, which he addressed by noting that "the physician and the philosopher can only come together if they both recognize that the term 'unconscious psychical processes' is 'the appropriate and justified expression of a solidly established fact'" (pp. 611–612). He asks: "What, then, can a philosopher say to a theory which, like psychoanalysis, asserts that on the contrary what is mental is in itself *unconscious* and that being conscious is only a *quality* which may or may not accrue to a particular mental act" (1925, p. 216).

Freud criticized the philosophical and introspectionist psychological overvaluation of consciousness and argued that this "symptom" occluded unconsciousness. He accomplished his critique by reducing consciousness to a transitory quality that might or might not be present at any given moment. This maneuver simultaneously raises unconsciousness to monolithic status. He observed that "the unconscious is the true psychic reality; in its *innermost nature it is as much unknown to us as the reality of the external world ...*" (1900, p. 613, emphasis in original).

Freud departed radically from his contemporaries. He proposed and described psychic processes regulated by laws that operate independently as "a consciousness apart which has become detached and estranged from the bulk of conscious psychical activity" (1912a, p. 263). In response to the introspectionist critique of the dynamic unconscious, Freud clarified this distinction. He summarized the opposing position as follows:

> Just as there are processes which are very vividly, glaringly, and tangibly conscious, so we also experience others which are only faintly, hardly even noticeably conscious; those that are most faintly conscious are, it is argued, the ones to which psychoanalysis wishes to apply the unsuitable name "unconscious." (1923, p. 16, fn)

Freud then countered the introspectionists by arguing:

> This attempt to equate what is unnoticed with what is unconscious is obviously made without taking into account the dynamic conditions involved, which were the decisive factors in forming the psychoanalytic view. (p. 16, fn)

Freud launched his voyages into the unknown waters of the human psyche weighted by the anchor of 19th-century positivism, and he boldly stretched his moorings to the limits. His graphic descriptions of unconscious processes simultaneously meet the restrictions of scientific elementism with regard to precision and detail and take the reader into realms characterized by formlessness, ambiguity, uncertainty, and processes that operate according to a unique logic. He inferred this world beyond sense perception indirectly by slips of the tongue, lapses of memory, jokes, and remembered dreams, and he described the key to experiencing the world of the unconscious as "a bending toward" (1912b) of the analyst's and the analysand's unconscious. In this manner, he pointed toward unitive experiencing. He acknowledged the essentially unknowable nature of this connection by noting that "it is a very remarkable thing that the unconscious of one human being can react upon that of another, without passing through consciousness ..." (1915, p. 194).

Freud on the Centrality of the Dynamic Unconscious

Freud positioned the dynamic unconscious as the foundational corner-stone of the psychoanalytic process. He asserted that "in a psychology which is founded on psychoanalysis we have accustomed ourselves to take as our starting-point the unconscious mental processes with the peculiari-ties of which we have become acquainted through analysis" (1911, p. 218). This brief yet sweeping statement points at once to the centrality of uncon-sciousness, the fluidity of mental functioning, and the subjective experi-entially verifiable nature of psychoanalytic experiences. He continuously presents radical transformations of previous formulations of his theory of psychoanalysis. However, he simultaneously maintains unconsciousness as the nodal point and distinctive feature that threads together seemingly unrelated elements of the psychoanalytic inquiry at various and concep-tually disparate points throughout. Freud's descriptions of reversal, dis-placement, identification, and condensation consistently convey the sense of fluidity, motion, and impermanence characteristic of the unconscious processes that he so carefully identified.

Freud described unconsciousness as "a regular and inevitable phase in the processes constituting our psychical activity; *every* psychical act begins as an unconscious one" (1912a, p. 264). For instance, in a radical alteration of his earlier models, Freud (1923) wrote that "the division of the psychical into what is conscious and what is unconscious is the fundamental prem-ise of psychoanalysis; and it alone makes it possible for psychoanalysis to understand the pathological processes of mental life" (p. 13). Further on he emphasized the significance of unconscious factors in mental life:

> To put it once more in a different way: psychoanalysis cannot situate the essence of the psychical in consciousness, but is obliged to regard consciousness as a quality of the psychical, which may be present in addition to other qualities or may be absent. (p. 13)

Freud's reiteration demonstrates the strength of his conviction. He continued to retain a sense of process and motion implicit in his remark regarding what "may be present or absent." Freud concluded that uncon-sciousness is "the first shibboleth of psychoanalysis" (p. 13). He also viewed the unconscious psychic processes as primary, and he argued that the overvaluation of consciousness obscures this basic psychic fact. Initially, this developmental starting point, he wrote, was "the only kind of mental process" (1911, p. 219). "It is probable," Freud speculated, "that thinking was originally unconscious" (p. 221) and that "everything conscious has an unconscious preliminary stage" (1900, p. 612).

Freud's theory and technique betray the positivist influence with its emphasis on accumulating bits and pieces of knowledge. Yet, he simultaneously, repeatedly, and consistently displays his sensitivity to the limits of consciousness and the vastness of unconsciousness. For instance, he noted that "the unconscious is the larger sphere which includes within it the smaller sphere of consciousness" (1900, p. 612). His writings reflect a consistent awareness of the ultimate ineffability of psychic experience. For example, he notes that "reality will always remain 'unknowable' ... the core of our being, then, is formed by the obscure *id*, which has no direct communication with the external world" (1938a, pp. 196–197). Despite his acknowledgment of an ultimate and unknowable reality, Freud's primary psychoanalytic endeavor emphasizes making the unconscious conscious.

Despite the distinctions and areas of divergence between science and the spirit evidenced throughout Freud's writing, we don't have to look too far for evidence of the fluidity of unconscious processes and for descriptions of experiences that mystical traditions frequently take for granted. Perhaps psychoanalytic thinkers following Freud have needed to make deeper distinctions between science and the spirit than Freud originally intended. The richest source of evidence derives from Freud's elaboration of unconscious processes. The operations of reversal and condensation, for example, are most basic to psychic life. The pervasiveness and centrality of psychotic processes, for example, make it clear that reversal, as Michael Eigen (1986a) asserts, "seems to antedate the development of the usual defenses" (p. 35). This places reversal as an unconscious process, in a position most influential of psychic life. The manifest ubiquity of both reversal and condensation does not seem to be adequately addressed in contemporary clinical practice. A dualist perspective and an associated search for the "meaning behind" can veil obvious expressions of both reversal and condensation. Similarly, a contemporary emphasis on relational aspects of the psychoanalytic encounter can result in losing sight of specific unconscious meanings that language can reveal.

Considering the nature and primacy of condensation, latent and manifest, can easily become the same. Similarly, condensation becomes "compressed" (Freud, 1900) into reversal and vice versa. For instance, with regard to schizophrenia Freud (1915) observes that words "undergo condensation, and by means of displacement transfer their cathexis to one another in their entirety. The process may go so far that a single word, if it is specially suitable, on account of its numerous connections, takes over the representation of a whole train of thought" (p. 199). The following vignette illustrates the above processes.

Avoided

Abby complains of feeling depressed and talks primarily of her father's decision to leave town. She says, "I feel that he avoided me." Abby normally speaks rapidly. However, we slow things down a bit. I stretch *avoided* into *a-void-de(a)d*. A silent pause ensues. I now reverse the phrase to *a dead void*. Abby becomes silent. Earlier in the session, when she complained of the depression, she talked about lying on her *living room* couch immobilized. In retrospect, Abby notes, "I have positioned myself on my back like a corpse in a coffin with my hands clasped together at my *waist*." She says that much of her identity revolves around taking care of her father and now he will be gone. Abby and I can wonder along together: Is her life *wasted* or is there still *room for living*?

The Unconscious Monolith

Despite Freud's sensitivity to and repeated articulation of the fluidity and transient qualities of psychic life, the momentousness of his discovery of the dynamic unconscious and unconscious processes over time has transmuted into a rock-solid monument of monolithic stature that has stifled creative transformative movement. The structure aspects of the unconscious in reified form, for the most part, have predominated developments in mainstream psychoanalysis since Freud. Internal mental processes, as Zenists observe, tend toward solidifying or reifying experiences. Reification generates a preoccupation with the unconscious and casts an almost impenetrable shadow on unconsciousness as fluid process. For instance, D. T. Suzuki (1972a) warns that "the conception of the unconscious leads to many wrong interpretations when it is taken as pointing to the existence of an entity to be designated 'the Unconscious'" (p. 71). However, despite this caution, D. T. Suzuki points to the identity of the relative and the absolute and notes that "no-mind" and "no-thought" carry the dual meaning of "the Unconscious" and "being unconscious." An overemphasis on structural notions in psychoanalytic thought frequently results in losing sight of this primary ongoing movement through the infinite range provided by a conscious/unconscious dynamic. The preoccupation with synthesis, structure, development, and maintaining distinctions creates an imbalance between the identity of the relative and the absolute aspects of being and conceals the formless, opening, spacious quality constitutive of healthy emotional life that Zen practice promotes in an ongoing questioning of reification processes. Freud's thinking remains largely undeveloped in this area; however, he demonstrates an implicit sensitivity to formlessness as expressed in his experiential observations. For instance, he notes that "a state of consciousness is characteristically very transitory; an idea that is conscious now is no longer a moment later, although it can become so again" (1923, p. 14). Similarly, with regard to theory, Freud (1900) conveys this same sense of fluidity and notes that "we must always be prepared to drop our conceptual scaffolding if we feel that we are in a position to replace it by something that approximates more closely to the unknown reality" (p. 610).

The intellectual climate of the time, as noted above, required that Freud make a sharp distinction between philosophical notions of unconsciousness and his radical new proposal. D. T. Suzuki makes a similar distinction regarding no-mind. Despite these important philosophical and theoretical distinctions, one notes unconscious operations implicit in the explicit expressions of Zen doctrine and technique. The apparent surface gap widens between the spirit of the science and the science of the spirit through Freud's initial need to situate psychoanalysis on the map of the Enlightenment secular universe. The positivist emphasis exerted an influence on Freud's approach that continues to guide the psychoanalytic inquiry in the present. For example, the search for latent bits of content in manifest expressions can result in missing the impact of the ongoing operation of unconscious processes. As a result, psychoanalysis, for the most part, addresses the repressed aspects or the "dynamic" unconsciousness that dominated his attention. However, Freud (1915) repeatedly reminds the reader "that the repressed does not comprise the whole unconscious. The unconscious has greater compass, the repressed is a part of the unconscious" (p. 161). Freud clarifies this distinction later in the same article:

> The unconscious comprises, on the one hand, processes which are merely latent, temporarily unconscious, but which differ in no other respect from conscious ones and, on the other hand, processes such as those which have undergone

repression, which if they came into consciousness must stand out in the crudest contrast to the rest of the conscious mind. (p. 172)

Later, Freud (1923) adds that the entire unconscious is not repressed or simply latent. Nevertheless, with few exceptions, the dynamic repressed unconscious dominates the psychoanalytic endeavor. The dynamic or repressed unconscious becomes, in Freud's words, "our unconscious." Psychoanalysis, prior to Bion and Matte-Blanco, has, for the most part, "forgotten" the "greater compass" that Freud alludes to in the above passage.

Structure and Process

Contents might or might not be conscious or unconscious at any given moment. We might be able to shed light on things that can become conscious or remain hidden in the darkness of unconsciousness. However, regardless of whether contents are conscious or unconscious at any given moment, they are subject to different processes or rules. It is this distinctive feature of Freud's unconscious that holds relevance in this context. Freud makes the distinctions between conscious and unconscious processes clear in his descriptions. For example, he says, "It must not be forgotten, however, that we are dealing with an unconscious process of thought, which may easily be different from what we perceive during purposive reflection accompanied by consciousness" (1900, p. 261). Additionally he notes that "the governing rules of logic carry no weight in the unconscious; it may be called the Realm of the Illogical" (1938a, pp. 168–169). However, despite the distinctions that he makes, Freud recognizes their arbitrary nature and never loses sight of the fluidity of the psyche. For example, regarding the dissection of the personality Freud (1933) writes that "we cannot do justice to the characteristics of the mind by linear outlines ... but rather by areas of color melting into one another.... After making the separation we must allow what we have separated to merge together once more" (p. 79).

In this discussion the term *unconsciousness* addresses the tendency toward reification and calls attention to the open-ended fluid interplay between both the conscious and unconscious dimensions of experience. Reification results in the perception of unconsciousness as a thing, entity, or territory to be conquered, colonized, and tamed through knowing. Depending on one's point of view, this territory takes on the characteristics of a "mythical kingdom" or a dark and dangerous place populated by gods, demons, selves, objects, some-things, and no-things—a dark abyss made visible through the light of consciousness. The army of Freud's ego marches into a wild and uncivilized territory in an expansionist effort. In this respect, Freud's notion "where id was shall ego be" becomes the slogan for a psychological imperialism. Alternatively, viewed from the other side, Freud (1938a) wrote that

> the frontiers of the ego are safeguarded against the id by resistances ... [in] a state of conflict and uproar, when the conflicts of the unconscious id have a prospect of forcing their way into the ego and into consciousness and the ego puts itself once more on the defensive against this invasion. (p. 165)

Despite the compelling and dramatic topographic metaphors sprinkled liberally throughout his writings, Freud continuously cautions the reader of their limitations. He describes the topographical model as "misleading" (1900). This "finger pointing," to use an applicable Zen teaching metaphor, can dominate the student's attention and eclipse a clear view of the moon. Freud realized that this particular artifact lost its usefulness as an effective pointer. He thus dropped his conceptual scaffolding and developed alternative representational models.

From the Zen perspective, we might speculate that the topographical pointer became reified from artifact to solid fact. Freud's sensitivity to the hazards of reification led him to conclude that "these images derived from a set of ideas relating to a struggle for a piece of ground, may tempt us to suppose that it is literally true that a mental grouping in one locality has been brought to an end and replaced by a fresh one in another locality" (1900, p. 611). With the above cautions and concerns behind him, Freud continues, "Nevertheless, I consider it expedient and justifiable to make use of the figurative images of the two systems" (p. 611). Again, Freud (1915) repeats: "It will, however, be useful to remind ourselves that as things stand our hypothesis set out to be no more than graphic illustrations" (p. 175).

We find this ongoing concern, mind's tendency toward reification, echoed six decades later by Bion (1962b), who comments on the ambiguous nature of the terms *conscious* and *unconscious*:

> I do not mean "the conscious" or "the" unconscious because that would imply that an observer would be required to differentiate two objects. Yet I do not wish to exclude that shade of meaning because when elements have been differentiated, some becoming conscious and some unconscious, it is reasonable to say there is an unconscious if such a concept is valuable. (p. 100, n 7.3.1)

Both Freud and Bion demonstrate a marked sensitivity to the issue of reification. However, by maintaining the structural notion they avoid the pitfall of nihilist extremism. In their own unique ways, based on their experiences, without the benefit of the Buddhist training, they seemed to have found the "middle way" so essential to Buddhist theory and practice. Implicit in their cautions we get a sense of the inextricable intertwining and identity of relative and absolute truth. They thus avoid the Scylla of eternalist extremism and the Charybdis of utter nihilism. Mark Finn (1992), in a discussion on the relationship between Winnicott's notion of transitional phenomena and Buddhist practice, summarizes this relationship as follows:

> The central assumption of Buddhist logic is the inseparability of the two truths: relative and absolute. Relative truth is the truth of conventional reality … categorized distinctions.… Absolute truth is the truth of radical unity … no distinctions, no conditionalities.… One cannot take absolute truth without relative truth, yet absolute truth is in fact absolute. (p. 113)

The light of consciousness blinds one to unconsciousness. From the no-mind perspective D. T. Suzuki (1972a) observes that "the attempt to reach light by dispelling darkness is dualistic, and this will never lead the Yogin to the proper understanding of the mind. Nor is the attempt to annihilate the distinction the right one" (p. 37). Preoccupations on what is and is not unconscious overlook the fundamental nature of mind. This point has both technical and theoretical implications, which we will return to below.

Matte-Blanco's Reformulation of the Freudian Unconscious

One common strand that winds its way through psychoanalysis and Zen and that threads together divergent themes centers on the fluidity of unconscious processes that Freud identified. For instance, Eigen (1992) writes, "Perhaps nowhere is the radical plasticity of self more emphasized than in Freud's conception of a timeless-spaceless unconscious" (p. 31). He adds that "this timeless-spaceless unconscious connects with Matte-Blanco's symmetrical unconscious, and … provides a privileged point of contact … through which the psyche plugs into divinity with special intensity" (p. 41). Eigen's observation serves to segue into Matte-Blanco's work, which in turn provides an entry into the Zen unconscious and its relation to psychoanalysis.

Matte-Blanco (1975, 1988) uses mathematical-logical principles to develop an extensive and thorough reworking of Freud's original formulations. Rather than proposing a critique of Freud's explorations into the unconscious aspects of the human psyche, he sets out to "recover the essentials of Freud's contribution" (1988, p. 6). With a movement away from the unconscious, which Matte-Blanco observes to be often the case, he contends that psychoanalysis has not "made use of its revolutionary impact" (p. 3). This distancing stance spills over into the literature on Buddhism and psychoanalysis in general and into the discussions on technique in particular. We will return to the neglect of the unconscious evident in the technical literature on Buddhism and psychoanalysis in Chapter 7.

Matte-Blanco's bimodal formulation charts a multidirectional movement that includes consciousness and unconsciousness as natural and necessary aspects of an ongoing process. Without diminishing the significance of Freud's discovery, he makes the following qualification:

> Freud's fundamental discovery is not that of the unconscious, not even in the dynamic sense (however important this may be) but that of a world ... ruled by entirely different laws from those governing conscious thinking. [He adds that Freud was] ... the first to describe this strange "Realm of the Illogical," which he found in an extraordinary stroke of genius. (1975, pp. 93–94)

In summary, Matte-Blanco (1975) views "the unconscious" as a misleading term that obscures the significance of "Freud's greatest discovery" (p. 133), which Matte-Blanco describes as "a *mode of being* and its characteristics" (p. 133). We will explore below how this mode of being functions in Buddhist soteriology as well, but first, a brief explication of Matte-Blanco's ideas will help set the stage for this exploration.

Matte-Blanco argues that, for the most part, psychoanalysis has not taken full advantage of the "momentousness" of Freud's discovery. His explication of the principles of symmetry and asymmetry directly relates to what might initially appear as incomprehensible, irrational, or mystical in Zen discourse. He offers promising insights into what Freud found so remarkable about unconscious communications between human beings.

Symmetrical and Asymmetrical Modes

Matte-Blanco explores the relationship between asymmetrical and symmetrical modes of processing. He refers to this dual processing as "bi-logic" and observes specific perceptual and experiential alterations related to the varying levels of conscious/unconscious operation. He describes two modes of being—the symmetrical and the asymmetrical—and he uses these terms to redefine and elaborate Freud's original formulations regarding conscious and unconscious processes. Rayner and Tuckett (1988) note that Matte-Blanco "works with one arm as it were, in psychoanalysis and the other in the concepts of basic mathematical logic" (p. 3). Asymmetrical and symmetrical relations and the distinctions between them form the cornerstone of Matte-Blanco's work. Here is a brief outline that defines Matte-Blanco's basic thesis and the terms that he uses.

Matte-Blanco views all relations as triadic. The triad consists of a subject, an object, and the relation between them. Asymmetrical relations move in only one direction and lack the quality of reversibility. Speaking of asymmetrical relations, he observes, "The relation and its converse are not identical" [and are] "always different from its converse" (1975, p. 38). We can say, for instance, "Jane reads this paper." However, the reverse statement, "This paper reads Jane," drastically alters the relation to something that appears impossible, at least from the perspective of asymmetrical relations. (We will put aside for the moment the emotional truth implicit in such a statement.) Asymmetrical relations characterize bivalent or everyday logic. This nondual both/and logic finds expression liberally and repeatedly in the Zen narrative. For example,

> Nevertheless, in the regular lectures which monks receive from their *rōshi*, they hear constantly phrases that refer to the nonduality of subject and object: "The well looks at the ass; the ass looks at the well" [and] "look at the flower and the flower also looks." (Hori, 2000, p. 289)

> Not to have is to have; silence is thunder; ignorance is enlightenment; the holy disciples of the Purity-path go to hell." (D. T. Suzuki, 1972a, p. 53)

Matte-Blanco (1975) describes symmetrization as "the most formidable departure from logic upon which all scientific and philosophical thinking of mankind is based" (p. 38). Symmetrical relations, in contrast to asymmetrical relations, according to Matte-Blanco, move in both directions with equal validity. He observes that "the relation that exists between them is symmetrical because the converse is identical with the direct relation" (p. 38). From the perspective of ordinary thinking, we encounter asymmetrical relations more frequently than symmetrical relations. While equally present, the symmetrical aspects of experience remain formless in the darkness of unconsciousness. For Matte-Blanco, symmetrical relations more accurately describe unconsciousness than the term *uncon-scious*. He argues that the relationship conscious/unconscious identifies only one of many aspects discovered and described by Freud. Freud also describes dimensions of time/timelessness, space/spacelessness, inside/outside, psychic/external reality, and the juxtaposition between them due to processes such as condensation and displacement. For Matte-Blanco, condensation explains Freud's use of the term *unconscious* to subsume all of the operations that he described. Matte-Blanco refers to the "mysteri-ous" and contends that both forms of logic operate in everyday thought and to varying degrees at different levels of the unconscious. On this basis, he argues that the unconscious functions through what James Grotstein (2007) describes as "a binary-oppositional structure known as 'bi-logic'" (p. 80). Bi-logic combines both forms. Asymmetrical relations predominate conscious secondary process thinking. Symmetrical relations character-ize primary processes and unconscious operations that appear less fre-quently. We can get a sense of the relation between symmetrical being and asymmetrical being from the following passage: "Symmetrical being is the normal state of man. It is the colossal base from which consciousness or asymmetrical being emerges. Consciousness is a special attribute of man, which looks upon the (infinite) base and makes attempts at describing it" (Matte-Blanco, 1975, p. 100). Matte-Blanco further notes that "asymmet-rical relations are something that emerge from and come out of the sea of symmetry; they are like limited 'incarnations' of a vast reality" (p. 104). Matte-Blanco (1988) contends that both types of relations function to unify "the forms of thinking and not-thinking which are fundamental to the characteristics of the unconscious" (p. 20). The principle of symmetry explains the presence of symmetrical relations and from the perspective of unconscious processes applies to "*any* relationship that we might have in mind" (Rayner & Tuckett, 1988, p. 20). Matte-Blanco (1975) notes that the principle of symmetry functions "as a unique and all-embracing principle of logic [that] completely dissolves all logic" (p. 54). What might appear enigmatic and far-fetched can also be experienced as obvious and "close to home." In this regard reversals become identical. For example, a patient who has lost his sense of self hears the analyst's assertion "There is noth-ing I can tell you" as "I can tell you there is no I-thing." Symmetrization increases at deeper levels of the unconscious. The predominance of either asymmetrical or symmetrical relations defines what Matte-Blanco refers to as levels or strata of the unconscious.

Matte-Blanco observes an infinite number of strata of unconscious operation; however, for the purposes of discussion he outlines five basic levels. He identifies the various strata by the degree of asymmetrical or symmetrical logic in operation at each distinct stratum. At the surface, the stratum of "conscious and well-delimited objects," we see a predominance of asymmetrical logic in operation. Total symmetrization characterizes the "indivisible mode," which is the deepest level in Matte-Blanco's scheme. At this stratum, according to Matte-Blanco (1975), "the endless number of things tend to become, mysteriously, only one thing" (p. 54). Similarly, Hori (2000) notes that "in this realm, what we normally take to be opposites are made identical: form is emptiness and emptiness is form; the delusive passions are at once enlightenment; samsara is nirvana. These statements appear to conventional understanding as examples of a different kind of logic" (p. 289).

Compare Matte-Blanco's observation with the following passages from Hui-neng: "The Unconscious means to be conscious of the absolutely one; to be conscious of the absolutely one means to have all knowledge" (D. T. Suzuki, 1972a, p. 64).

D. T. Suzuki, Hui-neng, and the Zen Unconscious

Nowhere in the Buddhist literature do we find as explicit an expression of the Buddhist unconscious than in D. T. Suzuki's explication of Zen Buddhism. Here we encounter what Matte-Blanco described above as the "mysterious" most directly stated in the accounts of spontaneous gestures attributed to various Zen masters. Dramatic descriptions of *mondo*, or question-and-answer dialogues between teacher and student, live on in abundance, sprinkled throughout the Zen literature. D. T. Suzuki's observations and insights into no-mind, the Zen koan, satori, and related aspects of Zen experience (1949, 1960, 1972a, 1972b, 1994) serve to weave together various strands in psychoanalysis that are relevant to the present discussion. Most notably, his detailed discussion of Chinese Zen Buddhist Hui-neng's no-mind doctrine clearly explicates the Zen unconscious (1972a).

D. T. Suzuki observes that the Zen notion of unconsciousness is not psychological in its intent. He makes this distinction based on a classical psychoanalytic understanding of Freud's conception of a dynamic unconscious. However, this distinction on D. T. Suzuki's part precedes Matte-Blanco's reformulation and Bion's extension, both of which in different ways bear important similarities to Hui-neng's no-mind doctrine and, as noted above, clearly move psychoanalysis in a mystical direction that radically departs from Freud's emphasis on knowing. Yet, at the same time, D. T. Suzuki points to a forgotten Freud caught between an ebbing earlier idealism, a priori philosophical notions, and the rapidly rising tide of scientific positivism. D. T. Suzuki's account, without losing sight of Zen's salvational aims, moves the spirit in a psychological direction that is personal, experiential, and iconoclastic.

Despite the distinction D. T. Suzuki makes between the psychoanalytic and the Zen unconscious, he asserts that Zen emphasizes experience, which is primarily a psychological concern. In this regard, D. T. Suzuki points to experience, a most crucial aspect of psychoanalysis, and he parallels Freud (1915), who observed that "to have heard something and to have experienced something are in their psychological nature two quite different things, even though the content of both is the same" (p. 176). Similarly, Bion (1965, 1967, 1970) emphasizes the primacy of experience in his discussion of "beening," "intuiting," "participation in hallucinosis," negative capability, and "relinquishing memory, desire, and understanding."

D. T. Suzuki's nondualist understanding of wisdom moves away from distinctions, qualifications, and conditions, and toward unitive experiencing that parallels Matte-Blanco's "invisible indivisible" unconscious, where, as described above, everything becomes everything else. Similarly, Bion (1970), as noted above, also speaks of "at-one-ment" as a desired goal of psychoanalytic experience and "without which no analysis can be considered complete" (p. 33).

D. T. Suzuki's Nondualistic Perspective

D. T. Suzuki, not unlike Bion and Matte-Blanco, addresses the issue of consciousness and unconsciousness from a nondualistic perspective. D. T. Suzuki's thinking parallels Freud's notion of consciousness and unconsciousness as qualities of a larger true psychic reality. He notes:

> When the sun rises, brightness fills the world, but space itself is not bright; when the sun sets, darkness fills the world, but space itself is not dark; Brightness and darkness are conditions, replacing each other; as for the characteristic vast vacuity of space, it remains ever unchanged. (1972a, p. 131)

From the Zen perspective of the identity of the relative and the absolute, the notions of the unconscious as structure and unconsciousness as process are both necessary and mutually coexistent. This coexistence extends to the fluidity between unconsciousness and consciousness and reflects the interplay between symmetrical and asymmetrical modes of being. We mediate experiences both ways. However, access to the nonsensual aspects of experience requires that we temporarily relinquish knowing processes. Reengagement with knowing processes provides a vehicle to negotiate a relationship in a world of self and other. Matte-Blanco captures the essence of this coexistence with the metaphor of a balloon that is necessary to contain oxygen. The foundational Buddhist doctrine of emptiness and dependent arising addresses this same coexistence. Japanese philosopher Gadjin Nagao (1989) uses the metaphor of a swimmer without water to underline the need for a material base with which to mediate nonmaterial ineffable experiences. Similarly, Hori (2000), with respect to language in Rinzai Zen study and practice, notes the necessity for conceptual and dualistic notions to address nonconceptual and unitive experiences. From a perspective that integrates Buddhist and psychoanalytic perspectives, Mark Finn warns of the danger inherent in overlooking this inextricable relation between absolute and relative truth. He comments on what he describes as "a typical symptom of an immature intoxication with Buddhism," which, according to Finn (1992), becomes expressed in "a sort of nihilism based on the notion that Buddhism abolishes all distinctions" (p. 113). Finn argues cogently and convincingly that this assumption is not correct. He concludes: "Thus the relative psychological world and the absolute spiritual world are inseparable. Buddhist practice sets as its goal the collapse of such dualities as sacred versus profane, psychological versus spiritual, while recognizing the relative truth of the distinctions themselves" (p. 113).

Knowing provides definition and form to the formless infinite. Experiences move in and out of form, often with catastrophic abruptness. The present form (thought, feeling, wish, memory, sense perception) moves toward formlessness. Freud was keenly aware of this interplay, which is most evident in his vivid, detailed, and dramatic descriptions of the functions of condensation and displacement in dream processes. Despite radical changes in his views, he expresses clear notions of the relationship between form and formlessness in mental functioning four decades later. "No; being conscious cannot be the essence of what is mental. It is only a *quality* of what is mental, and an unstable quality at that—one that is far oftener absent than present" (1938b, p. 283). He adds, "We all know what is meant by ideas 'occurring' to one—thoughts that suddenly come into consciousness" (p. 283).

Formlessness evolves into form. This evolution requires distinctions and categorizations into what is and what is not. Distinctions relate to asymmetrical aspects of experience. Unconsciousness moves toward symmetrization, dissolves distinctions, and generates deepening unitive experiencing.

The Buddhist prayer "The Identity of Relative and Absolute," authored by 8th-century Chinese monk Sekito Kisen, captures this relationship: "In the light there is darkness, but don't take it as darkness; In the dark there is light, but don't see it as light" (S. Suzuki, 1999, p. 21). Darkness requires, according to Bion, the "act of faith" that tolerates sitting still in darkness and allowing the experience to unfold. With regard to approaching ultimate reality, Bion (1970) observes: "Upon his ability to approximate to this will depend on his ability to achieve 'blindness' that is a prerequisite for 'seeing' the evolved elements of O" (p. 58). The effort to shed light on darkness dissolves darkness. When the light of consciousness disappears, darkness reappears. In darkness, we conjure up both gods and demons. We make distinctions that become visible in the light. This conjuring trick results in self-constructed fabrications that take on an "own life" quality, whether saints or demons, selves or objects. We forget their initial sense-making function and their fabricated nature. This dark night of the soul generates both terror and delight. Darkness transforms ropes into poisonous snakes that tempt the seeker to bite from the fruit of knowledge. However, knowledge obtained in the sense world removes one from the undifferentiated, formless darkness.

Nina Coltart (1992) describes what she refers to as the "sheer unconsciousness of the unconscious" (p. 3). This terse statement acknowledges the coexistence of form and formlessness. The relationship between synthesis and analysis, the initial distinctions between Bion's K and O, the Buddhist notions of emptiness and dependent arising, and the coexistence of the relative and the absolute—all express and point toward the invariant in Freud's "unknowable," in Bion's "ineffable," and in Suzuki's "unattainable" experience.

The Inside-Out Shirt

The following example clarifies the paradox that Matte-Blanco describes as the irreconcilability of this unitive relationship between consciousness and unconsciousness. On the outside, a shirt appears neat, finished, and everything in place. On the inside, seams overlap, and rough and unfinished edges, and labels become visible. This reveals a very different image of the shirt. However, both the inside and the outside consist of the very same fabric. The one fabric creates the inside and the outside. Certain individuals experience themselves as if wearing the shirt inside-out. When, during analysis, the analyst points out unconscious meanings and motivations hidden behind manifest expressions, such individuals have specific reactions. Jean, for example, would irritably say: "So what's so new about that!" "You think you are telling me something!" "I have been telling you this all along, you just got it?" Jean simply doesn't express the genuine surprise, embarrassment, or interest that other people might should they discover suddenly that their shirt was on inside-out. In fact, she might wonder why my shirt is not on inside-out. This creates a different situation clinically. For example, rather than looking for latent elements in manifest contents, which will actually blind us to the inside-out nature of the shirt, a reversal in perspective renders latent as manifest and manifest as latent. Thus, the surprise in these individuals stems from looking directly at what might appear obvious to the analyst but not to the patient. The following clinical example illustrates the consciousness and unconsciousness coexistence in which consciousness becomes an external variant of unconsciousness.

The Eternal Moment: Timelessness and Time

John attempts to reify an "eternal moment." He confuses the experience of timelessness, of impermanence, in his attempt to destroy time. He thus insulates himself from the intense anxiety associated with the reality of impermanence. The resulting internally reified state of mind becomes projected onto the external environment. He thus attempts to deal with fundamental anxiety by "freeze framing" the external world. However, John's futile attempt to produce a heaven condemns him to hell. Sooner or later the sounds of life's daily rhythms intrude. Hammering and drilling in the adjacent building, birds chirping gently in the backyard—both feel jolting, noxious, and eternal. At the extreme, a split-second sound becomes an excruciating eternity and intrudes into and disrupts the peace and hoped for solitude. In this way John experiences all sounds as eternal. To feel otherwise would be to admit his humanness and the reality of aging and death. The frozen now imprisons both John and the sound together. During sessions, sounds become overwhelming attractions and distractions. He has frustratingly frozen the "wrong" moment. No "right" moment exists for John. The moving reality of all sounds serves as thorny reminders of impermanence. Reality eventually intrudes. He expects me to shut it off, to relocate my office, or to call him in advance to cancel or postpone our session should I become aware of the intrusive sounds prior to his arrival. He expects me to save him from his own life and death. I fail miserably repeatedly and for better or for worse wake John up to his life.

Zen and Aggression

Zenists understand aggression as a distortion of reality. This distortion derives from the notion that everyone and everything are separate and independent. Deep analytic penetration through meditation practice dissolves aggression. Dissolution results from uprooting the perceptual causes and enables the practitioner to experience the undistorted perception that we are ultimately not as separate as we thought. This suggests that the continued operation of predominantly asymmetrical functions results in a distortion of our fundamental "indivisibility" or "oneness," and that increased symmetrization promotes dissolution. Movement occurs in both directions. If this were not the case, we would not be able to conceptualize the actual experience through transformations into language and derive thoughts about indivisibility or oneness. Both Suzuki and Matte-Blanco describe perceptual alterations in oscillations between definite and infinite, separateness and unity, and form and formlessness. Dissolution generates increased symmetrization. A fundamental implication relevant to this discussion is that symmetrical processes become more accessible during meditation. The perceptual alteration associated with increased symmetrization results in a different relation to reality. Aggressive feelings are not simply dissipated through the application of palliative methods. Rather, a radical psychic transformation occurs with an accompanying alteration in perception. From Matte-Blanco's (1975) point of view, "aggression ... after having passed through levels of infinite magnitude, begins to recede into the background" (p. 5). In this respect, zazen relies on unconscious processes to promote psychic transformations.

"Rose Is the Mother of Mary"

Matte-Blanco considers the statement "Rose is the mother of Mary." The principle of symmetrization attributes equal validity to the statement "Mary is the mother of Rose." Such statements, he continues, place us "like Alice in Wonderland" in "very unfamiliar territory." According to

Matte-Blanco, this is precisely the territory of the unconscious. The logical leap through Alice's asymmetrical looking glass requires an "act of faith." Suzuki describes the leap as "abrupt," and Bion as "catastrophic." Both intend to bridge the gap between the relative and the absolute. D. T. Suzuki (1972a) describes the abrupt nature of the enlightenment process as "both logical *and* psychological" and says:

> The logical leap is that the ordinary process of reasoning stops short, and what has been considered irrational is perceived to be perfectly natural, while the psychological leap is that the borders of consciousness are overstepped and one is plunged into the Unconscious which is not, after all, unconscious. (p. 54)

He proposes that the leap "is attainable only by transcending our everyday experience of sense-intellect, that is, by an existential leap" (p. 48). Buddhist practitioners find the territory beyond Alice's looking glass to be quite familiar. Suzuki observes, for example, that the irrational is an "essential in most religious propositions." The Zen master can say, "I hold the spade in my hand, and I am empty handed" (p. 23).

The belief in reincarnation, for example, results from the symmetrical relation between birth and death. The principle of reincarnation renders equally valid the statement "Birth results in death" and its reversal, "Death results in birth." This relationship requires some elaboration. The cause-and-effect relation from the Buddhist point of view is not linear and sequential. Both birth and death interact mutually and simultaneously. In this respect, both are necessary conditions for the ongoing rising, enduring, ceasing, dissolving, and emerging of both. Both factors arise interdependently and thus function as cause *and* effect. Again, we see the subtlety and importance of symmetrical relations in Buddhist thought. Buddhist teachers exploit the principle of symmetry in their techniques. For example, meditation on the statement "All sentient beings are our mother," at least for Tibetans, serves to generate infinite compassion for all beings.

Bion and Conscious/Unconscious Complementarity

Bion, through an act of faith, enters into and participates in the movement charted by Matte-Blanco's bimodal nondualistic formulation. He charts a multidirectional movement that includes consciousness and unconsciousness as natural and necessary aspects of an ongoing process and brings attention to the overshadowing of consciousness by the primacy of the unconscious in psychoanalysis. By conceptualizing a complementarity between conscious and unconscious he criticizes the value Freud places on knowing. He asserts: "I don't think this idea of the unconscious or even the idea of unconscious thoughts or ideas extends far enough" (1980, p. 20). His preference for the infinite extends psychoanalysis into the area of mystical experience and thus generates a restoration of the spirit into psychoanalysis. This maneuver opens Bion's discussion to both asymmetrical and symmetrical processes.

An overemphasis on knowing (asymmetrical logic) generates the gap that Bion speaks of. Similarly, D. T. Suzuki (1972a) observes that "the bifurcation is the work of the intellect, and inasmuch as we cannot get along in our practical life without resorting to it, we make full use of it, but we must not let it intrude into our spiritual realm" (pp. 29–30). Satori, or enlightenment, appears to become manifest with increased symmetrization, which occurs experientially. D. T. Suzuki elaborates the point that intellectual activity maintains distinctions. He says that "the gap between Satori and rationality could never be bridged by concept-making and postulation, but by an absolute negation of the reason itself, which means an 'existential leap'" (p. 69). The existential leap through "participation in hallucinosis" moves Bion from "knowing about" to "being O." Bion speaks of the ineffable quality of experiencing O. Not unlike Bion's effort to intuit the ineffable, D. T. Suzuki comments on the Zen "retreat to our inner self in which no bifurcation has yet taken place ... to reach the undifferentiated continuum itself" (p. 70). The Zen master's technique attempts to reveal the symmetrical mode that Matte-Blanco observes operates invisibly behind all conscious experience. D. T. Suzuki continues that they "wish to see into the unconscious-consciousness which accompanies our ordinary dualistically-determined consciousness" (p. 80). The Zenist moves from asymmetry to symmetry by responding that the person is both real and unreal and by arguing that any attempt to answer such an irrelevant question will only perpetuate ignorance. Here again is a symmetrization of what appears initially as contradiction. In this respect the notion of the identity of the relative and the absolute maintains the distinction between *ultimately* unreal and *relatively* real—neither as real nor as unreal as we sometimes tend to think we are. Thus, Zen accepts deepening symmetrization but questions confusing condensations.

Anna: "I Don't Exist"

Anna, an extremely isolated young woman who received very little parental attention as a child, consistently asserts, "I don't exist." Her "I don't exist self" feels consistently solid, concretized, intractable, and impenetrable. Who is the self who makes this observation? The enlightened capacity for simultaneous awareness of both ultimate and relative existence expresses the balance between and transcends existence and nonexistence. *Sunyata*, as noted in previous chapters, defines the ultimate unreality of existence. For Anna, this unreality is the no-thing that has become reified into an "I don't exist self." As she and I look for this "I don't exist self," what will we find? The no-thing has the same solidity as a some-thing. Ultimately, a some-thing is as insubstantial as the no-thing. Both some-thing and no-thing can equally saturate psychic space and obscure intuited experience. This holds disastrous consequences for Anna, her life, and her relationships. We are looking for sense and finding non-sense. Our attention is on the some-thing, not the no-thing. Both some-thing and no-thing, if we look for them, are ultimately nonfindable. Paradoxically, Tibetan Buddhist scholar Jeffrey Hopkins (1987) emphasizes how this nonfindability requires an intensification of awareness and deep involvement with objects.

Anna and I search together for the some-thing, for the no-thing, and we do not find any-thing substantial, independent, or permanent. Anna begins over time to feel some psychic space, which begins to reflect interpersonally in newly forming relationships. She begins to experience herself as "lover," "good friend," "colleague," and the many other ways that her sense of self becomes defined in newly developing relationships.

Ellie

This example further clarifies the direct clinical relevance of the reified some-thing and no-thing. Ellie, who is used to being engulfed and suffocated, devalues me. The analytic space becomes saturated with the no-thing that she never gets. There is no room here for Ellie to experience the some-thing even if for her; the no-thing is the some-thing that I can give her.

Reality "known" is "unknown" because the experience of being real becomes embedded and therefore hidden from experience in the act or doing of "knowing" (no-ing) *about* being real. However, the knowing about is no less real than the direct experience of being real.

Implications and Conclusions

Matte-Blanco (1975), as noted above, attempts to add dimensions to the psychoanalytic point of view that make it "possible to realize something which at a lower dimension is experienced as a separate object, becomes at a higher dimension, a constituent of the Whole" (p. 4).

The implication of this phenomenon of movement between distinctions and unity with regard to integrative studies can be summarized as follows: Whether or not an individual chooses to notice or to concentrate on sameness or difference, convergences or divergences, or identities between psychological and spiritual disciplines, we find ourselves faced with various aspects, perhaps starting points of relationships. In the case of Zen and psychoanalysis these relationships continuously form and dissolve between two highly subjective disciplines. For example, one might insist on the separation between the spirit and the science. Currently the trend is toward a deepened awareness of identities. Despite this trend, contemporary studies tend to ignore unconscious processes and miss what is most essential to the psychoanalytic inquiry. In this respect such studies represent a specific instance of the more general trend in psychoanalysis that Matte-Blanco observes. He writes "that psychoanalysis has neglected to a considerable extent its initial purpose of exploring the psychology of the unconscious, and of that mysterious world where everything is different from what we see in conscious life ... [thus] psychoanalysis has lost its most distinctive characteristics" (1975, p. 9).

Throughout the above discussion, we moved freely between what appears to ordinary sense as opposites. Such movements are natural whether smooth and continuous, or abrupt and catastrophic (more likely both). In either case, they transcend ordinary logic. However, the non-sense logic is not, as D. T. Suzuki (1972a) notes, "a kind of dialectic whereby contradictoriness becomes logically tenable ... satori is existential and not dialectical," and thus expresses, according to Suzuki, "a direct statement of their [Zen masters'] living existential experience" (p. 47). For example, as noted above, doing is undoing, dissolving is solving, seeing requires blindness, latent is manifest, and being is nonbeing. Considering the nature of unconscious processes such statements are neither contradictory nor complementary. They function more as mutually coexisting, each causing and affecting the other. The term *unconscious processes* in itself implies a contradiction. Matte-Blanco (1988) observes that processes imply the notion of time. However, he points to Freud's observation that timelessness is a basic characteristic of the unconscious. We nevertheless feel comfortable with thinking and talking about various unconscious processes. Interestingly, meditation teachers note that meditation practice often goes well when the practitioner loses awareness of time passing.

Rayner and Tuckett (1988) note that "although the logic of the unconscious is used intuitively in daily clinical work, we do not often stop to consider the fundamental and disturbing implications of the concepts employed" (p. 5). The contradictory nature of the simultaneity of being and nonbeing, for example, implies symmetrization. For instance, the notion that emptiness is exactly form and vice versa translates existentially into the seemingly paradoxical statement that "being is nonbeing." This statement seems implausible from the perspective of asymmetrical logic. However, the principle of symmetrization renders it acceptable and inevitable. From the Zen perspective the dread of existential anxiety associated with the threat to a permanent and separate sense of self can account for the therapist's resistance to primary process, symmetrization, unitive experience, overreliance on cognitive, secondary process, intellectualization in the form of hasty, well-practiced interpretations, and ultimately, the patient in treatment. Experiential realization of the identity of the relative and the absolute and associated ramifications for interpersonal relationships make such states, such as unitive experiencing, for instance, less threatening and engenders a more balanced relationship, or as Zenists would describe, a "middle way," that integrates relative and absolute through an alteration in the practitioner's perception.

Freud described psychoanalysis, in part, as a science of unconscious motivations. Symmetrical logic and the process of symmetrization become increasingly more important the more deeply we immerse ourselves in unconscious experiences. However, considering again the deepest level of symmetrization, we are confronted with the merging identity of consciousness and unconsciousness. In this respect, as noted above, the unconscious in opposition to consciousness maintains distinctions at the most asymmetrical points. On the other hand, the flow in and out of consciousness and unconsciousness addresses the deeper levels of symmetrization. Now these distinctions are somewhat artificial. For example, with regard to the dialectic between asymmetrical opposing processes and structures we can locate underlying, if not hidden, symmetrical operations.

While emptiness characterizes all phenomena, this awareness is not accessible to ordinary perception. Perception must be trained and transformed. As noted, Zen training exploits unconscious processes and generates a conscious intuited awareness of symmetrization. Additionally, outcomes such as the merging of subject and object, the eventual identity of discursive and concentrative meditation, the realization of the simultaneity of relative and absolute, the experience of the emptiness and dependent arising of all phenomena, including life and death, are fundamentally different experiences than those that imply pathology associated with regressive merger characteristic of "oceanic feeling," described by classical psychoanalysts to understand meditative states.

These contradictory states are inferred in the Buddhist realization of ultimate and relative reality, the notion of omniscience, the merging of concentration and discursive meditation, and the statements of the Heart Sutra that we touched on above. We have also noted that there appears a contradictory relation at the surface levels of thought. However, following Matte-Blanco's thesis, the apparent contradictions tend to dissolve at the deeper levels. One aspect of basic experience centers on expressions of unification, at-one-ment, indivisible-invisible, unconscious. We find expressions of such experiences in descriptions of enlightenment and the accompanying theory of emptiness and dependent arising, Freud's descriptions of unconscious processes, Matte-Blanco's explication of symmetrization, and Bion's observation of the intuited ineffable formless O. This creates an interesting situation in terms of the possible levels of perception and expression of experience. What appear, at first glance, to be different, separate, and unrelated, merge together into the formlessness, accessible through deeper levels of experience. Consider the expression "Let's not confuse apples and oranges." Apples are apples and oranges are oranges. Let's not confuse apple pie and orange juice. However, apples and oranges are both fruits and fructose is fructose. The Zen master transforms this understanding of distinction and nondistinction into a lived experience. "Bite the apple! Taste the orange! That mind, that mind be that mind!" (Zen Master Richard Shrobe, personal communication).

7

The Crazy Cloud of Attention and Inattention:
Meditation Review

One day a man of the people said to Zen Master Ikkyu: "Master, will you please write for me some maxims of the highest wisdom?" Ikkyu immediately took his brush and wrote the word "Attention." "Is that all?" asked the man. "Will you not add something more?" Ikkyu then wrote twice running: "Attention. Attention." "Well," remarked the man rather irritably, "I really don't see much depth or subtlety in what you have just written." Then Ikkyu wrote the same word three times running: "Attention. Attention. Attention." Half-angered, the man demanded: "What does that word 'Attention' mean anyway?" And Ikkyu answered gently: "Attention means attention."

—*Zenso Mondo* [Dialogues of the Zen Masters] (Kapleau, 1966, pp. 10–11)

Introduction

The above *mondo*, or question-and-answer dialogue between a student and a Zen master, points to the importance of attention in Buddhist practice. Attention techniques engender an "alteration in perception" (Klein, 1986) whereby, according to Buddhist thought, the transparency and insubstantiality of what appears permanent, solid, and eternal becomes exposed. This wisdom cuts through everyday sense and thought perception and is described as *prajna* ("quick knowing" or intuitive understanding).

In this respect Buddhism functions as a perceptual psychology. Alterations in perception engender a liberating knowledge of reality as a result of a clearing away of the perceptual distortions. The alteration of attention in meditation allows insight into the false perception of reality that is grounded in subject/object dichotomies, distortions that engender endless grasping, greed, envy, exploitation, and at the extreme, the horrors of war, genocide, terrorism, and holocaust. Perception interacts with attention. This relationship between perception and attention renders Zen master Ikkyu's enigmatic response to his student's queries understandable. The systematic training of attention to the present moment is central to Zen practice.

Psychoanalytic Attention

Despite shifts in emphasis over the years since Freud's first formulations, the psychoanalytic inquiry shares with Zen praxis the systematic application of subjective attentional processes as its primary experiential technique. Freud (1914) speaks of free association to the contents and flow of mental processes as the "fundamental psychoanalytical rule" (p. 147). He defines the optimal stance of the analyst as "evenly hovering attention" and asserts that this stance aims "to create for the doctor a counterpart to the 'fundamental rule of psycho-analysis' which is laid down for the patient" (1912b, p. 115). Freud describes the analyst's stance as a complement to his directive to the analysand. He writes:

> Just as the patient must relate everything that his self-observation can detect, and keep back all the logical and affective objections that seek to induce him to make a selection from among them, so the doctor must put himself in a position to make use of everything he is told for the purposes of interpretation and of recognizing the concealed unconscious material without substituting a censorship of his own for the selection that the patient has forgone. To put it in a formula: he must turn his own unconscious like a receptive organ towards the transmitting unconscious of the patient. (p. 115)

Wilfred Bion (1970), who is often quoted in the literature on Buddhist meditation and psychoanalytic attention, and Heinz Kohut (1971, 1977) both make radical departures from Freud in unique and diverging directions. However, like Freud, they both place attention at the center of the psychoanalytic inquiry. Freud, Bion, and Kohut all credit a special attentional focus in the psychoanalytic process. They advise that the psychoanalyst must "see" beyond the senses in order to capture and understand the essence of human experience, to promote psychic change, and to alleviate suffering. Freud describes a "bending toward" of the unconscious of both the analysand and the analyst. Bion speaks of "intuition" that facilitates the experience of "at-one-ment." Kohut places "empathy" with the inner life of the analysand at the center of the psychoanalytic inquiry. He argues that empathy, or vicarious introspection, with the patient's inner life serves as the only true source of psychoanalytic data. Despite differing formulations, bending toward, at-one-ment, and empathy all point to a temporary dissolution of the subject/object dichotomy not unlike that described in Zen notions of nonduality. This point holds important implications for understanding limitations in the contemporary literature on the use of Buddhist meditation to promote psychoanalytic attention.

From the Buddhist perspective, therapeutic listening, not unlike all other phenomena, is transitory, transparent, and insubstantial; lacks any permanent, solid, or eternal quality; and arises, changes, and falls within the context of the therapeutic encounter. At any given moment, the psychotherapist might be more or less attentive to any given internal or external experience. What, then, are the essential qualities of attention from a psychoanalytic point of view, and how do these relate to attentional phenomena in Buddhist meditation?

Bare Attention

The effort to understand the relationship between Buddhist and psychoanalytic practice is reflected in the increasing number of papers on the technique of Buddhist attention that have appeared in the psychoanalytic literature since the mid-1980s. One predominant theme in this conversation centers on Freud's (1912) description of evenly hovering attention and the Theravada Buddhist meditation technique of mindfulness, or "bare attention" (Coltart, 1992, 1996; Epstein, 1984, 1988; Rubin, 1985; Speeth, 1982). One consistent point of convergence between the two techniques centers on the shared emphasis on an essentially passive, nonjudgmental stance. Speeth (1982), for example, observes: "Freud described the inner work of free-association as the twofold effort of paying attention to the process and the content of the mind and simultaneously eliminating all criticism or censorship of what arises. The requirement for lack of censorship makes this practice akin to Buddhist mindfulness" (p. 153).

Consider the following oft-quoted definitions of these two attention strategies. In his influential and popular book *The Heart of Buddhist Meditation*, the Theravada meditation master Nyanaponika Thera (1973) writes:

> Bare attention is the clear and single-minded awareness of what actually happens *to* us and *in* us, at successive moments of perception. It is called "bare," because it attends just to the bare facts of a perception as presented either through the five physical senses or through the mind which for Buddhist

thought, constitutes the sixth sense ... attention or mindfulness is kept to a bare registering of the facts observed, without reacting to them by deed, speech or by mental comment which may be one of self-reference ... judgment or reflection. (p. 30)

Similarly, in his discussion of psychoanalytic technique, Freud (1912b) writes:

The technique is a very simple one. It disclaims the use of any special aids ... and simply consists in making no effort to concentrate the attention on anything in particular, and in maintaining in regard to all that one hears the same measure of calm, quiet attentiveness of "evenly-hovering attention".... All conscious exertion is to be withheld from the capacity for attention, and one's "unconscious memory" is to be given full play; or to express it in terms of technique, pure and simple; One has simply to listen and not to trouble to keep in mind anything in particular. (p. 112)

Freud's instructions for evenly hovering attention and Thera's definition of bare attention clearly demonstrate the descriptive parallels between the two techniques. The recommendation that bare attention practice can enhance the therapist's capacity for therapeutic listening derives from these comparisons. For example, Rubin (1985) writes that "meditation can be of immense value to psychoanalysis in general and psychoanalytic listening in particular, providing a systematic and efficacious technique for cultivating precisely the capacity and state of mind that Freud recommended for optimum listening" (p. 602).

The effort to find relevance for psychoanalysis in Buddhist meditation practice represents a positive shift in the psychoanalytic response to Buddhism. However, to reduce the complexity of psychoanalytic awareness to evenly hovering attention does not do justice to the psychoanalytic process. Indeed, just as Buddhist meditation develops discriminations with regard to the phenomena of consciousness that are not apparent to the untrained meditator, psychoanalytic training develops an awareness and sensitivity of the many constantly occurring intrapsychic and interpersonal phenomena that demand the analyst's attention. Therefore, at issue is not merely a flexible mind-set that hovers evenly over the subjective landscape of the mind. The analyst must develop the capacity to access and understand both the conscious and the unconscious aspects of the psychoanalytic encounter. To reduce psychoanalysis to the technical dimension of mindfulness is to fail to take into account the complexity of the unconscious processes that, as discussed in Chapter 6, are central to the theory and practice of psychoanalysis. Likewise, to reduce Buddhist practice to the technical dimension of mindfulness neglects the function of meditation, which supports the salvational aims of Buddhist practices that are geared toward the experiential insight that all phenomena are empty of any permanent quality or essence and arise subject to causes and conditions.

This essential oversimplification, as I see it, inhibits our progress in understanding the internal integration of Buddhism and psychoanalysis by individuals engaged in both practices. From this perspective it is incorrect to think that Buddhist practices such as meditation function simply as "add-ons" to psychotherapeutic technique. Further implications extend this basic conclusion to key treatment issues such as the clinical use of unconscious processes, the conceptualization and use of the transference and countertransference dynamic, the shifting object of analytic attention, and the understanding and processing of the therapist's experiential states. Clinical material presented below demonstrates these important points.

For instance, if one considers lapses of attention on the part of the analyst to be merely the result of inadequate listening skills or the lack of attentional focus, one will assume that shifts between attention and inattention are to be regarded exclusively as interferences with therapeutic efficacy. Thus, one will miss out on understanding that unconscious processes in the analyst may represent, for example, a form of empathic attunement to the analysand's unconscious communications. For example, the analyst's "inattention" with a particular patient, upon deeper scrutiny, can reveal an early object relation involving an inattentive parent (Cooper, 1999, 2002b). We will return to this issue below. For psychoanalysis, the unconscious, and the experience of the analyst's own analysis, provides the matrix for this exploration. When excluded from the discussion, this oversight results in a view of psychoanalysis as limited, lacking, or deficient, and Buddhism as adjunctive.

In sum, an exclusively technical emphasis on evenly hovering attention ignores the complexity of attentional states in psychoanalysis. Contemporary theorists have painted a picture of the psychoanalytic process that involves a multicolored palette of attentional states; they have elaborated the broad brush strokes of Freud's early understandings into the larger canvas envisioned but left incomplete by Freud. A description of subjective experience in psychoanalysis or Buddhism that includes only evenly hovering attention forecloses the wider dimensions of subjective experience that both disciplines have the potential to address. Such an approach amounts to an implicit or explicit devaluation of either Buddhism or psychoanalysis (or both), by reducing Buddhist soteriology to a "relaxation response" or "attention device," and by reducing psychoanalysis to a symptom-relieving-based psychotherapy. As a result, the potential radical transformational capacity inherent in both systems becomes overlooked.

The Role of Unconscious Processes

This stance posits a deficit in psychoanalytic technique and relies on a faulty argument. For example, assume for the moment that psychoanalysis offers no systematic method for training the candidate's attention. Writers, who advocate exploiting mindfulness meditation, embrace this point of view. This standpoint leaves too many readily observable questions unanswered. Most pertinent to this discussion, one might profitably ask: How does one account for those highly attuned and sensitive therapists who have no interest in spirituality or meditation practice? How did these individuals develop listening skills? Clearly, Buddhist meditation practice does not serve as the sole avenue to psychoanalytically attuned listening. The answers to these questions lie within the analyst's own analytic process and experience. The requisite training analysis addresses the psychoanalytic candidate's unconscious issues and can account for the high degree of attunement enjoyed by many nonmeditating analysts. Hopefully, psychoanalysts undergo a "good enough" analysis and develop through this requisite process the capacity for adequate therapeutic listening skills. However, not unlike the unconscious, the candidate's requisite training analysis, which, not unlike Buddhist meditation, functions as an experiential nodal point of psychoanalytic training, has been consistently neglected in the literature on the use of Buddhist attention strategies to improve the analyst's capacity for evenly hovering attention.

As noted in Chapter 6, experience suggests that meditation practices that evoke the necessary alterations in perception associated with Buddhist notions of salvation do rely on the unconscious *processes* that they unlock. Nina Coltart (1996), for example, observes:

> During meditation, there is a lowering of the threshold of consciousness, and in the steady inward looking that accompanies conscious focusing on the breath, the energy withdrawn from our usual centre of consciousness, the ego or I, activates the contents of the unconscious ... being unhampered temporarily by conscious assumptions, we can see the law of "Dependent Origination." (p. 132)*

---

* "Dependent Origination" refers to the contextual arising of all phenomena. That is, phenomena do not exist inherently, but arise subject to causes and conditions.

Coltart makes a distinction between conscious and unconscious processes and implies that meditation accesses the latter. She writes, "The conscious intellect may have knowledge, but it is the great sea of the unconscious that is the source of wisdom" (p. 133).

The meditative and psychoanalytic unlocking of unconscious processes also generates an alteration of perception and an accompanying processing and experiencing of the treatment in unique and often dramatic ways. Variations are evidenced, for example, in the writings of Bion (1970) and Milner (1987). The following vignette demonstrates how unconscious factors can interfere with the therapist's capacity for attention.

Meditating Therapist

A meditating therapist who consulted with me described feelings of extreme dread and intense anxiety stemming from what she described as "witnessing my client's graphic descriptions of physical and sexual abuse." Further, she found herself consistently "actively and intentionally moving my conversations with my patient away from this disturbing material." As a result, she reported feeling "guilty" and "inadequate." Further exploration of her inner states revealed her own aversion to this material and resulting loss of attention that was in part rooted in childhood traumas that she had to suffer and was forced to keep to herself. Once her own traumatic experiences were brought into consciousness, and her need to defend against her own inner feelings were dealt with, continued work led to the awareness of the "induced" (Roland, 1981) aspect of her countertransference reaction. That is, a collusive parent refused to "hear" or respond to the patient's complaints and pleas for help during childhood. By not listening to the patient, the therapist was acting in the role of the patient's inattentive parent. This cocreated relation was now manifesting in the treatment. This example graphically illustrates how unconscious dynamic issues can impede effective and clear psychoanalytic listening. The point here, which we will explore more deeply below, has to do with internal, often unconscious, factors that can enhance and block an individual's attentional capacity and that have nothing to do with any technique for enhancing attention that these authors imply result from the practice of bare attention.

Confrontation With Self-Experience

As noted above, confrontation with the false perception of an inherently existing self forms the center of the Buddhist analytic enterprise. This Buddhist formulation makes it clear that the analyst's resistance can function as an avoidance of the catastrophic, albeit requisite, confrontation with self. Ignorance, or *avidya*, a process that actively and ruthlessly maintains separation, is not readily relinquished despite one's conceptual understanding or through an inventory of learned techniques. In contrast to the above articles, in an article on "free-floating attention," Langan (1997) looks beyond technical recommendations and captures the sense of the fundamental anxiety of being as a source of resistance that interferes with the analyst's capacity for maintaining attention. On this point he writes:

> People spend their lives treating their quotidian concerns as if they were matters of life and death, and so they avoid the looming presence of Life and Death.... Most of the time, perhaps to avoid the awe and dread of that brimming presence, we forget about it and live instead like sleepwalkers in paradise (or is it zombies in hell?). (p. 828)

From an integrative stance, self-confrontation requires a more comprehensive view of evenly hovering attention than Freud developed. This is not simply a pragmatic issue. Awareness of the analyst's identification with the patient's self states requires an approach that simultaneously supports and places on equal footing a constructive use of countertransference and a constructive response to the dissolution of relative subject/object separation. When unobstructed, analysis moves toward unitive experiencing and the possible dissolution of boundaries. This requires the analyst's willingness to allow and acknowledge identification with self and object representations that constitute the patient's self states. The analyst must remain open enough to *become* one with the patient. In Zen parlance, we might speak of *being* both the "one *and* the two" of the patient.

This stance informed by these foundational Buddhist principles departs radically from Freud's assumptions and an accompanying working approach that entails the tracking down of the fragments and pieces of content in an effort to uncover the latent meanings of manifest content. The above studies neglect this fundamental emphasis both in the Buddhist literature and in contemporary psychoanalysis.

Being Conscious

One might profitably question the value of being more conscious. Bion (1980), for instance, argues that this state of mind may not suffice to unfold the evolving Truth of the analysand's inner experience. He notes:

> We try to be as conscious as wide awake, as logical as we know; to have all our wits, all our experience about us to do the work of psycho-analysis. But is that the state of mind one which can make contact with a different state of mind? (p. 20)

For Bion, the requisite state of mind entails a leap of faith. He confronts both the analyst's and the analysand's resistance to experiencing at-one-ment. He "participates" with the patient by facilitating the "existential leap" that finds liberal expression in the Zen literature. D. T. Suzuki (1994), for example, provides a gripping description:

> At first the seeker knows of no way of escape, but get out he must by some means ... before him there yawns a dark abyss. There is no light to show him a possible way to cross it ... the only thing he can do in this crisis is simply to jump, into life or death, but living he feels to be no longer possible. He is desperate, and yet something is still holding him back; he cannot quite give himself up to the unknown.... Here begins a new world of personal experiences, which we may designate "leaping" or "throwing" oneself down the precipice! (p. 52)

Pushing Edges

What will emerge if one pushes edges out of what Ron Sharrin (2002) describes as "the Procrustean bed of Western psychology" (p. 1) and beyond the narrow perimeter of technique? For example, what is the experience of the analyst who attempts to or succeeds to give himself over completely to his unconscious memory as Freud suggests and to leap off of the precipice described by D. T. Suzuki? Would the analyst become subject to the sway of unconscious processes and access radically different experiences? One could reasonably argue that such a leap would result in a potentially creative and transformational impact on *both* analyst and analysand. Most significant to this discussion is the movement toward unitive experience.

For example, as noted above, Bion (1970) describes a process of "intuition" that results in "at-one-ment" with the experience of the patient. As analysts we must asked ourselves: Are we willing to get "in to it" with each individual patient? Bion's recommendations to eschew memory, desire, and understanding and to participate in hallucinosis become increasingly relevant. He addresses the dualistic value judgment implicit in the notion that listening and distraction are fundamentally different, the latter being separate and contraindicated. What do listening and nonlistening mean? What functions do attention and inattention serve at any given moment? What relationships might evolve out of attention and inattention?

The Shape of Attention

Meaning, despite its importance, functions as one narrow current in the wider stream of potential experiencing. We have observed in the previous chapters that in koan work, meaning is stripped away repeatedly. The pursuit of latent meaning with certain patients at certain stages of psychotherapy, not unlike premature interpretations, can foreclose valuable experiential states and might be indicative of the analyst's resistance to deepening unitive experiencing.

Pushing the edges of attention and inattention requires the simultaneous awareness of both form and process. The analyst's associations and impressions take on specific "shapes" with different patients. These shapes, when examined holistically, can reveal the patient's self and object identifications, associated affects, and accompanying relationships. More importantly, they reveal the patient's present state. Much of what one needs to communicate might not be accessible to free association or language. For the individual who does not have the capacity to free associate, what initially might appear as associations, upon deeper examination of their wider shape and form, constitute fragments of inner reality. The following case illustrates this point.

Ben's World

At 50, Ben presents as a little boy struggling to connect, be heard, understood, and most importantly, exist. Ben looks like a "falling apart" person. He is disheveled, clothing not fitting right, shirt not quite tucked in or out; books, magazines, papers seem to fly everywhere. He clumsily knocks things over as he enters the room for his sessions. While marital strains brought Ben into treatment, he complains primarily of "a falling from grace" in his political organization. Ben lost his position as staff writer and lecturer due to budget cuts.

Ben speaks of radical politics. During his sessions he has a captive audience. His monologue dominates and saturates the space. Our initial meeting leaves me feeling stupid. Over time my stupidity intensifies. The stupider I feel, the more treatment seems to progress. Ben frequently interrupts himself to say, "You know what I mean." He understands his question more as a statement. "A psychoanalytically trained therapist," he says, "would know the latent meanings behind my manifest words." This becomes a double-edged sword. I could rescue him from his life and his problems. However, this assumes the existence of a rescuer and someone to be rescued. With Ben one can't make this assumption. It is not clear that Ben's mother could provide him with what is necessary for a self to emerge. He appears to remain in an unintegrated state characterized by the scattered and diffuse fragments of both his inner and outer experience. His father rescued him from a series of foster care situations after his mother was rescued from herself through permanent institutionalization for paranoid schizophrenia when Ben was nine.

Actually, I have no idea what Ben talks about most of the time. I do not feel like a rescuer. Ben's narrative keeps him in control and nulls me out of the space. Unlike his father, Ben is helpless and passive. Ben was the passive, almost inert recipient of the care-taking ministrations of both his wife and the political organization. His wife takes care of the household, their child, and the family budget. The political party arranged his job and his family housing. Ben holds a graduate degree. However, he works as a laborer. He was hired as a technician, became overwhelmed by the responsibility, and was quickly reassigned to a less demanding custodial task.

Ben did not have the capacity for free association. When put to the task, he became anxious. He would draw a blank, become increasingly hostile, and would eventually withdraw completely. Despite Ben's inability to free associate, I noticed what initially appeared as my associations to his narrative. This experience took on a chaotic form with specific contents emerging in a circular process that frequently left me feeling bewildered. My associative process entailed assigning meaning terms to the contents of Ben's political analysis. First there would be an elaboration of a rudimentary meaning system of parallels. When he talks about the dialectic, I would posit, he is feeling ambivalence. Jane is his mother. When he speaks of A, he really is talking about B. Mary is Ann and his nephew is his father. Ben's child becomes himself. The inner process would expand, mushroom, explode, and recycle.

A system of private meanings developed. I would think at these times, "What is he really talking about?" "How can I formulate an interpretation?" I would then ignore his narrative and only hear instantaneous translations into this internal meaning system. We get stuck. Time goes by. He leaves no openings. There is no contact. I begin to feel lost following my associations and translating his language into my inner constructions. My efforts do not further the treatment. Intense drowsiness and drifting set in. This preoccupation derails the possibility of connection and of dialogue. I feel lost and overwhelmed in this inner world. My feelings shift rapidly between interest and disinterest, alertness and drowsiness, attention and preoccupation, claustrophobia and diffusiveness.

Over time, I begin to question my inner reaction to his narrative. Initially, I attribute my lack of understanding to the reality of my inexperience as an analytic candidate, disinterest, lack of understanding of political issues, and an unstated difference of opinion. I feel persecuted by internal pressures. I live in a political vacuum. I should understand these things, and then I could help Ben. However, I am stuck and can't respond. Ben's remarks "You know what I mean?" might more accurately be translated as "You *don't* know what I mean!" My insights remain isolated and trapped within this idiosyncratic and convoluted meaning system.

Stepping back, the larger shape of these internal associations resembles Ben's experience of his mother. She lives trapped within what Ben refers to as "the confines of a paranoid delusional system." He says: "She experiences life in a vacuum." Ben recalls his mother's breakdown. His world fell apart. Both Ben and his brother were placed in a series of stormy and unhappy foster care situations. This was horrible for Ben. He remembers and longs for his mother's love and caring before her deterioration. He decides to call her and reports that she said, "I am not in this world." He recalls his experiences during her episodes that she seemed to operate from her own reality. He says: "This had nothing to do with the real world." The larger shape of my free-associative process revealed this identification with his mother and his own self-experience in relation to her. My initial preoccupation, in retrospect, seemed to function as an enactment of the early mother/son relation. The contents of my evenly hovering attention are not amenable to free association in the sense described by Freud. It is not clear that there exists the capacity for containing meaning. They might be fragments of a catastrophe of what might have been—but has not evolved into a cohesive form.

The larger shape and my emotional reactions reveal the image of his internal mother. Ben holds on to this image and to his lost mother. The appearance of what initially seemed to be free associations represents the fragments of his mother as object and with Ben as self, contained in my mind both as one and in pieces. Opening into the experience and to the impact reveals my emerging internal experience of Ben's self and object world.

Implications and Conclusions

The implication of the movement between distinctions and unity, charted in both Zen experience and psychoanalysis with regard to integrative studies and in terms of clinical experience, such as described above, can be summarized as follows: Whether or not one chooses to concentrate on identities or differences, between psychological and spiritual disciplines, and associated techniques such as evenly hovering attention and bare attention, the Buddhist/psychoanalytic conversation is faced with various aspects, perhaps starting points of fluid relationships. These relationships appear to continuously form and dissolve.

Recently, the trend has shifted increasingly toward an emphasis on identities. However, authors who focus exclusively on comparisons represent an unsettling trend in psychoanalysis that, as noted in Chapter 6, neglects the unconscious and exemplifies Freud's (1933) earlier criticism when he speaks "of the embarrassment that still comes over us when, accustomed as we are to the atmosphere of the underworld, we move in the more superficial, higher strata of the mental apparatus" (p. 68).

My point can be further clarified by going back to the relationship between *avidya* and impermanence. Both Buddhist and psychoanalytic thought demonstrate sensitivity to the fluidity of psychic life. The conversation between Buddhism and psychoanalysis, in as much as it is a human conversation, is not immune to reification processes. Thus, similarities and differences can easily become absolutized. However, when taken out from behind an exclusively scientific lens and given equal footing in the conversation, different images emerge.

Outcomes such as merging and interchangeability of subject and object, the realization of the simultaneity of ultimate and relative existence, are experiences that speak to this fluidity. They are fundamentally different experiences than those that imply pathology associated with regressive merger characteristic of the oceanic feeling, traditionally used in the early psychoanalytic literature to describe meditative states. This realization renders moot the point made by contemporary writers that bare attention and evenly hovering attention bear certain similarities. Considering the identity of the relative and the absolute, and from the point of view of unconscious processes, same or different is not the issue. Both aspects of experience are relative, highly subjective, and fluid. Identity serves as a poor rationale for ripping a technique such as bare attention from the larger fabric of Buddhist experience and attempting to make a technical and conceptual imposition into a seemingly "deficient" psychoanalysis.

This approach renders an incomplete picture of meditative processes and functions. From a psychoanalytic perspective, Rayner (1995) argues in a similar vein that *same* and *different* can function as obstructions. While useful to a point, this emphasis ignores the role of primary processes or unitive modes of being (processes that Buddhists acknowledge by statements such as "same *and* different") and their influence on meditative states of consciousness. Considering the fluidity of psychic processes, perhaps it would be more accurate to view bare attention and evenly hovering attention as elements of an equivalence class or set with certain similarities, differences, and identities, rather than describing them simply as "identical states of mind." This conceptualization more accurately describes and validates the experiences of Buddhist meditators as depicted in Buddhist texts, as observed in my own meditation practice, and as reported by patients, colleagues, and peers.

Analytic reductionism results in an incomplete picture of Buddhist meditation practices. However, critics of the early psychoanalytic view of meditation as solely indicative of pathology rely on a faulty argument. This argument hinges on distinguishing between good and bad meditation forms. Simply stated, "insight, good—bliss, bad." This creates a dichotomized and hierarchical ordering of meditation techniques that ignores conscious and unconscious dynamics so essential to the psychoanalytic inquiry. This position thus maintains distinctions between pathological and nonpathological meditation techniques and depends exclusively on secondary processes. An exclusive reliance on secondary processes conceals underlying identities. When practiced improperly, meditation can engender the difficulties that Freud identified. However, one might profitably argue that the problems are not inherent simply in the meditation techniques but are mediated by the student's and the therapist's relation to the method.

The articles discussed in this chapter, with the exception of Langan (1997), utilize a language that attempts to fit or translate Buddhism into the linear terms of psycho-"logical" scientific discourse. The endeavors to equate bare attention with evenly hovering attention, while of value in such a context, serve as an example. As a result, this series of articles are a product of the scientific-logical discourse. While fully respecting and understanding the need for such linguistic and conceptual modifications, the result is a loss of access to the nonlinear, intuitive, and creative value of a hybrid Buddhist and psychoanalytic discourse.

.

8

Sense and Non-Sense

Introduction

Wilfred Bion's elaboration and use of the notion of "invariance" (1965, 1970) serves as a point of departure for this chapter. For Bion, invariance refers to that which remains unaltered when a basic experience becomes transformed into a communication of that experience. Bion uses the example of the transformation of a landscape into a painting. The invariant quality of the actual landscape is also present in the painting. This invariant quality, according to Bion, makes the landscape recognizable in the painting. The patient's communication to the analyst is a transformation of an actual emotional state or experience. The Zen student's response to a koan functions as a transformation of experience by which the teacher gauges the student's depth of understanding. Invariant qualities present in both account for the recognition of the experience in the resulting description. Bion contends that different areas of inquiry require different invariants. The invariants present in the painting of a landscape, he argues, differ from the invariants in a photograph of the same landscape. Invariance, then, for Bion, refers to the unaltered aspect of a transformation. What remains unaltered by the transformation allows for recognition of an experience in the resulting expression. The principle of invariance applies to religious experiences and their subsequent communication. For example, Buddhist scriptural depictions of emptiness* make the experience or religious practice, such as *kanna-zen* or *shikantaza*, comprehensible and recognizable to the student of meditation.

Both Zen practice and psychoanalysis function through primarily experiential and highly subjective processes. The practitioner's experiences in both traditions require transformation into language. The patient

---

* See Chapter 2.

uses language to communicate inner experience to the analyst. The analyst uses language to communicate to the patient, colleagues, and students.
The Buddhist student and teacher also rely on language to point toward
experience. The psychoanalytic experience undergoes transformation
into interpretations, case studies, or theoretical papers. Zen experience
transforms into scriptural texts, doctrinal studies, debate, question-and-
answer dialogues, and through koan study. For example, D. T. Suzuki
(1994) describes the Zen koan as "the expression of a certain mental
state (Enlightenment)" (p. 77). Bion would refer to the verbal and written communications of Buddhism and psychoanalysis as transformations.
He observes that the medium of expression influences transformations.
Within a given context the transformation will reflect, for example, the
difference between a Freudian and a Kleinian analyst or, in the context
of the present discussion, the differences between Zen and other religious
perspectives. However, despite any possible differences, the expression
attempts to make definite and speakable what is infinite and ineffable. The
constraints of ordinary language and logic can foreclose understanding
experiences that are not limited by the bonds of ordinary logic. As a result,
we can easily fail to trace the invariant from the transformation back to
the actual experience.

This teaching story illustrates the problem. A master points to the sky
and to the moon. The student can only focus on the tip of the master's
finger and fails to see the moon in the sky. He thus remains ignorant of
the truth to which the master points. Similarly, both psychoanalysts and
spiritual seekers can become preoccupied with a theory, philosophy, technique, or the contents of a teacher's or patient's expressions and fail to
grasp the actual experience that they attempt to convey.

Non-Sense

This description of *non-sense* remains intentionally loose. Too much
detail might oversaturate psychic space that would be better left open for
the reader's creativity. Therefore, the reader is encouraged to pay attention
to the experience of reading and to follow one's own associations (particularly in areas of text that seem vague or confusing) and observe what
emerges. In this sense the content serves a secondary role not unlike the
finger pointing at the moon in the above teaching story. Here we depart
from Bion's view that different systems require different invariants to render recognizable transformations. This inquiry delves into the pervasive

and unitive aspects of experience that I address through the notion of non-sense. In this context, non-sense functions as an invariant that identifies what is experientially essential to both Zen and psychoanalysis. That is, non-sense refers to those aspects of experience common to both disciplines. The invariant principle becomes more obvious in areas where Zen and psychoanalysis converge. For example, the psychoanalytic technique of evenly hovering attention and various forms of Buddhist meditation share observable descriptive similarities. As noted in Chapter 7, reviews of descriptions of psychoanalytic listening and Buddhist meditation reveal striking parallels. Comparative studies on Buddhism and psychoanalysis tend to use the sense aspects (ordinary logic) of both experiences to make comparisons about non-sense. The tendency to use sense in this way ignores and obscures non-sense. Emphasis tends to center on the object to the neglect of the experience of the subject in relation to the object. That is, the transformation product (artifact) absorbs attention rather than the initial experience. Further, the claim that non-sense permeates all experience requires that we also acknowledge its operation in areas where Zen and psychoanalysis diverge. This is not quite as easy to see because of the vast seemingly irreconcilable differences between both. However, the differences in the resulting transformations, whether defined as Zen or psychoanalysis, are as striking and necessary as the similarities in the actual experiences. Movement constantly oscillates in and out of divergence and convergence. The definite and the infinite depend on where one stands and what one is willing to sit with at a particular moment. In psychoanalysis we can think of the pervasive unconscious background of experience that, while invisible, is present in all manifest experience despite the level of health or pathology. In religion, non-sense can refer to the "ineffable" or the "cosmic." The Buddhist concept of emptiness represents an epistemological formulation of non-sense. Non-sense functions provide a neutral way to talk about diverse transformations and expressions of a basic experience that cuts across both disciplines and refers to what is pervasive despite our present capacity or incapacity for perception or discussion of the actual experience. Based on Bion's definition, this pervasiveness qualifies non-sense as an invariant. As an invariant, non-sense functions as a useful tool for exploring convergences and divergences between Buddhism and psychoanalysis. Perhaps we can move beyond the initial constraints of what we define as Buddhism and psychoanalysis. At the least, we hope to eliminate biases that might occur by using terms specific to either discipline to guide our exploration. Whether non-sense finds expression through an "indivisible" yet "invisible" unconscious, as

Matte-Blanco (1988) suggests, or is simply not presently ascertainable to "ordinary non-analytic perception" (Hopkins, 1983), as Buddhists posit, it remains constant and basic to all experience. Whether attributed to an incapacity for non-sense, to unconscious resistances, to the operation of *avidya* (innate ignorance), to all, or to none of the above, it represents a force active in both psychological and spiritual traditions.

Non-sense derives from making at least enough sense to establish a necessary ground. We can relate non-sense to what Bion (1970) refers to as the non-sensual data of psychoanalysis and to the area of experience where psychoanalysis increasingly diverges from medicine. The movement is away from the facts and hard data of physical science and toward what can be intuited. Movement away from the sensual data, in this context, facilitates access to non-sense. Non-sense both transcends and permeates sense and no-sense, pathology and health, ignorance and enlightenment. Non-sense constitutes the experiences of both self and no-self. Non-sense is reflected in the Buddhist conceptualization of the mutuality of relative and absolute existence. From the point of view of nonanalytic or ordinary commonsense perception, what appears as a contradiction becomes perfectly acceptable in relation to non-sense. For instance, from the non-sense perspective, discussions *about* the integration of Buddhism and psychoanalysis can function as an unconscious resistance to the *experience* of the integration of Buddhism and psychoanalysis. As I have elaborated in previous chapters, fundamental anxiety fuels this resistance. Resistance to being relates to the threat of I-sense becoming no-sense. As I noted in the introduction, I-sense refers to a contextually emerging fluctuating sense of self that interacts with unconscious reification processes, resulting in the lived experience of an abiding and separate sense of self. In the context of this chapter, sense and no-sense represent two prototypical forms of an infinite range of I-sense.

Nonanalytic perception confuses no-sense with non-sense. The Buddhist confronts sense (and no-sense) with non-sense, not with no-sense. Psychoanalysts have acknowledged non-sense through a careful mapping of unconscious processes. However, as a whole, as Matte-Blanco (1988) observes, "Analysts have tended not to consider the matter or have moved their discipline towards conventional psychology and conventional logic" (p. 5). The distinctions between non-sense, no-sense, and sense require further clarification.

No-Sense

No-sense in relation to non-sense functions to maintain the distinction between madness and enlightenment. We can entertain the possible truth that enlightenment can be maddening and that madness can be enlightening. Perhaps from the perspective of unified nondifferentiated awareness that might be associated with certain notions of enlightenment experience, we can agree with such statements. However, for the enlightened individual, unitive experience paradoxically accompanies a deepening capacity for differentiation. Buddhist descriptions of enlightenment experiences suggest that what occurs is an intensification of both aspects of experience. The progressively deeper layers of unitive experience accompany a retrospective capacity to generate increasingly more rarefied and subtle distinctions in experience and meaning. For the enlightened being, the idea that "everything is everything else" is not the same experience typically associated with madness. Madness often destroys any capacity for differentiation and meaning. The Buddhist notion of omniscience refers to the capacity to live in the relative and the absolute and to experience the unity and separateness of life simultaneously. Omniscience magnifies and reveals. Madness nullifies and blinds. Non-sense alludes to an opening into reality and a deepening of directly lived experience. Hopkins's (1987) description of the Buddhist analytic process makes this distinction clear. He writes: "This analysis is not a vague process of turning your mind away from events. When you analyze, you are more engaged than you ever were before in your life. It is said, 'One who knows emptiness is aware, more perceptive, more awake, more conscientious ... more into objects ... more familiar ... brilliant ... clear'" (p. 197).

Regarding the issue of the relation between enlightenment and madness, Bion (1970) observes that "it would be more true to say that psychotic mechanisms require a genius to manipulate them in a manner adequate to promote growth or life" (p. 63). He uses the terms *genius* and *mystic* interchangeably. A similar transformation appropriate to the present discussion would be Buddha (literally "one gone thus"). This transformation generates different associations and requires elaboration. The implication in this reading is that psychosis requires a particular context and relation for consideration as indicative of pathology. The pathology arises through a lack of capacity to use psychotic mechanisms or to resist the possibility of churning no-sense to the nth degree and accessing non-sense and the infinite. Tibetan Buddhist teacher Chogyam Trungpa (1967) describes the "manure field of Bodhi." We can use our "neuroses," says Trungpa, to generate and reveal "Buddha nature." The unenlightened tendency maintains a flight into sense. We can thus avoid dirtying our hands in the manure. From Trungpa's point of view we can hypnotize our selves with the promise of enjoying the beauty of the rose, not getting cut by the thorns, and remaining clean. He writes: "We would prefer to approach Buddhism as if picking flowers in a beautiful garden, but we then miss the richness of life" (1976, p. 1). Lightness requires acknowledging darkness. The genius here of "one gone thus" relates to a willingness to belly down and crawl around in the mud, manure, and mess, get cut by the thorns. Jesus' crown of thorns epitomizes this willingness. Crucifixion precedes transcendence. However, this approach assaults the basic human need for form since the situation is always messy, muddy, and unclear. In this context no-sense maintains the finite and refers to a closing off from reality and to a loss of connectedness. Bion (1959) refers to the psychotic's "attacks on linking." Such individuals tend to destroy both internal and external connections and meanings. They engender no-sense and experience a false sense of grounding. These individuals become sealed off, lost in space, and presently removed from contact with the ground and from the open-ended aspects of experience. Edna O'Shaughnessy (1988) observes that in this state "the psychotic is in despair, imprisoned in his bizarre universe" (p. 180). We need to avoid the confusion between the psychotic closing off from experience and the opening to experiences associated with enlightenment. Fusion from the perspective of the open system becomes a diffusion into freedom. By contrast, fusion from the perspective of the closed system represents a "re-fusion" or a refusal to open into life and results in imprisonment. The terms no-sense and non-sense help to keep this important distinction in mind. No-sense refers to the pathological, regressive, and imprisoning aspects of being and maintains the distinction between "one gone thus" and "too far gone," although the two aspects of experience are not necessarily mutually exclusive. Non-sense, on the other hand, refers to what can be healthy, progressive, and liberating.

Sense

Experiencing requires a certain amount of sense. However, too much sense making also becomes a resistance to non-sense and, like no-sense, a form of imprisonment. The high diver climbs the ladder one step at a time. However, the moment arises when he needs to let go of the rail, step out to the edge, and dive into the cool waters below. Initially, we need a certain amount of ground to stand on. Distinctions require reasoning and thinking processes and create the ground from which potential openings take place. For example, the Tibetan middle-way Buddhist practitioner begins with study, reasoning, and debate. These activities generate enough sense to know about being. Through meditation practices they exploit sense to "simulate" the experience of non-sense. Continued practice gradually transforms the simulation into direct experience. By contrast, the Zen master in the Rinzai tradition creates an abrupt awakening by derailing the student's rational thought processes. He thus engenders the non-sense experience within the student. Both arrive at non-sense through different maneuvers. The psychoanalyst makes sense through a process of exchange that includes understanding, reasoning, explaining, interpreting, and tolerating not knowing. The analysand, gaining assurance and some familiarity with the process, becomes able to take steps toward tolerating not knowing. The analyst and the analysand thus create the ground for moving from no-sense or sense into non-sense. The need for this distinction arises from the notion that unitive experience results in a state of nondivisibility. Non-sense functions as background for both sense and no-sense. Therefore, we use sense and no-sense to find an entry into non-sense. Through unitive experience non-sense makes contact with no-sense and creates the possibility for sense. For example, when there is no experience of being at all, merger states might represent a progression from nonexistence to being. Merger requires a you and a me to merge. Considering this possibility, can we continue to view merger exclusively as pathological or regressive? On the other hand, not everything needs to make sense. Consider those patients who torture themselves trying to make sense out of everything. One patient, for example, relates hearing as a child: "Go to your room and don't come out until you figure out what you did wrong." He finds his way to the consultation room still attempting to figure things out. Such individuals attempt and frequently succeed in recruiting the therapist into the process. They become buried in the ground. The sense-making activity can become punitive, perhaps revealing a tie to a punitive internal parent image. Sense making can also evolve into a resistance that reveals the fear of leaping into the unknown. At the extreme, sense, like no-sense, becomes another form of imprisonment and a closed system that prevents contact and opening into directly lived experience. In this sense, non-sense functions as a source of liberation. Buddhism teaches that we instinctively attempt to make sense by formulating and solidifying an I-sense. However, Buddhists argue that from the non-sense perspective, I-sense ultimately makes no sense.

The Ground and the Groundless

Psychoanalysis from this perspective emphasizes non-sense at the expense of what makes sense. The accompanying feeling of groundlessness can become uncomfortable. We move in unknown territory. Ordinary logic does not always work for us in the uncharted areas that we explore as therapists or spiritual seekers. This becomes more likely as we move from the ground to the groundless and from sense or no-sense into non-sense. We need the sense (no-sense) to reach non-sense. Without the solid ground of reason and of what makes sense, we risk falling from the groundlessness of non-sense, into the closed state, and out of contact. Both sense and non-sense are vital forces. In this respect, the ground and the groundless are fundamental to human experience. We require a runway for the jet to take off and land. However, we don't take the runway with us. That would impede the flight. We need to trust that the ground will be there at landing time. If we can risk discomfort, then we can create the possibility for spontaneously lived experience and genuinely creative transformation. In this respect, non-sense, sense, and no-sense refer to experiential states. The ground and the groundless relate more to levels of structure and relatedness that provide experiential access into and out of these states.

Some Comments on Analysis

Analysis derives from the Greek word *analusis*. This term refers to a dissolving, an undoing, or a taking apart of a whole. When applied to psychoanalysis this meaning refers literally to a dissolving, undoing, or taking apart of the psyche. However, the practice of psychoanalysis, for the most part, tends toward developing, building up, and strengthening. In this sense, psychoanalysis tends toward solving, doing, and synthesizing. Therefore, there is an implicit value on knowing, building ego structure, developing a more cohesive self-structure, using higher-level defenses, and moving toward separation and autonomy. These outcomes relate more to sense making. The need for I-sense, from the Buddhist point of view, deflects fundamental anxiety and generates this overemphasis on sense making and the natural human tendency to reify experience. This unconscious need becomes embedded in psychoanalytic theory and technique and moves toward sense and away from non-sense. Perhaps this sense-ground appears safer, constant, solid. However, Trungpa (1976) observes: "Constantly, we find ourselves suddenly slipping off the edge of the floor which appeared to extend endlessly, then we must save ourselves from death by immediately building another extension" (p. 20). As psychoanalysts we can easily resist this inevitable slipping off the edge by continuing to build more ground through sense-making activity. We can break the flow safely before we reach non-sense, which Bion (1990) notes "remains unconscious" and becomes "a source of speculation and disturbance" (p. 11).

Freud left plenty of room for non-sense. As elaborated in Chapter 6, this is implicit in his discovery and exploration of the unconscious and its laws and in his complementary techniques of free association and evenly hovering attention. Psychoanalysis addresses unconscious motivations and requires some way to conceptualize the unconscious aspect of experience. The unconscious is implicit in both psychoanalytic theory and technique. Processes such as projection, displacement, and condensation assume an unconscious that operates through laws and principles that assault what logically makes sense. When we explore the domain of psychoanalysis, for the most part, we talk about the unconscious and its processes. However, we do not always use these very same properties and functions to explore and discuss psychoanalysis. Matte-Blanco (1988) observes that with few exceptions, the non-sense aspect of Freud's work remains undeveloped. While the above-noted sense-making therapeutic goals have obvious benefits, it seems that from the point of view of non-sense, other outcomes occur. These outcomes relate to letting go, dissolving, and undoing. At the less differentiated levels of unconscious operations, says Matte-Blanco, being and non-being become condensed. Similarly, we can say that dissolving is solving, undoing is doing, and analyzing is synthesizing. When non-sense becomes truly experienced it makes its own sense. From this point of view, psychoanalysis functions to dissolve and undo obstructions to what I like to think of as creating more emotional elbow room. This requires that we undo preconceived and erroneous notions of how we experience our self and ourselves in relation to others. This undoing process requires identifying, examining, scrutinizing, and questioning our self-constructed and reified self deceptions. As noted above, the primary self-deception that requires analysis is the I-sense. Not any I-sense. Rather, the I-sense that implies an inherent, absolute I operating independently of any causes or conditions. In terms of the psyche we could say that for creative transformations to occur, we need to get past what we think we know and allow ourselves the space to not know. Our theories and philosophies, the contents of our patient's communication, and the hard facts can saturate our mental space and make not knowing seem virtually impossible. Freud makes this clear in his technical recommendations. He warns physicians to avoid "deliberate attentiveness" and selectivity. Freud (1912b) says that "if one's expectations are followed in this selection there is the danger of never finding anything but what is already known" (p. 118). In a similar vein, Bion (1980) adds, "What you have seen before doesn't matter. What does matter is what we, the analyst and the patient, have *not* seen before" (p. 13, emphasis in original). The psychoanalytic endeavor, at least from Bion's perspective, requires that both the analyst and the analysand tolerate not knowing and an accompanying unsettled feeling. As Bion (1990) puts it,

> in psychoanalysis: when approaching the unconscious—that is, what we do *not* know, not what we *do* know, we patient and analyst alike, are certain to be disturbed.... If they are not, one wonders why they are bothering to find out what everyone knows (pp. 4–5).

In summary, this operational definition of psychoanalysis requires that we dissolve any notion of self as we presently experience and understand it. The Zen master put it this way: "Be the I don't know mind!" This endeavor generates anxiety. However, if we allow it, this anxiety fuels the flight from the ground to the groundless.

The Spiritual Dimension of Psychoanalysis

For the purposes of the present discussion remarks regarding the question "What is spiritual?" are limited to what might be considered spiritual in the therapeutic situation. The term *spiritual* here refers to those moments that occur during therapy sessions that are characterized by a distinct sense of simultaneous connectedness and separateness. During these heartfelt moments both individuals relate from the depth of their being with a feeling of fullness and wholeness. As one patient put it, "I really *feel* myself." This experience of the depth and fullness of being occurs through a spontaneous gesture. Such spontaneous gestures carry a full sense of lived presence and an intensified awareness and acceptance of self and other. The feeling of connectedness does not compromise the sense of separateness, of individual integrity, wholeness, and uniqueness. The accompanying experience of separateness is without a loss of relatedness and connectedness with the other. During the treatment process such moments seem to transcend the days, weeks, months, and even years of sense-making activities. While the day-to-day sense-making work dissolves in the wake of these spontaneous moments of raw, fresh experience, sense making often creates the necessary ground for their occurrence. As noted above, ground creates a starting point to launch into such experiences. The groundless by definition implies a ground. This becomes a "grounded groundlessness." We distinguish this experience from the disconnected groundlessness of the psychotic experience. Experiences of "grounded groundlessness" might evolve out of a spiritual context. More often than not, they don't. Here is an example.

Carl

Carl is floating. He has found himself floating before. Usually he floats alone in space, disconnected from the ground, as a reaction to his anxiety and as a reaction to the anxiety of those afraid to float with him. However, now we are floating together. When he gets too uncomfortable, he lets me know through a heavy obsessive monologue. If I lightly point to the ground through an interpretation, he can allow himself to continue to experience what he describes as a "newfound freedom." He laughs and says, "I am embarrassed with the simplicity of it all. There is nothing behind it—just laughter. No reason, no explanation—just laughter." I nod. He continues to laugh. His laughter is gentle, deep, and catching. The laughter is not the previous strained anxious laughter that we are both familiar with. The silences between feel light and airy, like open space. Not the dreaded dead spaces where he describes suffocating in a bottle. This is not the heavy defensive silence that previously occurred in the dead spaces between his obsessive lists, explanations, and explications of "profound truths." I laugh too. We both laugh together. He begins to break the laughter and the silence with the observation that he suddenly feels anxious. He feels compelled to give me an explanation for his experience, feelings, and behavior. He is anxious at not having an explanation. None exists. He just feels good. I again point to the ground and say, "Oh, like with Dad." He responds "yeah" and laughs again. We both laugh. The laughter is gentle and connected. This event occurs two years into the treatment. It did not just magically happen one day. We spent considerable time talking *about* his relationships with Dad, Mom, lovers, and me. We both understand a few things *about* his life and his self in relation to his life. These sense-making activities provide entry into non-sense and into *being* his life in the present moment. A failure to let go at the appropriate time and continue with sense would foreclose the non-sense experience. This would constitute a resistance to being on my part. This example, in my opinion, speaks to what is spiritual with regard to psychoanalysis.

In summary, except for the preparation (sense making) and the actual experience (non-sense) of such moments, we do not know what can be considered spiritual. For, if the spirit, if you will, is all pervasive, then how can we imagine anything not being spiritual? One answer is that the spirit requires a material base that becomes manifest in the relation of sense and non-sense. Through the mutual interaction of both therapist and patient resistances, the non-sense can become hidden in the sense-making activity. In this respect, doing becomes undoing. The possibility for non-sense becomes undone. Revealing non-sense results in directly experienced moments of simultaneous connectedness and separation. We experience a momentary emotional truth of being in relation to our self and of our self in relation to the other.

Faith

Both Zen and the area of psychoanalysis that I have emphasized throughout the chapters in this book center on a faith-driven experiential perspective. Faith, from this vantage point, relates to the experientially based feeling of conviction. This sense of conviction generates the motivational force necessary for pursuing lived spiritual and emotional truth. This faith transcends the "blind faith" typically associated with religious dogmatism. Bion (1970), who emphasizes faith, "craves something better ... [than]. That is the truth accept it" (p. 63). This faith requires unrelenting scrutiny into the fundamental truth of evolving reality. Like Carl's floating described above, this truth must be lived.

The Buddhist view of faith finds expression in Robert Thurman's (1994) observation that the historical Buddha "was primarily a critic of religion. He critiqued its absolutist tendencies, its devaluation of human reason, and its legitimization of unreasonable, arbitrary, and oppressive structures of authority. Reality, as Buddha saw it, is beyond dogmatic theories, while freely open to unprejudiced experience" (p. 16).

For the Buddhist, faith in reality demands an emotional conviction. For example, reciting the "vows of refuge" comes on the heels of a dread of cyclic existence. This practice, "I take refuge in the Buddha, the dharma (teaching), and the sangha (spiritual community)," is a heartfelt urgent pursuit, not a dry intellectual or obligatory endeavor. It becomes a matter of life and death. From the psychoanalytic perspective Eigen (1991) describes faith as an "experiencing that is undertaken with one's whole being, all out, with all one's heart with all one's soul, and with all one's might" (p. 109). The co-requisite for this lived faith demands, as Bion put it, a relinquishment of memory and desire.

In summary, if we can maintain a sense of faith in the possibility for such lived truths, and if as therapists we pursue this possibility religiously and unrelentingly, within ourselves and with those who seek our help, then we can suggest that we have identified a primary experiential hub of psychoanalytic and spiritual integration. The following quote from Eigen (1985) serves as a relevant conclusion. "If his [the analyst's] sense is deeply rooted in the non-sense (F) beyond knowing (K), his work may have a resonance that makes a difference" (p. 221).

9

The Gap Between:
Being, Knowing, and the Liminal in Between

> When the hands are off the precipice,
> Conviction comes upon thee all by itself;
> Let resurrection follow death,
> And none can now deceive thee.
>
> —D. T. Suzuki (1994, p. 23)

Introduction

This chapter examines various relationships derived from the image of gap, precipice, and the abyss, with specific emphasis on interacting dynamics between being and knowing. While of significant value to psychoanalysis, I argue that symbolic meanings can occlude the actuality of the analysand's or spiritual seeker's affective experiencing, particularly concerning the human tendency to concretize experiential states engendered through meditation or the psychoanalytic encounter. I draw from Matte-Blanco's explication of symmetrical and asymmetrical perceptual modalities that we reviewed in Chapter 6 to highlight the fluid nature of spiritual experiencing, the paradoxical coexistence of ultimate and relative realities, and the reciprocal dynamics and identities between states of experiencing that might otherwise appear opposed. The primacy of experiencing for both disciplines, particularly concerning the experiencing subject's momentary state of consciousness, forms a central theme for both Zen and psychoanalysis. Clinical material supports and illuminates the points under discussion.

The gap appears as a perennial dilemma that reveals itself in many forms in the various world religions, philosophies, and psychologies. By definition, the gap includes precipice and abyss. Interpersonally or relationally, gap includes subject and object and what connects (separates) them. Connectedness implies separateness by definition. Psychologically, from a practical point of view, the gap points to the separation between different aspects of self and thus expresses the need for establishing or regaining wholeness through healing fragmentation. In this respect, Buddhism acknowledges the gap between subject and object. On this point Luk (1993) notes: "All of us are accustomed to the deep rooted habit of splitting our undivided whole into subject and object by clinging to the false ideas of the reality of an ego and phenomena" (p. 11). The gap symbolizes this rift. The need to cling to the precipice becomes a clinging to ego, which, as I noted previously, from the Zen perspective refers to false solidified ideas of who we imagine ourselves to be. In this respect, therefore, bridging the gap has to do with the experience of wholeness. Wholeness in this context requires acknowledging both unity and duality that transcend linear polemic notions of concretized subject and object.

The gap charts an exploration that simultaneously reveals and veils ultimate reality and addresses both real and imagined distinctions that apply equally to the various depictions of the dimensions of experience. The gap evolves in many directions, multiply layered with meaning and function. As symbol, gap might point toward womb, abyss, death, breast (nourishment, entanglement, suffocation, safety), or the unknown. Precipice might function to represent common sense, umbilical cord, the extent and limits of relationships, a closing off to the unknown, freedom, imprisonment, or clinging to life and death. Abyss might represent womb, depression, the object's narcissism, the path to creativity and freedom, or the unknown. The unknown permeates all formulations and symbols. Thinking about the gap exclusively as symbol for precipice and abyss might represent a resistance to the actuality of the gap itself and as a sign or expression of the futility of imprisonment, both psychically and as a human being caught in the space between life and death in the moment-to-moment drama of the multitude of lives and deaths of emerging, crystallizing, and dissolving psychic states.

The gap (precipice and abyss) functions as a metaphor for the relationship between being and knowing, which can become polarized and reified at extremes maintaining a state of fragmentation, alienation, and various sociocultural manifestations, such as phobias, chauvinism, racism, aggression, or holocaust. Each fragment might function like a still-frame snapshot of a moment of the natural flow between being and knowing when left to operate unfettered. This latter form constitutes the focus of this discussion, which explores converging and diverging expressions of the gap between being and knowing in the psychoanalytic writings of Wilfred Bion and in the Buddhist teachings of Zen master Hui-neng,* as explicated in the writings of D. T. Suzuki. Convergences provide points of entry that can be acknowledged, touched lightly, and let go. Divergences create openings. The tension between the two might promote vitality, continued growth of the individual, as well as the disciplines of Zen and psychoanalysis. In this respect, the gap demonstrates the close kinship between psychoanalytic and religious experiences and the simultaneously widening space between psychoanalysis and science if continued growth can be tolerated.

The gap, precipice, and abyss find expression in Bion's O and in the satori (enlightenment) experience of Zen. Both allude to and hint at the ineffable, unknowable, fluid, ever-evolving aspects of psychic life that D. T. Suzuki (1994) describes as "being-in-itself"† and Bion (1970) as "beening." Bion and Hui-neng both argue for the primacy of experience, but experience lived beyond sense, hearing, seeing, cognizing. Bion describes the experience of "at-one-ment," which is not buffered by sense (without which an analysis is not complete). As I noted in Chapter 8, sense maintains the subject and object dichotomy. Similarly, satori becomes experienced through the dissolution of dichotomous thinking. The following anecdote serves equally well to describe both Hui-neng's and Bion's shared stance regarding the primacy of experience:

> Self-realization never comes from merely listening and thinking.... In a great desert there are no springs or wells ... a traveler comes from the west going eastward; he meets a man coming from the east and asks him: I am terribly thirsty; pray tell me where I can find a spring and a cool refreshing shade where I may drink, bathe, rest, and get thoroughly revived?
>
> The man from the east gives the traveler, as desired, all the information in detail, saying: When you go further east the road divides itself into two, right and left. You take the right one ... you will surely come to a fine spring and a refreshing shade ... do you think that the thirsty traveler from the west, listening to the talk about the spring and the shady trees, and thinking of going to that place as quickly as possible, can be relieved of thirst and heat and get refreshed? (D. T. Suzuki, 1994, p. 13)

---

* Hui-neng (638–713), the sixth patriarch and founder of the Southern School of Chinese Ch'an (Zen) Buddhism. Hui-neng authored the Platform Sutras, which advocate the no-mind doctrine of abrupt awakening and criticize the fossilization that occurred as a result of philosophical and intellectual speculation and the mental death of "mirror wiping" mental stasis meditation.
† Being-in-itself refers to the experience of being stripped of the buffering of conceptualizing and reasoning processes. Bion uses the verb beening (1970) to refer to this state of being.

Being-in-itself and beening both keep in mind the active nature of psychic experience that can be destroyed by attempts at definition through the vehicle of ordinary language. In a similar indictment Suzuki describes meditative homeostasis as "psychic suicide." However, Bion also, through O and beening, reminds the reader of the paradoxical relationship between content and no-content, definite and infinite, or what Buddhists describe as the relative and the absolute reality. Paradox keeps things open. Perhaps in therapy by keeping open to the gap, precipice and abyss edges can be pushed to greater extremes.

Wisdom, for the Buddhist, usually means intuitive experiential wisdom or "quick knowing" (Evans-Wentz, 1954). The problem is that over time, the wisdom derived through the original experiences of geniuses like Hui-neng or Freud becomes codified, concretized, and intellectualized, and its potency tends to be neutralized "for it was identified with intellectual subtleties which dealt with contents and their analysis" (D. T. Suzuki, 1972a, p. 33).

Starting Points

Bion and Hui-neng work from different starting points. Bion deals with emotional pain and the growth of the psyche. Bion's dialogue attempts to connect, perhaps meeting at a preverbal (birth) state. His submergence in the psychic universe of the analysand ("participation in hallucinosis") attempts to bring the latter to life, back to the surface, and into the world. Bion's gap between being and knowing functions as a nodal point for his psychoanalysis.

For Hui-neng being *is* knowing. Knowing *is* being. However, fundamental anxiety perpetuates an ignorant vicious cycle of separation and reification. The dialectic tension between being and knowing serves as a connecting thread for both Bion and Hui-neng. Is it possible to live at the center of this tension of lived-in-the-moment truth while simultaneously pushing the edges? Is transcendence necessary or possible? Transcendence creates its own dualities; thus, Hui-neng speaks of a return to the ordinary. His movement is from the ordinary to the extraordinary and back to the ordinary. Ignorance is a human pathology that no one is immune from. Hui-neng deals with the relationship between pain and enlightenment. So perhaps they create a meeting point. Like "two arrows meeting in mid air" (Loori, 1994), the dialectic tension stemming from their differences explodes in infinite directions and possibilities. The simultaneity of identity and distinction of all phenomena are basic to a psychoanalysis viewed from a subjective and experiential perspective. On this issue Eigen (1986b) writes: "We cannot trifle with the gaps between and within us. We learn to live in the movement between face and facelessness, at the point where union and difference cocreate one another" (p. 242). The gap as an expression of simultaneity provides a vehicle for discussing the integration of Buddhism and psychoanalysis.

Both Bion and Hui-neng view ultimate truth to be beyond the reach of ordinary knowledge and argue that a search for knowledge obscures lived ultimate truth or its own O-ness. Sense making creates its own resistances to experience by attempting to foreclose the infinite. Bion remains open to the fluid unknown that is at the center of his psychoanalytic endeavor. Hui-neng discovers the unknowable in the basic facts of human existence: He speaks of the pain of a slap on the face, a kick in the shin, the coolness of a drink of water, the shade of a tree, a proper cup of tea. Both invite the individual to participate in the humanness of life with all of its terror and delight. Bion endeavors to stimulate the analysand's birth, rebirth, or growth. Perhaps the latter will engage or reengage the world of self and other, perhaps for the first time stepping out from a self-imposed prison. Hui-neng locates the extraordinary in the moment-to-moment being in the ordinary world. If Bion addresses the null dimension, Hui-neng addresses the dull dimension. At the level of discussion that Bion and Hui-neng address, alterations in psychic structure demand coming to terms with the paradox of the simultaneity of identity and difference. Failure to face this paradox reifies fragmentation and forecloses wholeness.

What parallels and distinctions exist between O and satori, being-in-itself and beening? What techniques do Bion and Hui-neng offer to engender psychic transformations that render these alternate realities accessible? What roads do they invite the reader to take? Does the "reality of sameness" (D. T. Suzuki, 1994, p.13) have the same meaning and requirements as Bion's at-one-ment? If so, facing the gap, whether illusion or actuality, becomes a primary concern for both analyst and meditator alike. Suzuki writes that the task of Zen has been "upholding satori against ritualism and erudition and all forms of mere philosophizing" (p. 16). Similarly, Bion (1970) argues and cautions of the hazards of rote interpretations. He writes "his 'habits' will lead him to resort to instantaneous and well-practiced saturation from 'meaning' rather than from O" (p. 51).

In explicating the gap, neither Bion nor Hui-neng engages in philosophical speculation. They concern themselves in a highly pragmatic way with ultimate truth and the reality of human suffering. Both provide difficult yet engaging solutions. One area of practicality includes the provision of a system and associated techniques that have the potential to relieve individual suffering. Their radical solutions simultaneously require that the system employed (psychoanalysis and Zen) remain alive and vital. Similarly, Zen concerns itself with both the causes and the antidotes to suffering and provides a most radical and dramatic account of breaking through the unconsciously self-imposed and imprisoning veil of illusion to being-in-itself. Hui-neng and Bion both address the gap between words (theory, interpretation, philosophy, dogma) and experience (evolving lived-in-the-moment truth). They confront the gap between the ongoing actuality of experience of ultimate truth and the formulations designed to contain, restrain, or disavow the experience "in the minds of ordinary people" (Bion, 1970, p. 85). Bion writes: "As my practice with more disturbed patients increased, it became evident that more rigorous formulation of theory was needed if the gap between representation and realization was to be bridged by the analyst's inter-pretation" (p. 9).

The Limits of Comparison

Paradoxically, comparisons that trace observed similarities between Buddhist meditation and psychoanalytic attention inadvertently serve to set them apart and maintain the gap. Discussion of similarities and differences between the Southeast Asian Theravada Buddhist technique of mindfulness meditation or "bare attention" and the classical psycho-analytic attentional stance of evenly hovering attention that I reviewed in Chapter 7 has dominated the recent literature on Buddhism and psycho-analysis. However, such comparisons do not represent accurate and stable estimations of the convergences and divergences between the two systems. Any point of view simply represents a point along a continuum of experi-ence and is by definition too limited to embrace the actual experience. Intuitively speaking, for example, I have often felt a close kinship and less of a psychic and emotional distance with individuals whose points of view (Kaballah, Celtic mysticism, for example) are unfamiliar me. Conversely, a seemingly unbridgeable distance can exist between individuals who might share the identity of psychoanalysts, Zenists, or both.

Bion

Bion expands the borders of psychoanalysis beyond the boundaries of the Cartesian dualistic pragmatism that characterized early psychoanalysis. He takes the reader into the ever-evolving realm of the mystical infinite. Bion moves freely and comfortably between the definite and the infinite. This realm of experience embraces what might be arbitrarily defined and known and what can only be intuited and lived through direct experience. Bion's forays into the non-sense aspects of experience, which for him comprises the true realm of psychoanalysis, become most evident in *Transformations* (1965) and in *Attention and Interpretation* (1970). The notion of gap constitutes one strand, among many, that threads its way through both of these works.

What I found to be most intriguing at the time that I encountered his work were the variety and diversity of responses to his ideas on attention written during what Gerard Bleandonu (1994), Bion's biographer, describes as his "epistemological period." Bion's writings during this period have elicited comments that span the gamut from extreme criticism to utter praise. He has been described as a mystic by some and written off as demented by others (Grotstein, 2007; Lopez-Corvo, 2006). Some critics believed that Bion's writings during this period should be "dismissed as the ramblings of a senile man" (Symington & Symington, 1996, p. 10). What was also striking and hard for me to understand at the time was the conspicuous absence, with few notable exceptions (Coltart, 1992, 1996; Eigen, 1998; Grotstein, 1981; Rhode, 1994, 1998), of any depth discussion of Bion in the literature on mystical experience, religion, and psychoanalysis beyond his basic technical recommendation to relinquish memory, desire, and understanding.

Bion's Postulates

Bion's postulates provide a loose framework to point toward the experience of, into, and beyond the gap. His axiomatic explication of the gap makes visible a series of relationships and themes common to both Zen and psychoanalysis. This holds equally true both conceptually and experientially. For Bion, the gap becomes objectified in the distance between heaven and earth, the person and God, the sinner and the state of grace, subject and object, consciousness and unconsciousness, physical medicine and psychoanalysis, representation and realization, the sensuous and the nonsensuous, and K (knowledge) and O (ultimate truth). Here we follow and comment on two of Bion's axiomatic explications of postulates that unfold the gap.

The Gap Between Phenomena and the Thing-in-Itself

Bion (1965) writes that "my theory would seem to imply a gap between phenomena and the thing-in-itself" (p. 147). Here he criticizes the limits imposed on psychoanalysis by the scientific materialist matrix, concerned with sense and critical of non-sense that both spawned and impinged upon Freud's thinking. He observes: "From this conviction of the inaccessibility of absolute reality the mystic must be exempted" (p. 147). Bion argues that reliance on mystical experience can move psychoanalysis beyond the restrictions of enlightenment secularism. However, a basic human need for protection generates its own resistance to ultimate truth. Regardless of an individual's conscious beliefs, he observes that "the remainder of us believe it unconsciously but no less tenaciously for that" (p. 147). Human nature both craves and resists truth.

The Gap Between Reality and Personality

Bion raises the stakes with geometrical logical precision and simplicity. The honesty and straightforwardness of his message become occluded by our own terror and disbelief. On this issue Eigen (1985) writes: "One does not want to hear or bear or believe Bion's message" (p. 211). The intrinsic need to maintain the gap at the cost of psychological freedom and creativity operates fiercely. Bion (1965) moves from phenomena to personality and from the thing-in-itself to reality. He postulates "the gap between reality and the personality" (p. 147). Does Bion dare imply that the personality is unreal? He equates personality with unreal phenomena. The latter opposes the reality of the thing-in-itself. Here we find in Bion's thought the confrontation with self, the central feature and purpose of Buddhist analysis. The Buddhist practitioner asks: "Are self and phenomena existent or nonexistent?" The seemingly enigmatic answer, "both real and unreal," expresses the fundamental unsolvable paradox. We find no shade of gray here. Bion continues by noting "the gap between 'knowing phenomena' and 'being reality'" (p. 149). This distinction sets reality as direct experience apart from phenomena known (and thus the personality) through the limited vehicle of the senses. The person as phenomena becomes unreal and the insubstantiality of the person/self phenomena becomes the truth. He at once demonstrates the limits of enlightenment secularism and departs radically from Freud's use of knowledge, which true to his positivist orientation can provide layer upon layer of data about phenomena such as the person but seals off access to ultimate truth and the direct experience of being. The prospect of experiencing the ultimate insubstantiality of self produces existential terror and, therefore, requires rationalist protection.

Hui-neng

Hui-neng speaks of the gap in relation to light and dark, day and night, the intellect and experience, the problem and the solution, the opposition of consciousness and the freedom of unconsciousness, between actual experience and ideology. The seeker bursts through the illusion of duality, he writes, "by making no distinction between confusion and enlightenment, by paying no attention to the presence or absence of a thought, by neither getting attached to nor keeping oneself away from the dualism of good and bad" (D. T. Suzuki, 1994, p. 58). Hui-neng's revolutionary impact on Buddhism addresses healing this split and teaches that "the main point is not to think of things good and bad and thereby to be restricted, but let the mind move on as it is in itself and perform its inexhaustible functions" (D. T. Suzuki, 1972a, p. 36). Healing the split in Hui-neng's sense is not limited to the intrapsychic. Perceptual origins extend to all phenomena and address the essential connectedness and interrelatedness of all beings and phenomena. The foundational principle of dependent arising expresses this experience. Without this experiential realization, alienation, grasping, and aggression continue. D. T. Suzuki (1972a) asks: "How is it possible for the human mind to move from discrimination to nondiscrimination, from affections to affectionlessness, from being to non-being, from relativity to emptiness, from the ten-thousand things to the contentless mirror-nature or self nature" (p. 52). This task might appear extreme. Actually, it is, since relative ordinary dualistic commonsense knowledge is governed by the restrictions of secondary processes. Consciousness tends toward the relative and hence the gap. Ultimate knowledge derives from unconsciousness, and "to be back in the unconscious," according to D. T. Suzuki, "is to attain Buddhahood" (p. 76). For Zen from D. T. Suzuki's interpretation of Hui-neng, the Zen unconscious functions free from memory, desire, understanding, and sense-mediated data. The Zen practitioner relies on intuited experiential wisdom, not empirical consciousness or the six senses. That is, as D. T. Suzuki notes, "when both memory and intelligence are forgotten" (p. 76).

From the Zen point of view, D. T. Suzuki observes that "we can't know what is fundamentally ultimate and intrinsic to our nature as human beings through the senses" (p. 59). He adds that ultimate reality (not unlike Bion's O) "is not subject to the laws of relativity, and therefore cannot be grasped by means of form" (p. 59).

D. T. Suzuki provides gripping descriptions from the Zen perspective of resistance in relation to the gap that vividly portray experiences familiar to psychotherapists who venture into this realm. For example,

> At first the seeker knows of no way of escape, but get out he must by some means … before him there yawns a dark abyss. There is no light to show him a possible way to cross it … the only thing he can do in this crisis is simply to jump, into life or death, but living he feels to be no longer possible. He is desperate, and yet something is still holding him back; he cannot quite give himself up to the unknown … Here begins a new world of personal experiences, which we may designate "leaping" or "throwing oneself down the precipice." (1994, p. 52)

The dilemma that D. T. Suzuki's seeker finds himself in requires an active effort to resolve. D. T. Suzuki writes:

> It is distinctly understood that this period of incubation, which intervenes between the metaphysical quest and the Zen experience proper, is not one of passive quietness but of intense strenuousness … it keeps up an arduous fight against all intruding ideas … an intense seeking, or steady looking into the abysmal darkness is no less than that. (p. 53)

Bion demands a similar effort to relinquish memory, desire, and understanding. According to Bion (1970), this strategy enables the analyst to achieve "artificial blindness" (p. 41). He writes "by rendering oneself 'artificially blind' through the exclusion of memory and desire, one achieves F (Faith); the piercing shaft of darkness can be directed on the dark features of the analytic situation" (p. 57).

Zenists acknowledge this basic human habit of mind that both craves and resists truth in the notion of *avidya* (ignorance, unknowing). As I noted in the introduction, *avidya* refers to a ruthlessly active not-knowing that resists truth and maintains the gap by generating a perceptual separation between subject and object. However, not unlike the neurotic defenses

described in the psychoanalytic literature, the inadequate functioning of
ignorance creates its own set of problems and perpetuates grasping, longing, aggression, and the repetition of cyclic existence. Ignorance as a habit
of mind resists truth, maintains a self-constructed deception, and reifies
the experience of lived truth. This unconscious, albeit active, not-knowing
maintains the gap. The effort to fill in the gap through a futile pursuit of
sense, the ongoing expansion of the territory of ego ("Where id was shall
ego be"), the endless accumulation of solid ground to stand on, the failure
to maintain the solidity of what is essentially fluid, and the need to exclude
the infinite from the definite paradoxically increase the gap and deepen
the abyss.

On this point, D. T. Suzuki (1972a) writes:

> Even when they are told that every being is endowed with Buddha-nature and
> that they are Buddhas, even as they are, they keep themselves from Buddha-
> hood by reason of their own discriminative understanding, which creates an
> artificial barrier between themselves and Buddha. (p. 82)

Zen attempts to destroy this illusion between discriminative understanding and lived Buddha-hood. Hui-neng observes that "from the
first not a thing is." No gap, no barrier, no self, no understanding,
no Buddha. No crystal ball. Pop! No bubble; only being-in-itself. He
approaches this task by creating an abrupt awakening into satori by
stripping away the buffers of logic, intellectual understanding, and
reasoning processes. His purpose is to generate a radical transformation of consciousness, and he speaks of a turning back or turning over
at the basis of consciousness. D. T. Suzuki (1994) describes this radical transformation of consciousness as follows: "By this the entirety of
one's mental construction goes through a complete change. It is won-
derful that a satori insight is capable of causing such a reconstruction in
one's spiritual outlook" (p. 17). Zen functions to transform knowledge
and philosophical reasoning about emptiness into lived experience.
Therefore, as D. T. Suzuki notes,

> Emptiness is not at all the outcome of intellectual reflection, but simply the
> statement of direct perception in which the mind grasps the true nature of exis-
> tence without the intermediary of logic.... We may say that here a perception
> takes place in its purest and simplest form, where it is not at all tainted by intel-
> lectual analysis or conceptual reflection. (pp. 47, 48)

Thus, the seeker moves from *about* to *being* because "what one thinks or reads is always qualified by the preposition 'of' or 'about' and does not give us the thing itself" (p. 48). Suzuki describes the transformation of consciousness associated with the satori experience as a movement from an intellectual analysis to Zen consciousness, or the "final explosion." Therefore, we find the master responding to the student's question, as the following vignette reveals, by twisting the nose until tears fall from the eyes.

> Shih-kung … wishing to see what understanding of Zen his head monk had, proposed this question: "Can you take hold of vacant space?" … The monk thereupon, extending his arm, made a grab at empty space. Remarked the master: "How can you take hold of space that way?" "How then?" retorted the monk. No sooner was this said than the master grabbed the monk's nose and pulled it hard. The monk cried aloud, saying: "This is altogether too hard; you will pull it out!" The master concluded: "In no other way can you take hold of empty space." (1972a, pp. 81–82)

How does the analyst "twist the nose" of the analysand until tears fall? Bion's way entails formulating interpretations that promote O and not simply add knowledge. The latter only strengthens the barrier of discursiveness and deepens the gap. How then does Bion evoke such an interpretation? He recommends suspending memory, desire, and understanding and having faith that the ineffable truth of the session evolves (1967, 1970). This procedure, according to Bion, enables the analyst to participate in hallucinosis and experience at-one-ment with the evolution of the session. Suzuki would say "being-in-itself." That is, according to Suzuki, when the unconscious is present everywhere, or in Bion's terms, when the infinite or what we don't know evolves. We can also ask: "How does the Zen master approach O?" Initially *mondo* (the ongoing dialogue between master and student) served this purpose. The koan system developed, as I noted in Chapter 3, when *mondo* evolved into another form of resistance through speculation, discursive reasoning, and intellectual dogmatic pursuit.

Bion, by arguing for a psychoanalysis of being before knowing, calls for a restoration of vitality into psychoanalysis. Similarly, prior to Hui-neng, Buddhism in China was limited to the privileged classes, remained orthodox, scholarly, and demanded much erudition. Hui-neng, by contrast, relied on his intuition. Thus, satori and O become the guardians of psychic life. They keep their respective systems moving, alive, and vital by honoring what cannot be known in the ordinary sense of the term and what objectification destroys. Definition kills the infinite. They both remind us that consciousness is not a thing that can be studied like an artifact of a dead civilization or like a scientific specimen. Hui-neng's Zen and Bion's psychoanalysis both honor and respect the moving, living, breathing being-in-itself/beening quality of psychic life. As D. T. Suzuki (1972a) notes, "The main point is not to think of things good and bad and thereby be restricted, but to let the mind move on as it is in itself and perform its inexhaustible functions" (p. 36).

Unconsciousness and Enlightenment

Bion has little to say about unconsciousness. He "prefers the infinite" and writes that "the differentiating factor that I wish to introduce is not between conscious and unconscious but between finite and infinite" (1965, p. 46). However, we can observe trends in Bion's descriptions of O that point toward the Zen unconscious. After all, the Zen unconscious in many respects is the infinite. This connection between unconsciousness and O becomes clear in similar trends in D. T. Suzuki's (1972a) writing on satori and in his discussion of Hui-neng's no-mind doctrine. Hui-neng discusses *tzu-hsing*, a Chinese philosophical term that D. T. Suzuki translates as "self-nature" or "being-in-itself" (p. 40). Not unlike Bion's O, *hsing*, according to D. T. Suzuki, "is something ultimate in the being ... though it must not be conceived as an individual entity, like a kernel or a nucleus which is left when all outer casings are removed, or like a soul which escapes from the body after death" (p. 39). Such conceptualizations would only serve to maintain the gap. D. T. Suzuki continues his description of *hsing* by noting that "this mysterious *hsing*, however, is not a logical *a priori* but an actuality that can be experienced," and further, D. T. Suzuki notes, "it is not mere being, but knowing. We can say that because of knowing itself it is; knowing is being, and being is knowing" (p. 40). Hui-neng, as D. T. Suzuki observes, calls for a different kind of seeing and knowing that not unlike Bion's intuition pierces the veil of sense and reveals non-sense as a directly lived experience. He notes that "to be itself is to know itself.... Hands are no hands, have no existence until they pick up flowers and offer them to the Buddha" (p. 42).

Not unlike Bion, who points out serious limitations stemming from the classical psychoanalytic emphasis on knowing, Hui-neng criticizes the seeing related to classical Buddhist notions of wisdom. This sense-dominated dualistic perspective advocated by Freud keeps the analyst "removed as a surgeon" from the analysand's experience and maintains the gap. The following passage from D. T. Suzuki has relevance with respect to the affinity between Bion's approach and Hui-neng's. Both represent radical departures from the roots of their respective disciplines while simultaneously cutting through obstructions to the very same roots. For instance, D. T. Suzuki (1972a) writes:

> When we say, "See into thy self-nature," the seeing is apt to be regarded as mere perceiving, mere knowing, more statically reflecting on self nature.... But as a matter of fact, the seeing is an act, a revolutionary deed on the part of human understanding whose functions have been supposed all the time to be logically analyzing ideas, ideas sensed from their dynamic signification. The "seeing," especially in Hui-neng's sense, was far more than a passive deed of looking at a mere knowledge obtained from contemplating the purity of self-nature: The seeing with him *was* self-nature itself, which exposes itself before him in all nakedness, and functions without any reservation. (p. 42, emphasis added)

Technical Implications

Hui-neng's critique of the "mirror wiping" meditation with its dualistic implications, and Bion's critique of Freud's dualistic model with its emphasis on a return to homeostasis as a desired outcome have far-reaching technical implications. D. T. Suzuki (1994) describes the Zen experience as a "psychological process of 'self-forgetting' and 'cutting off both the past and the future'" (p. 62). In the same vein, Tai-hui, the 12th-century Chinese Zen master, provides the following admonition:

> The truth (dharma) is not to be mastered by mere seeing, hearing, and thinking. If it is, it is no more than the seeing, hearing and thinking; it is not at all seeking after the truth itself. For the truth is not in what you hear from others or learn through understanding. Now keep yourself away from what you have seen, heard, and thought and see ... why? Because this is the abode where the senses never reach. (p. 87)

Bion concerns himself with the effectiveness of psychoanalytic interpretation. He argues that effective interpretation should bridge the gap between knowledge learned and truth lived. Within the context of this gap between reality and unreality he, unlike Freud, contends that "the interpretation must do more than increase knowledge" (1965, p. 148), and he asks, "Is it possible through psycho-analytic interpretation to effect a transition from knowing the phenomena of the real self to being the real self?" (p. 149). "Interpretations that simply increase knowledge maintain 'the inaccessibility of "O"' [and] 'postpones "O" indefinitely'" (pp. 147, 149). From Bion's point of view, accumulations of empirical knowledge function to occlude truth. Clinically, the analyst can offer interpretations that are true to the facts, but that block the unfolding at-one-ment with the ultimate emotional truth of the patient. (See the vignette of Ben below.) For Bion, effective and accurate interpretations result in transformations in O (ultimate reality, truth), not simply in K (knowledge). They require a capacity in the analyst for at-one-ment because it (O) cannot be known.

Practice Parallels

Consider the following meditation instructions. Note the parallels with Bion's stance regarding memory, desire, understanding, and sense data. Both Bion's and Tai-hui's technical instructions stem from nondualist assumptions. They both require temporary disengagement from and reengagement with the phenomenal world. Circular movements occur between sense and non-sense. Both experiences result in an intensification and involvement with reality and an ever-widening spiral of expansion from the definite to the infinite. Ultimately, the definite is infinite and the infinite definite. They transcend the gap. D. T. Suzuki (1972a) provides the following meditation instructions:

> Purge your mind thoroughly of thoughts—thoughts about all things, thoughts about goodness and badness of things. Events past are already past; therefore have no thoughts of them, [for Bion, this would include factual information about the analysand, such as marital status, etc.] and your mind is disconnected from the past. Thus past events are done away with. [Suzuki adds the following footnote: "Events to come are not yet come do not seek for them. Thus your mind is disconnected from the future."] (p. 66)

D. T. Suzuki continues:

> Present events are already here before you; then have no attachment to them. Not to have attachment means not to rouse any feelings of hate or love. [Bion observes that hate and love, not unlike K, can saturate psychic space and obstruct the awareness of evolving truth.] Your mind is then disconnected from the present, and events before your eyes [sense data related to K] are done away with. When the past, present, and future are thus in no way taken in, they are completely done away with. When thoughts come and go, do not follow them, and your pursuing mind [Desire] is cut off. When abiding (with thoughts) do not tarry in them, and your abiding mind is cut off. When thus freed from

abiding (with thoughts) you are said to be abiding with non-abiding [for Bion at-one-ment or participation in hallucinosis]. If you have a thoroughly clear perception as to the mind having no abiding place anywhere, this is known as having a thoroughly clear perception of one's own being.... All this is understood when the unconscious is in evidence anywhere. (p. 66)

Similarly, Bion (1970) advises:

It is necessary to inhibit dwelling on memories and desires. They are two facets of the same thing: both are composed of elements based on sense impressions.... If the mind is preoccupied with elements perceptible to sense it will be that much less able to perceive elements that cannot be sensed. (p. 41)

Further, he states:

To repeat: the capacity to forget, the ability to eschew desire and understanding, must be regarded as essential discipline for the psychoanalyst. Failure to practice this discipline will lead to a steady deterioration in the powers of observation whose maintenance is essential. (p. 51)

Further on Bion offers the following technical description. Note the parallels to the D. T. Suzuki no-mind meditation instructions presented above.

To attain the state of mind essential for the practice of psycho-analysis I avoid any exercise of memory; I make no notes. When I am tempted to remember the events of any particular session I resist the temptation. If I find myself wandering mentally into the domain of memory I desist. In this my practice is at variance with the view that notes should be kept or that psychoanalysts should find some method by which they can record their sessions mechanically or should train themselves to have a good memory. If I find that I am without any clue to what the patient is doing and am tempted to feel that the secret lies hidden in something I have forgotten, I resist any impulse to remember what happened or how I interpreted what happened on some previous occasion. If I find that some half-memory is beginning to obtrude I resist its recall no matter how pressing or desirable its recall may seem to be. (p. 55)

Bion outlines a similar procedure with regard to desires. He writes:

I avoid entertaining desires and attempt to dismiss them from my mind.... Such desires erode the analyst's power to analyse and lead to progressive deterioration of his intuition. Introspection will show how widespread and frequent memories and desires are. They are constantly present in the mind and to follow the advice I am giving is a difficult discipline. (p. 56)

The no-mind school and Bion, as evidenced in the above technical instructions, both develop a position that transcends the linearity of dualism and nondualism. Considering the pre-Buddhist Indian Vedanta tradition that touched Bion during his early life and influenced both Bion's and Hui-neng's Indian ancestors, we can suggest that they represent branches of one root planted in the same soil. We become more entrenched in Freud's dualism when we view Bion as true to Freud or simply a supplement, as some authors suggest (e.g., Epstein, 1984, 1988; Rubin, 1985). Further, it would seem reasonable to argue that previous discussions on psychoanalytic evenly hovering attention and Theravada bare attention are limited to technical comparisons, in part, because of a discrepancy that results from differing basic assumptions.

Freud's efforts to squeeze his theory and technique into the Cartesian dualistic frame would appear to be dissonant with the basic monoistic assumptions that drive the Buddhist system. This would appear to create a state of dissonance regarding the internalization of the two systems for individuals involved in both. Limiting the discussion to either same or different comparisons by focusing on the specific parallels and the relation to elements of technique avoids internal dissonance and therefore wards off catastrophe and terror that both Bion and Suzuki speak to with regard to authentic transformation. However, this stance reflects and supports the gap.

It seems reasonable to speculate on the nature of the influence of Bion's early life in India and the resulting internalization of those experiences that eventually emerge in his theory. Bleandonu (1994) comments on Bion's interest in Eastern philosophy. "Bion," he writes,

> describes psychological states which are not unlike those encountered in yoga. He was certainly very interested in the Orientalism which flourished in Western culture in the 1950s and 1960s.... Bion spells out his sense of recognition as he finds aspects of his work confirmed in the Bhagavad-Gita. (p. 285)

Bion (1970) also advises the reader that "no one who denudes himself of memory and desire, and of all those elements of sense impression ordinarily present, can have any doubt of the reality of the psychoanalytical experience which remains ineffable" (p. 35). However, confrontation with the ineffable, or as D. T. Suzuki puts it, the "unobtainable" or "unknowable," is "catastrophic" (Bion, 1965, 1970) and "terrifying" (D. T. Suzuki, 1972a, 1972b). The analyst who practices Bion's recommendations, when met with any degree of success, experiences a catastrophic threat to the sense of self that accompanies the resulting state of consciousness. Bion thus draws attention to a basic source of resistance. He says, "Resistance is only manifest when the threat is contact with what is believed to be real.... Resistance operates because it is feared that the reality of the object is imminent" (1965, p. 147). Reality becomes a source of terror and delight. From the Buddhist point of view Nagao (1989) notes that "by making one constantly look into the abyss of nothingness and confront the death of the self, emptiness becomes an object of human dread ... emptiness was a dreaded reversal ... an overturning of the ground of selfhood" (p. 4). Fueled by anxiety the individual maintains the gap and remains imprisoned in the reified world of sense-mediated experience. Dissolution of the gap simultaneously deepens symmetrization and intensifies lived experience. The imminent reality of the object "anything whatever—its reality" (Bion, 1965, p. 147) is in this formulation, its ultimate unreality. What is wholeheartedly believed to be a solid crystal ball in reality is a bubble. Pop!

Knowledge produces more ground and restricts freedom that remains embedded in the sense/ground. We crave solid ground to stand on. However, we constantly find ourselves slipping off the edge. We thus construct castles made of sand on which to stand. They dissolve, washed over by the shifting tides of ongoing movement between the definite and the infinite, sense and non-sense, consciousness and unconsciousness. Bion and D. T. Suzuki both continuously point to this faulty foundation. Therefore, Bion (1970) notes that "O does not fall in the domain of knowledge or learning save incidentally; it can 'become,' but cannot be 'known'" (p. 26). Knowing based on sense creates and perpetuates the gap. Consistent with Bion's thinking on non-sense, D. T. Suzuki (1972b) remarks: "To know means to set the object of knowledge against the knower. Knowledge always implies a dichotomy and for this reason can never be the thing itself. We know something *about* it" (pp. 118–119, emphasis added). D. T. Suzuki further notes that: "As far as knowledge is concerned, it stands outside the thing, can never enter into it, but to know the thing really in the true sense of the term means to become the thing itself, to be identified with it in its totality, inwardly as well as outwardly" (p. 119).

Duality/Unity: Necessary Illusion

From Bion's psychoanalytic perspective and from Hui-neng's Zen perspective the gap functions as a necessary illusion. The gap appears when asymmetrical processes predominate and provides tenuous protection from the terror of being-in-itself or beening O. However, this faulty protection forecloses the possibility of delight, joy, and a fully lived life. This ultimate illusion holds very real consequences for the seeker who finds his way to the edge.

The gap as artifact reflects the reification of the experiential extremes of nihilism and eternalism—a freeze-frame moment of the natural psychic movement between being and nonbeing, or as Bion depicts, in the ongoing come-together-break-apart flow. In a fundamental theoretical and philosophical break from Freud, who attempts to stop the movement with a return to homeostasis, Bion intends to free up blocks to this natural infinite rhythm. In this regard, Hui-neng's criticism of "tranquilization" that he equates with psychic death applies equally to Freud as to his Buddhist opponents.

Paradoxically, the self-protective reification creates the illusion of the gap and the fear of the abyss by enlarging the gap. We prefer a sanctified heaven and a demonized hell to remain oceans apart. Deepening symmetrization dissolves the illusion that asymmetrization crystallizes. Continuous movement prevails. Things are not as solid or as permanent as we think (or need to think) they are. As unconsciousness manifests, the illusion, the form of the gap, becomes revealed. What occurs as abyss, Matte-Blanco would attribute to the subject's incapacity to perceive dimensions of experience not ordinarily accessible to asymmetrical consciousness. Consequently, Hui-neng speaks of an abrupt awakening. The following vignette exemplifies this perceptual state.

Ben

Ben describes himself as a gifted psychic healer who I have seen in psychoanalysis for 14 years at the time of this writing. However, he rarely practices. He expresses fear of his gifts and abilities. "To make them known," Ben says, "would make others unbearably uncomfortable that I can see so deeply into their being." I raise the question of possible connection between his hesitancy to practice and the possible threat to the emotional tie to his father and possibly to me. This transference formulation constitutes an important treatment theme and appears in many guises. The demands and restrictions of this tie determine Ben's "permissible" range of creative movement and emotional expression. Ben's father, a man of science and very restricted himself, criticized his son's creativity, spontaneity, emotional expressivity, and intuitive powers. For example, Ben reports, "I would have to pretend not to have any feelings or sense of what was going on between my parents in relation to their troubled marriage." "I had to be blind and act like nothing was wrong." Ben described his father as "obsessively analytic and antiemotional." He was punished for writing songs and improvising or being a creative and feeling person in general. These restrictions had the effect of making him feel like his arms were cemented to his body. He would become enraged. His contained rage would erupt in the form of hives, mostly on his hands and spreading up his arms. They dissipated once he allowed himself free expression of his rage. "I would like to strangle him to death for choking me." Hands could both create and destroy. I equated his healing powers as "creative, intuitive, and as an expression of his empathy." He disagreed and remarked that "it only appears so because of its highly nuanced nature." He continued to explain: "It is like a magician who knows the technique and makes a series of highly technical maneuvers that appear like magic to the audience."

Ben's need to maintain a logical stance with me and an accompanying anxiety that I was questioning his state of mind were obvious and perhaps accurate to a certain extent. However, something else was evolving that demanded my acceptance despite my lack of understanding. He could perceive a dimension of experience not accessible to others who had not bridged this gap. For him, logic and intuition become merged into a unitive experience.

This situation creates a dilemma. Should Ben's comments or my reasoning be viewed as resistance to the offered observation? Where is the line drawn between pathology and genuine mystical experience? Do I have the capacity to make such distinctions and choices? Are these arbitrary distinctions necessary? If existing formulations, as Bion argues, do not contain this experience, I can only perpetuate a gap by attempting to fit it into existing formulations. Does he need to insist on the nonintuitive so as not to threaten the tie to his father (myself)? This becomes a source of dissonance, which stems from reification and a resulting polarization. The distance between theory and experience, between what one learns to expect and what actually happens, becomes infinitely vast. Does one hide at the edge of the gap and run into the safety of existing formulations that both illuminate and obscure? Or, can we leap into the abyss trusting intuition and the message that both Bion and Hui-neng articulate so clearly? From the level of symmetrization that Ben reaches, he experiences intuition and logic as the same. If I can't allow that due to my own anxiety, I will continue to stand firm with my "transference interpretation" and

Ben's "resistance." This is not to say that this would be invalid. However, the opportunity exists that supports a continued evolution, one that at least momentarily dissolves the need to maintain the gap that leaves us both standing at opposite edges of a precipice separated by a bottomless abyss. What is at stake? Do I wish to "save" Ben from his delusion and pull him back to sense? What does he want? Can I follow his lead and participate in freeing us both from fears evoked by and that militate against evolving truth? Can we together realize and transcend the limitations on our experiences imposed by the illusion of the gap? Is it an illusion? If so, do we both for our own reasons, need to collude?

Leap of Faith

It is difficult to talk about Bion or Hui-neng without some reference to faith. Faith becomes essential for plunging into the depths of the seemingly infinite gap between reality and phenomena. Without faith the relinquishment of sense-mediated knowledge, according to Bion (1970), results in "a simultaneous apparent deposition of the reality principle" (p. 48). This generates terror and facilitates resistance to lived truth. Faith facilitates the existential leap from "knowing about" to "being O." D. T. Suzuki observes that strong faith engenders a "spirit of inquiry" and generates the capacity within the practitioner required for "throwing oneself down the precipice" and into the abyss created by the gap. Sense occludes faith and faith allows for freedom from sense.

   Consider the following graphic description of the Zen student's confrontation with the gap. Through a continuous struggle with a koan, the student comes to the edge of a precipice and faces a life-and-death struggle not unlike the catastrophic confrontation with being that Bion describes when the analyst attempts to move beyond memory, desire, and understanding and stretch beyond the self-imposed restrictions of theoretical limitations toward O.

> If you want to get at the unadulterated truth of egolessness, you must once
> for all let go your hold and fall over the precipice.... What does it mean to
> let go your hold on the precipice? Suppose a man has wandered out on the
> remote mountains, where no one else has ever ventured. He comes to the
> edge of a precipice unfathomably deep, the rugged rock covered with moss
> is extremely slippery, giving him no sure foothold; he can neither advance
> nor retreat, death is looking at him in the face. His only hope lies in holding
> on to the vine which his hands have grasped; his very life depends on his

holding on to it. If he should by carelessness let go his hold, his body would be thrown down to the abyss and crushed to pieces, bones and all. (Suzuki, 1994, p. 64)

The nightmare that Suzuki's seeker faces holds relevance and functions as a useful model to explore existential gaps in the psychoanalytic situation. Consider the following vignette.

Ethan's Gap: Muddy Ditch/Bottomless Canyon

Ethan glides through life not living, tiptoeing around dancing about on eggshells, always with regret as an afterthought. Ethan exists outside the mix. What was a separating "brick wall" according to him is beginning to feel more like a thin membrane. Awareness of how he keeps himself from breaking through is becoming torturous. Deadly to remain, deadly to break through. The gap fluctuates like a nightmare from what Ethan describes as a "shallow ditch and a bottomless canyon." Is the abyss his widowed mother's depression swallowing him up, or is it a measure of a much needed, yet feared, separation? The struggle is between life and death. All the while Ethan observes his dead life trickling away. The human condition—the inevitability of our mortality—looms large. The omnipresent cloud hanging overhead becomes an enveloping fog. Both analyst and analysand alike are vulnerable to the vicissitudes of the human condition. We can collude to escape the dread of death. Collusion feels like a safer death. I can offer interpretations that function as a buffer that cushions us both and keep us both oblivious to the needed inevitable fall into the abyss. We are at a point of birth of emerging feelings. Ethan fidgets nervously. His body expresses his silent vulnerability as he feels me honing in on his feelings. Should he be "found out," he says, "would be both a horror and a relief." Ethan says, "If only I could give up this fight, lay down and cry." Ethan uses the language of armed conflict. He speaks of "defeat," "losing my battle with you," "letting up my guard, giving up my watchful defense." His language points toward his relation to the gap. Ethan clings so close to the edge of a precipice, afraid to let go his hold, afraid and full of regret not to. Meanwhile, passing time gnaws away at his hold. It is truly a matter of life and death. Their paradoxical mutuality looms large. Ethan is caught.

Gap as Actuality/Gap as Symbol

Ethan finds himself victim to the existential pathology that Hui-neng attempts to heal through an abrupt awakening. Human nature reifies either pole and dulls awareness that ultimately life is death, death is life, and either is neither. The gap, as I noted above, can represent many things. However, symbol risks becoming another form of reification that resists the painful stark reality of this existential dilemma. Ethan hangs off the precipice-fraying vine, rats gnawing away, tiger above, lion below. Symbols risk not hearing Ethan's pleas for help. He gestures with his hand held Buddha-like, with barely an inch of distance between the tips of his arched forefinger and thumb. He says, "I feel that close to breaking through."

Speaking of a spiritual breakthrough, D. T. Suzuki (1994) writes:

> It is the same with the student of Zen. When he grapples with a Koan single-handedly he will come to see that he has reached the limit of his mental tension, and he is brought to a standstill. Like the man hanging over the precipice he is completely at a loss what to do next. Except for occasional feelings of uneasiness and despair, it is like death itself. All of a sudden he finds his mind and body wiped out of existence, together with the koan. This is what is known as "letting go your hold." As you become awakened from the stupor and regain your breath it is like drinking water and knowing for yourself that it is cold. It will be a joy inexpressible. (p. 94)

Can we as analysts let go our hold on our symbols and theories of what we imagine should be and allow ourselves to experience the ever-evolving truth being-in-itself? Can we let go and then let go of letting go before it becomes another restricting force creating an endless repetition of gaps?

10

Unitive Experience and the Pervasive Object

Introduction

This final chapter details an 18-year psychoanalytic treatment of a neurologically impaired, severely depressed Orthodox Jewish woman and, through an in-depth case study, demonstrates, synthesizes, and operationalizes the various abstract ideas discussed in the previous chapters.

Buddhist teachings posit that due to countless births all sentient beings are mother to all other beings. This sentiment, together with associated meditation practices, Buddhists believe, engenders compassion for all beings. Ideally, from this perspective, love and regard for one's mother should guide all human relations. Matte-Blanco (1975, 1988) would view this perception, that all beings are mother, as was described in Chapter 6, as an example of the deepest level of "symmetrization," where "everything mysteriously becomes everything else."

This sense of at-one-ment or unitive experiencing, where boundaries between subject and object become blurred or completely dissolved, contains both light (positive) and dark (negative) aspects. Zenists speak of the sky that is neither dark nor light, just sky, and observe that when it is night, darkness fills the sky. During the day, light fills the sky. However, the sky is neither dark nor light. Similarly, unitive experiencing describes a neutral condition. From this perspective all mental states are fundamentally neutral. Negative and positive aspects stem from the projection of the subject's perceptual coloration.

Freud makes a similar observation regarding psychic states. Positive and negative valuations stem from the individual's perceptual coloration of psychical processes. Freud (1900) asserts that "thought-processes are in themselves without quality, except for the pleasurable and unpleasurable excitations which accompany them" (p. 617). The latter condition renders unitive experience subject to the same fluctuations. From the religious perspective, descriptions abound of the joy associated with realizing at-one-ment with humanity, nature, spirit, cosmos, the divine, and the universe. Thomas Merton, for example, writes that "in the embrace of mystical love we know that we and He are one. This is infused or mystical contemplation in the purest sense of the term" (Gunn, 2000, p. 156). Speaking from the Zen perspective, in a commentary on the *Heart Sutra*, Soeng (1996) notes that "Mahayana sutras thunder again and again against philosophers ... who are disposed to freeze reality into a categorical permanence and to discriminate between subject and object" (p. 7).

Despite individual differences, unitive experience constitutes a desired outcome within the context of spiritual/mystical praxes. Religious traditions frequently tend to privilege and emphasize the light aspects of unitive experience while simultaneously expressing an aversion to darkness. Sanctified heavens and demonized hells necessarily remain infinities apart. Expressions such as "entering" or "gathering" the light reflect this positive valuation of unitive experiencing.

Zen Buddhists, on the other hand, demonstrate an understanding of the value of darkness as the state of formlessness, where all creation emerges, where unitive experiencing deepens as utter darkness dissolves distinctions. It is in the dark where relative merges with absolute, where the "ten thousand things" become the "One," where ever-present stars become visible in the night sky.

In sharp contrast to spiritual traditions, psychoanalysis, with few exceptions,* attributes pathological motives to unitive experiencing. Traditional psychoanalytic thinking, as noted in Chapter 2, typically associates unitive experiencing with the analysand's regressive pathological narcissistic merger needs or the analyst's unresolved countertransference issues. The negative evaluation to the mystical state of merger with the divine first described by Romaine Rolland as the "oceanic feeling" constitutes a significant and well-known example of such pathologizing (Kovel, 1990; Parsons, 1999).

Freud (1930) addressed unitive experiencing in terms of the oceanic feeling as "the indissoluble bond of being one with the external world as a whole" (p. 65). He attributed this feeling to pre-oedipal infantile states in which distinctions between self and object have not yet developed and noted: "An infant at the breast does not as yet distinguish his ego from the external world as the source of sensations flowing in upon him ...

---

* For example, Bion (1970), Cooper (1997, 1999, 2000a, 2001), Eigen (1983, 1992, 1998, 1999), Milner (1987), Rhode (1994, 1998).

originally the ego includes everything, later it separates an external world off from itself" (pp. 66–67).

Freud attributed the reappearance of unitive experiencing in adult life to the psychoanalytic discovery that "it is rather the rule than the exception for the past to be preserved in mental life" (p. 68). For example, the Mosaic command "Thou shall love thy neighbor as thyself" implies a blurring of the distinctions between self and other in very much the same way as the Buddhist assertion that "all beings are our mother." Freud viewed this form of unitive experiencing as regressive and related to primary narcissism. This ethic, advocated by Buddhist and Mosaic law, according to Freud, reflects an inappropriate privileging of early infantile states.

The necessary but somewhat artificial distinctions between light and darkness noted above fail to do justice to the complexities of psychospiritual/mystical experiencing. Strands of each become intertwined within and between both disciplines. That is, the emphasis differs between the two disciplines with shades of gradation, depending on the individual or on the particular tradition.

An alternative view posits that both light and dark contain both negative and positive colorations. However, this perspective requires a different stance than that typically associated with traditional hard-line thinking articulated in either camp. For example, Eigen (1983), who treads both worlds, notes that "if a heightened sense of subject-object union is an illusion, it is a crucial one" (p. 159). Can light be acknowledged for what it is? Can shadows be exploited in the service of spiritual evolution or an analysis? Can pathological merger issues be separated out from genuine spiritual endeavors and associated realizations? Can a balance point be located that embraces both shadow and light in relation to at-one-ment?

Contemporary psychoanalytic formulations, despite the tendency toward a predominantly negative evaluation of religious experiencing, more than hint at the unitive aspects of being. For example, while not articulated in spiritual/religious terms, Kohut elaborates an experiential psychoanalysis of the unitive. His psychology of the self, a primarily deficit/developmental model with necessary linear implications,* nevertheless frees the psychoanalyst up from linear notions such as the premise that unitive experiences are exclusively pathological regressions. As a result, psychoanalysis can postulate a spiritual/transcendent sector of self-experience and associated object relations in nonreductionist terms (Roland,

---

* For a detailed discussion of the relationship between linear and nonlinear aspects of experience in relation to mystical and scientific models see Cooper (2000a).

1987). Spiritual selfobject needs and associated relations, such as to spiritual teachers, ideals, practices, scriptures, or gods, center on the capacity of the individual and the environment to mediate unitive experiences in a way that permits the individual to integrate such experiences into a cohesive sense of self. However, in certain instances, unitive experiences that operate in the absence of a cohesive and integrated or, at the extreme, any, sense of self promote anxiety and depression and limit the human potential for spontaneity and full creative living.

I have argued in Chapter 8 that a judgmental stance with regard to unitive experiencing can function as a resistance by the analyst to such experiencing. Additionally, psychoanalysis can study, nonjudgmentally, the various ways that an individual relies on spiritual practice or involvement with religious communities as a legitimate attempt to meet early and current needs. Alternatively, spiritual activity can function as an attempt to repair damage to other aspects of the self often related to unmet, destructive, nonexistent, or toxic experiences. The ongoing oscillation of past, present, and future needs creates a vehicle with which to escape classical notions of linearity while maintaining a model that addresses both progressive and regressive aspects of spiritual experience. The case of Sara, a psychotically depressed woman who has embraced the Judaic tradition, which will be discussed in this chapter, exemplifies this point of view and elaborates clinical implications.

With regard to the progressive function of religious experience, Lichtenberg (1991) writes that religious involvement and associated inner experiences are not necessarily or exclusively derived from early experiences or the lack of early experiences. With regard to spiritual experience, Knoblauch (1995) writes: "Nevertheless, the idea that selfobject experience can be derived from an abstract and internal source implies the potential for such experience to emerge without the presence of another as a trigger or a screen" (p. 209).

The relationship between the Zen teacher and the student exemplifies Knoblauch's observation. On the one hand, the teacher, through a sense of in-the-moment presence, centered focus, and equanimity, becomes a reliable external object with both mirroring and idealizing dimensions. The student can find validation and anchoring as a result. On the other hand, the teacher will demand that the student look internally for self-realization and accept no responsibility for the student's plight with such admonishments as "I am a worthless wretch and have nothing to give you" (John Loori, personal communication). Thus, the ethical master derails inappropriate idealizations while maintaining a supportive relational connection.

Kohut takes issue with organized religions and with religious leaders who foster or promote hasty overidealizations. In his view such tendencies, whether indulged in by religious leaders or by misguided psychoanalysts, interfere with a "spontaneous emerging" transference. He writes that "the active encouragement of an idealization of the analyst leads to the establishment of a tenacious transference bondage (analogous to attachments that are fostered by organized religions), bringing about a cover of massive identifications and hampering the gradual therapeutic alteration of existing narcissistic structures" (1971, p. 164).

Kohut's critique applies with equal validity to both certain so-called psychotherapeutic practices and certain behaviors of some religious leaders. Despite these cautions, Kohut acknowledges the validity of legitimate religious experience. He summarizes the latter poignantly in his conclusion to *Restoration of the Self* (1977). The "task" of modern man, he argues, is dealing with a "crumbling self." Regarding this preoccupation in contemporary art, he writes:

> And nowhere in art have I encountered a more accurately pointed description of man's yearning to achieve the restoration of his self than that contained in three terse sentences in O'Neill's play *The Great God Brown* ... "Man is born broken. He lives by mending. The Grace of God is Glue." Could the essence of pathology of modern man's self be stated more impressively? (p. 287)

It is noteworthy that Kohut turns to a spiritual metaphor with such a positive evaluation. However, this positive evaluation requires caution. Most notably, exclusive attention to self-experiencing overlooks object relational dynamics with underlying unitive dimensions that contribute to individual difficulties and, when not clearly understood or addressed, can lead to treatment impasses, or to an inadvertently pessimistic stance regarding prognosis. This concern will become clarified in examining what I describe as "pervasive object transference" through the binocular lens of Kleinian and Zen perspectives with regard to unitive experiencing.

Pervasive Object Transference

Kleinian formulations posit both primitive good and bad mother representations. Through projective/introjective cycles, the individual ideally integrates both sets of representations into a more stable and cohesive object world accompanied by a more or less stable and integrated sense of self with both good and bad aspects. M. Klein (1935) asserts that bad objects derive from the subject's murderous impulses that are projected into the mother. She writes:

> But it is because the baby projects its own aggression on to these objects that it feels them to be "bad" and not only in that they frustrate its desires: the child conceives of them as actually dangerous—persecutors who it fears will devour, scoop out the inside of its body, cut it to pieces, poison it—in short, compassing its destruction by all the means which sadism can devise. (p. 262)

Thus, for M. Klein, these images become gross "distortions" of the actual object that come to populate the subject's internal and external worlds. These distortions, according to M. Klein, derive from the infant's primitive projective processes. While not negating this crucial aspect of projection in the development of the infant's internal object world, this view fails to take full account of the failure of maternal reverie or the actuality of the mother's projection of bad objects and sadistic impulses into the infant. M. Klein describes these early cycles as "momentous" (p. 267) in that they exert a significant impact on the internalization and integration of one's psychic structure. M. Klein implicates "restrictions" in the projective/introjective processes with "the most severe psychosis." This underscores the importance of projective/introjective processes in normal development.

In the ensuing discussion I will elaborate one idiosyncratic permutation that sheds light on a specific spectrum of depressive symptoms accompanied by a specific, consistent, and tenacious transference/countertransference dynamic. The latter might best be described as "object pervasion" and manifests in analysis as "pervasive object transference." Object pervasion has been discussed tangentially elsewhere in a different context (Cooper, 1999). In that communication, regarding a blurring of boundaries, I wrote:

> This experience of both Adam and myself as mother represents a blurring of boundaries…. One manifestation of this blurring of boundaries took the form of what we describe as a pervasive object transference. With certain patients … at certain times in the treatment the affect becomes and *is* the expression of the object representation. The treatment situation becomes one in which *both* patient and therapist "become" and experience themselves as the object; for the patient everyone and everything simultaneously becomes the object. Interpretation during this phase of treatment requires recognition of this perceptual state and accompanying physical sensations, behaviors, feelings and thoughts. (p. 77)

Object pervasion addresses the destructive force and the ensuing damage to the nascent self related to both the fantasy and the actuality of the object. These processes can go awry, due to the mother's pathological projective excesses. At its most insidious level, object pervasion saturates psychic space and leaves no room for self-experiencing to evolve. At the extreme, the experience of no-self becomes concretized and extremely resistant to movements of any kind. Psychotic depression ensues as symptomatic of extreme object pervasion. The high level of toxic psychic saturation spills out and colors the entire environment and includes the analyst. Thus, both subject and object come to be experienced as the pervasive object. The space and time of the therapy session can also become manifestations of this dreaded and all-engulfing object.

The notion of object pervasion derives from clinical experience with psychotically depressed patients in the light of psychoanalytic and Zen principles. Specifically, the notion of projective identification coupled with the understanding of the identity of the relative and the absolute shed light on this particular variation of unitive experiencing.

M. Klein posits an "early aggression" that evokes guilt, and hence excessive attachment. This hypothesis assumes or implies an exclusively internal dynamic within the subject. As if mother had no role to play in this process of skewed development except to provide the instances of frustration that, according to M. Klein, engender the "perception" of a bad object. This stance further assumes that the mother is free of such attachments herself.

In the cases I have observed, without exception, the mother experienced severe trauma. Further, the psychic aspects of the trauma were not treated. Rather, they were split off from awareness and rigidly if not vehemently disavowed. Traumas included Holocaust survival, accidental blindness, and early object loss through death, sexual exploitation, rape, incest, and prolonged ongoing physical abuse.

In analysis, excessive projection by the subject accounts for elements of object pervasion. This situation requires attention through careful monitoring of countertransference states and careful interpretations. However, excessive and continuous saturation through the object's projection and actual interactions with the subject, the subject's introjection, and the latter's lack of any capacity to halt further saturation further contributes to the process of pervasion.

M. Klein (1935) notes:

> According to Freud and Abraham, the fundamental process in melancholia
> is the loss of the loved object. The real loss of a real object, or some similar

situation having the same significance, results in the object being installed within the ego. Owing, however, to an excess of cannibalistic impulses in the subject, this introjection miscarries and the consequence is illness. (1935, p. 263)

On the contrary, in the case of object pervasion there seems to be too much object. The subject's sense of self becomes lost. In this respect, depression can be conceptualized as symptomatic or indicative of the empty space where a self and the associated thought processes and affects should have been. From the perspective of the unitive, the nothing space manifests as depression—depressive symptoms, in actuality, empty, nothing ("No I thing"), a dead void, a black hole. Yet, shifts in perspective to a spiritual/mystical paradigm can attribute to this gap the potential for being anything and everything. From the Zen perspective the unitive identity of the relative and the absolute reveals "the 1 in the 10,000 things and the 10,000 things in the 1." Nominal becomes phenomenal, infinite is definite. An infinite universe includes a universe of possibilities. Bion tracks this ineffable universe of infinite possibility through ongoing cycles of O transforming into K or knowledge. As Eric Rhode (1994) notes, "It represents nothing and has a way of becoming everything" (p. 72).

The lack of an adequate supporting psychic structure results in this space collapsing in on itself. A state of internal suffocation ensues with psychic deadness as a predominant symptom. Thus, there is not enough of a self to mobilize the "cannibalistic impulses" that M. Klein posits. The object takes over in a parasitic (Bion, 1970) relationship to its host. Any bits and pieces of self that might appear become immediately devoured both by the internal object and by the real external object in actuality if that object is present. At the stage of object pervasion, cannibalism initiated by the subject would be a welcome development, as it would clear away space for the self to emerge and then occupy. Such efforts occur in sporadic spurts. The ongoing cannibalism in such patients can reflect the birth of a self or efforts to repel or counteract object pervasion. When pervasion subsides, there typically occurs a period of starvation reflected in the subjects efforts to restrict dietary intake, lose weight, and in the extreme, starve oneself.

Anna, an avid and dedicated yoga practitioner, for example, ate only one meal a day. This meal would always be the same without variation and went on for two months. Analysis revealed reaction formations to self-initiated cannibalistic urges, efforts to starve out the parasite, efforts to purify her insides or to liberate psychic space from occupation and exploitation. Religious dietary restrictions served the same purpose.

The terrifying implications of toxicity became so intense during this period of starvation that Beth would bag feces and soiled toilet paper in a plastic bag and dispose of it outside of her home. She perceived the plumbing in her home as part of her insides. Cara would consistently move her bowels prior to our sessions so as to leave her toxic insides outside of the consultation room. Dalia, on the other hand, would move her bowels after each session. Among the many symbolic meanings for Dalia's behavior that emerged during analysis, most significant to this discussion centered on her feeling that she could give birth to a self in the womb/room provided by analysis. However, fetus, through shifts in perspective, becomes feces, poisonous, dangerous, and must be removed, before it destroys the good object (analyst, office, womb).

In terms of structural theory the subject becomes, under adverse conditions, all superego constituted solely of internal bad objects. The latter, at the extreme, colonize, exploit, and denude the subject's (host's) inner landscape. The subject becomes an unwitting host for what is split off or disavowed in the object. Sara, who will be discussed in detail below, becomes a host, for example, for mother's aggressive and sadistic colonization of her psychic space in which case her own sense of self is either crushed, immobilized, or never developed. The remnants or vestiges of self live in a psychic "ghetto" reflected in the external world, such as in self-isolation, starvation (food, social contacts, emotionally), substandard living conditions, and a neurologically impaired body/mind.

Does Sara see her mother as all bad due exclusively to excessive projection of her sadism? Does M. Klein ignore the dependently arising possibility that some mothers are bad. Such mothers might be stuck in an early primitive state. Mother has "scooped out" Sara's insides to make room for herself—a womb/room that gets activated during sessions when Sara asserts: "I want to climb inside of you, be inside of you where I will be safe from harm." On the other hand, her expressions might reflect cries or pleas from a self attempting to be born. She desires a safe environment to incubate and to be born from.

Such individuals are unable to freely and spontaneously utilize the space/time of the session creatively. The room (womb) and time (gestation period) remain empty. They become locked in paranoid schizoid organization—oscillations derailed—living in fragments reflected in disjointed speech, stuttering; fragments dispersed into infinities of time and space reflected in silence. Thus, the possibility for psychic birth and wholeness remains foreclosed. In this respect the sessions become "failed starting points for birth; all that is left is an empty cocoon." Sara alternates between the wish to sit on my lap and be the suckling babe at her good mother's breast and sitting under my chair, a discarded feces. On my lap she is an acceptable infant. Under my chair she is expelled, degraded waste matter. Her assertion "I feel like a lump of shit" expresses the newness of birth. A formless lump, not unlike clay, has formative potential to be the anything and everything, to be the 10,000 things. Simultaneously, her expression reflects a movement from nonexisting to being and the destruction and elimination of what might have been a self, aborted and discarded.

Again, careful scrutiny of the patient's productions, coupled with close monitoring of the analyst's countertransference reactions, contributes to making the distinctions necessary for accurate and effective interpretations. With regard to object pervasion, both aspects require simultaneous interpretation to be effective as object infects and operates in both analysand and analyst simultaneously.

Failures in such psychic processing to accomplish a full integration of good/bad, object/self engenders other outcomes. For example, a mother with a brittle, rigid, fragmentation-prone sense of self might attenuate anxiety and mediate concern for her child by responding in a controlling, intrusive, and limiting manner that the infant experiences as suffocating, sadistic, and punitive. On the other hand, a truly sadistic and toxic mother might be perceived and experienced by the infant as loving and nourishing despite the toxicity of the proffered nourishment. Speaking of such a mother, Eva noted that "she was vicious, destructive and viper-like in her criticisms, all negating of another's personhood and being."

The Identity of the Relative and the Absolute: Clinical Implications

The identity of the relative and the absolute addresses both dualistic and unitive aspects of experiencing. S. Suzuki (1970) writes: "We are both one and two." When unitive experiencing is in the ascendance, the analyst becomes saturated with the pervasive object, as does the patient. However, the analyst then can communicate this experience in a usable form as an interpretation when dualistic experiencing ascends. Language both requires and creates definition and distinctions between what aspects of experience are chosen for articulation and what remains unstated and, hence, formless. The patient, without enough of an I-sense for dualistic experiencing to return, relies on the analyst to restore or engender a feeling of I-sense or to create enough space for I-sense to appear in the analysand through the analyst's interpretive expression. Thus, the projective identification is fed back to the analysand in a digestible and usable form and feeds and nourishes the nascent I-sense, or at least temporarily clears away the pervasion. An underlying masochistic "love" or imagined need for the object invites its return.

Extreme nihilism, a perceptual error of overnegation of self, results in the experience of no-self. Depression emerges as a symptom of the nihilistic obliteration of self and points to the space where a self might have been. In my own practice and in discussion with colleagues, the pervasion of the object seems to appear more frequently in women than in men. Without exception, women describe an emotionally unavailable father or a "wimp." The situation with men creates an all too easy oedipal victory and contributes to a brittle and precocious false self, but a self nonetheless. The woman, on the other hand, without the intervention of a strong father, or at least the fantasy of a strong father, to buffer the narcissistic demands of the mother, results in the defeat of normal Electra strivings. The impoverished self becomes more vulnerable to further saturation by the mother's needs. No support exists to mediate I-sense. In a sense, through intense and primitive introjective processes, the child, without a strong enough psychic structure to contain mother's primitive affects and projections, without the psychic equipment to support reverie, digestion, and return, becomes wiped out, overrun, destroyed. Nothing remains for I-sense to develop from. This results in a characterological mélange of unintegrated, fragmented primitive mother introjects that then determine the subject's mode of being in the world and associated I-sense. Virtually no capacity exists to mediate affect states. Overmedication frequently becomes a preferred alternative that functions as a substitute for psychic structure. Varying states of deadness ensue. The analyst must direct attention toward detecting manifestations of object pervasion in both crude and microscopic forms. The latter manifest in affect, thought, word, action, and attitude experienced and expressed both verbally and nonverbally by both analyst and analysand. An overemphasis on the subject's I-sense will obstruct this process. Thus, the patient might be deemed as unanalyzable.

Sara's Journey

Sara entered treatment at the age of 28 with complaints of depression and acute anxiety precipitated by the sudden and unexpected loss of a job. However, as she described it, "I have been feeling depressed most of my life." Sara stutters and has received speech therapy for her condition. The incidence and intensity of her stuttering have decreased and gradually become undetectable since the start of treatment. She typically speaks in an emotionally flat, almost mechanical voice that becomes inaudible at times. The initial phase of Sara's analysis, which at the time of this writing was in its 12th year of an 18-year analysis, was characterized by an almost exclusive emphasis on her self states. She initiated this dynamic by an ongoing query: "Am I stupid, lazy, worthless?" The unrelenting and abusive tenor of her continuous queries functioned as an initial expression of object pervasion that at the time escaped my understanding. However, as the analysis deepened, this particular style of relatedness, the accompanying locus of attention, and the associated affect states reflected specific familial interaction patterns that eventually emerged in the treatment. That is, her stated self-perceptions, both real and unrealistic, served as an outline for the narrow parameters that would ensure a minimal object tie despite the inadequacy and toxic nature of the connection. The price of relatedness left her feeling suspended on a thin tightrope, ever anxious of failing and falling.

Sara, at 40, had recently completed her undergraduate degree. Her education was delayed by serious neurological impairments that compromise her ability to function in academic, work, and social environments. She is somewhat clumsy in her movements, tends toward extremes, and becomes highly anxious and disorganized when there is any loss of predictability in her environment. She presents in a rather needy and cautious way and prefers (demands) that I be "the one who knows." She is used to compliance bordering on subjugation and finds herself terrified by the freedom that therapy seems to present, along with not knowing what I might expect of her beyond speaking freely. Therapy is an invitation to step off of the tightrope. However, she is fearful of what she describes as "stepping out on the thin ice of new experience." She fears falling into the abyss of depression. She would rather know exactly what I want, do it, and be done with it.

Sara, the second oldest of four siblings, grew up in an upper-middle-class, Jewish suburban community. Her parents, both of Western European Jewish descent, are well educated. Her father and mother work together in a successful professional practice. Her siblings are highly gifted intellectually. They all hold advanced college degrees, are married, and have children. She cannot compete with them. This has been a lifelong source of humiliation, frustration, envy, anger, and guilt. Her experience of her two younger siblings surpassing her during childhood has seriously compromised her self-esteem. She could not compete with them for her parents' attention or interest and often feels "invisible" at family gatherings. Sara fears that she will lose my attention. She laments: "You will reject me for being boring, lazy, stupid, and too slow and you will be more interested in your other patients." "They are more attractive, more intelligent, more interesting to be with." "I am a worthless lump of shit." "You will replace me."

Until about two years into the treatment, Sara's parents subsidized her rental apartment. She hid this fact during her initial intake interview, and as a result, she obtained acceptance for low-fee treatment through the consultation center that I was affiliated with during my training. While Sara denies any conscious intent on her part, she consistently and effectively uses her helplessness to her advantage. She frequently creates situations where she can become dependent and taken care of. For example, she lives in subsidized housing and receives an array of disability benefits. She responds with resentment to situations in which she is required to take care of herself. She resents me for, as she says, "putting things back on me." She becomes enraged when any caregiving or attention is withdrawn. For example, a friend invited Sara to stay with her family as a temporary measure when Sara lost an apartment. Sara managed to extend her stay for well over a year, despite the fact that the family lived in cramped quarters and initially planned on a brief stay as an emergency measure.

During a period of treatment Sara became enraged with me for refusing to take her constant telephone calls. My insistence that Sara leave promptly at the end of our sessions evoked intense rage, unrelenting demands, and increasing pressures that I experienced as inappropriate intrusions. Her expressions of extreme helplessness to the point of immobilization felt like sadistic attacks. Over time I began to understand Sara's reactions as manifestations of object pervasion. That is, Sara would experience me like her withholding and sadistic mother. Simultaneously, I would experience her as her pressuring, intrusive, sadistic, and demanding mother.

Religious Dimensions

Spiritual practice and religious involvement provide an external structure in the absence of a cohesively developed internal psychic structure. This structure also functions in part as a defense against anxiety-provoking affect states that seriously threaten Sara's fragile sense of being. However, she finds herself stuck in an extremely brittle archaic position that severely limits her functioning in virtually every area of her life.

Close scrutiny to how Sara relates to her spiritual practices and identification of specific aspects of the tradition that she became involved
with contributed to clarifying both adaptive and defensive functions. For
instance, Sara involved herself in a rigidly defined (more so by Sara than
by any dogma, creed, or teacher) orthodoxy in the Jewish tradition. Her
rabbi would frequently admonish Sara to "lighten up" when she would
seek his advice. She consciously understood her belief and accompanying practices as an attempt to get closer to her unavailable father. She also
became aware of her identification with an idealized image of her maternal
grandmother, whom she viewed as "holding the family together." In this
sense, religious observances could hold Sara together. Her grandmother,
now deceased, was a person who, in Sara's words, "always remained strong
in her convictions." Unconsciously, the external structures of her practice,
which Sara dutifully performed, also functioned as a rationalized voice
of support for her healthy autonomous strivings from her mother, who
Sara described as "harsh, domineering, controlling, sadistic, hypercritical, opinionated and engulfing." "Mom," according to Sara, "made me
feel small, tiny, worthless, and invisible." At times, Sara would "cease to
exist." Sitting with Sara frequently induces sadistic feelings. Unconscious
anger would then manifest in a feeling of withholding. Retrospectively,
the withholding would usually be appropriately consistent with standard
psychoanalytic practice; however, the sadistic feelings would linger. These
feelings later came to be understood in the context of object pervasion
and upon articulation would dissipate. They diminished consistently to
the extent that Sara could become conscious and articulate her aggression
and rage. At other times, I would feel removed.

Initially, I rationalized this stance as related to my growing capacity
for objective neutrality and in the best interest of the treatment. Later, we
discovered that Sara's parents would both withhold from her and make
similar rationalizations. For example, Sara's mother would not talk to her
for weeks at a time. While of the opinion that withholding was in her best
interest, such a stance would frequently have disastrous consequences. For
example, her mother's refusal to sign a document that would guarantee
Sara's rent resulted in the loss of her apartment.

Sara could rely on Judaic law to protect herself from her mother's
intense narcissistic demands and toxic saturation of her psychic space
that threatened Sara's healthy movements toward engendering an I-sense.
She could safely argue with her mother and express anger, disappointment, and other forbidden feelings. More importantly, Sara could assert
her own uniqueness, individuality, and independence through evoking

Judaic dietary laws or Sabbath rules and restrictions. For example, during the Sabbath Sara found it easier to say "No, I can't travel after sundown" than "No, I really don't want to see you." Or, "No, I won't let you put me up as your punching bag in front of the whole family." She could turn down a dinner invitation easier by saying "No, I can't eat in that restaurant, it's not kosher," rather than saying "No, I won't let you humiliate me in public." Or, "No, I don't want you intruding into my diet, stomach, digestive track."

Her father, who Sara described as a wimp, was not emotionally equipped or available to perform this much needed protective function for Sara, her siblings, or himself. He tends to withdraw into his work or denials. He prefers to "stick to the facts and details" than to relate to any feelings. As Sara exclaims: "Feelings are not appropriate, they only get in the way." This form of emotionally flat reporting of the facts characterized the treatment for many years and would often feel deadening. Not unlike her father, Sara can easily get lost in details. Sometimes I would find myself letting her, and not unlike her father, I would "space out." She would then become quite anxious when I would bring to her attention the distracting quality of such maneuvers. However, this rigid style of relatedness defines the narrow limits of her feeling of connection to father, mother, spiritual practices, and me. For example, the family-oriented synagogue or my interpretations were experienced by Sara in the same way she described her critical and demanding mother. She feels a need to endure the criticism, real or imagined. Even bad connections can create minimal sparks of life. Mother simultaneously enlivens and destroys her. Object pervasion, not unlike alcohol, initially enlivens but ultimately depresses through oversaturation and intoxication.

When Sara participated in family gatherings, she would become extremely fussy about food preparations, bring her own cooking utensils, call her mother beforehand to determine the source of the ingredients, and then call her rabbi or others in her community to verify that they were kosher. At other times, she simply would refuse to eat. She remained inflexible and thus could assert her existence and individuality and prevent further invasion. However, her self-assertion would be met with criticism, belittling, and result in humiliation and withdrawal.

Saturation of critical mother destroys nascent buds of psychic structure and leaves a barren, lifeless internal landscape that is experienced as depression. Fragments remain as the destruction process becomes internalized, thus insuring that no I-sense will develop. Excess fragments become projected into the analyst, who becomes another critical mother with the potential to further destroy emerging I-sense emanations.

During the third year of treatment, Sara related a tale from the family history. She was a low-weight baby. The family doctor recommended a rigid feeding schedule as Sara displayed very little appetite. This included a 2:00 a.m. feeding. Her mother deeply resented this chore and was quite vocal about it. Further, Sara typically refused these nocturnal feedings. Her refusal fueled her mother's anger and resentment. She would storm out of the bedroom leaving Sara awake and alone in the dark. "If mother was not going to do the job right," Sara queried, "why didn't she just let me sleep?" In the present, Sara would frequently experience terror at the close of our sessions and would have trouble leaving. She would also leave multiple messages on my answering machine in the middle of the night. In this context, it was as if Sara would be abruptly wakened from her sleep during the session by me (intrusive mother) and then suddenly be left to face the world alone. On the other hand, not unlike her intrusive mother, she could call (wake) me in the middle of the night and attempt to feed me a toxic formula of rage and helplessness.

Through our discussions, it soon became clear that Sara engaged exclusively in those aspects of her spiritual practice that would enable her to rationalize retreats and to maintain a safe distance from her mother and others whom she would imagine to be critical, judgmental, intrusive, or abusive. Her withdrawal would not, however, release her from the internal mother. Self-destructive processes would ensue. For example, she would rely on traditional customs to maintain a sense of control with men. On the one hand, she could safely keep a man out of her apartment and ward off any emerging sexual impulses. On the other hand, she could push an interested man away with sudden demands for the customary short courtship and a commitment for marriage. This dynamic would manifest during sessions in fluctuations between extreme withdrawals and intrusions that would leave me feeling either pushed away or running for cover. These extreme self state experiences recreate microscopically her I-sense in relation to both her father and her mother: "I feel like I don't exist" (father), "I feel inadequate" (mother). They can suddenly fluctuate, merge, separate, reverse: "I don't exist in your eyes." "You don't exist to me." "I am inadequate to Daddy, he wished for a son." "I don't exist in Mom's eyes. I am an inadequate extension of her." "I am her withered arm, and should be amputated." "You are inadequate, you don't help me." "You expect me to be perfect and you demand too much from me." "I am a burden to you.

I demand too much from you." Despite the myriad rapidly fluctuating per-mutations, object pervasion remained a consistent theme.

With regard to the larger religious community Sara would assert that "services are for families"; she would reiterate, "I should be married and have kids, I am not and don't; therefore, I am inadequate and have no busi-ness being there." "I can remain home and be observant."

During this phase of the treatment, Sara would frequently crouch down in the corner of the consultation room with her long, unkempt black hair covering her face and her face to the wall. She would repeat, "You think I am ugly, stupid, too slow." "You hate me and just want to get rid of me." On the other hand, she would lunge forward in her seat and repeatedly ask, "Do you think I am stupid?" "If you don't, then what do you think of me?"

This approach to dealing with her anxiety exacerbated Sara's feelings of self-isolation. However, the assumptions driving my therapeutic stance up to this point assumed enough of a self to be and experience isolation. Sara's self-imposed banishment becomes an external metaphor for her internal world. The pervasion of the object banishes whatever aspects of self might be available; perhaps fragments of what might have been a self, dispersed by the intense force of pervasion. As object occupies psyche, like some alien invasion force, saturation exploitation and subjugation leaves noth-ing left to work with. The emotional landscape is stripped and plundered of anything that supports the invader's life while the invader simultane-ously spreads and destroys. As a coping strategy, isolation did not work for Sara, she found herself feeling lonely, isolated, and depressed. Relationally, she was repeating a familial interaction pattern. Sara's mother would fre-quently not speak to her for weeks at a time. She understood her mother's behavior as an expression of rage for various slights, and she experienced my silent listening in the same way. I became Sara's angry, withholding mother. Sara's only recourse was to lock herself in her bedroom as a safe haven from mother's unrelenting emotional brutality. Now she was locked up inside herself, lonely, isolated, and frightened.

From the point of view of the pervasion of the object, I would respond: "You experience me as your withholding mother, but you pressure me in the same way that you described that she pressured you. We have Mom all over the place." It seems essential to respond to both aspects of the dynamic simultaneously. Both analyst and analysand hold pieces of the pervasive object.

Gradually, as our work together progressed, Sara began to question her rigidity. She noticed that she did not maintain the same stance with newly found friends. She had a variety of "loopholes" for dealing with both her food and Sabbath restrictions. She also realized that, for the most part, her friends simply did not treat her in the same way as her mother. Her relation to her religious experience also began to shift about this time. For example, she chose to break Passover to keep an important appointment, to study for an exam, and to come to therapy. While she did struggle with considerable anxiety, guilt, and ambivalence, she realized that she "did not have to chuck the whole thing." She could "always go back." She exclaimed, "My decision does not mean I am a hypocrite." Her choice of words is telling and relates to her mother's inappropriate use of Sara in an unconscious effort to address narcissistic trauma and associated unresolved issues related to her family's flight from religious persecution when Sara's mother was seven years old. There was no going back, no second chance. This wealthy family was forced to start over again as street vendors in New York City. They had chucked the whole thing.

Sara's spiritual needs in relation to her spirituality were changing radically. She said: "Blind faith is no longer a requisite for spiritual practice." "I do not have to swallow the whole thing and feel left alone in the dark if I don't." Again, her language points back to her early relationship with her mother with regard to the failed midnight feedings. In contrast to her strict observance to the rules discussed above, Sara would not participate in those aspects of her practice that were more informal and less rigidly defined. She avoided group activities. For example, she rarely attended services. When she did, she would not remain for social activities with the larger community after the close of the formal worship. She experienced the former as a threat to her self-esteem. The latter were "less personal, more predictable, and not so threatening." She described feeling safely contained by formal worship and prayer.* Her concerns centered around nonacceptance, criticism, negative judgments, and a resulting feeling that she does not exist. The whole congregation came to be viewed as bad mothers.

Sara also uses certain religious practices to modulate unmanageable affect states and to attempt to order and organize what can be at times a confusing perception of both her inner and outer worlds. For example, daily prayer recitation, which Sara dutifully performs at specific times, serves as an integral aspect of her daily practice. Prayer is Sara's meditation and, at times, leads to moments of deep peace and joy. These feelings would often be accompanied by unitive experiences.

---

* See Cooper (2000b) for a detailed discussion of the container and contained in relation to spiritual practice.

As she put it, "Everything just seems to fall into place and we are all part of it." Rare failures to exercise prayer practice would seem to derail her entire day and stir up feelings of inadequacy, failure, guilt, and anxiety. An intense oversaturation of these affect states would obliterate any sense of her skills, her abilities, and any positive sense of herself. At these times, practice became another harsh and demanding mother. Mother's presence, both within and without, would become intensely overwhelming. She would then experience herself as nonexistent. However, this "I don't exist self" was extremely solid, brittle, and resistant to any loosening.

Pushing Edges

I became aware and began to question an emerging and consuming intense desire to change Sara. Upon introspection, I decided to leave her be. Could she be exactly who she is in my presence independently of any activity or lack of any activity? Sara began putting me to the test by pressing the edges of my offered acceptance. Depression intensified. She started cutting classes, avoiding the synagogue, skipping prayer practice. She spent her days lying in bed or playing electronic games on her computer. Sara's anxiety and guilt intensified. She feared being dismissed by me. She imagined that, not unlike her mother, I would shun. She expected me to become impatient and criticize her for "being lazy and stupid." Instead, I expressed an interest in the computer games that were occupying her attention. She backed off on herself a bit and said that the games were probably therapeutic with regard to visual-motor training and eye-hand coordination. I agreed but also questioned her need to be rational, practical, and purposeful. The thought that she could simply enjoy the games just for fun seemed alien and threatening. She talked in a self-deprecating way about the time she spent watching television. Again, I expressed an interest in the types of shows that she enjoyed watching. These were light, refreshing moments in sessions that otherwise felt oppressive and heavy. Time could come to an unbearable halt. Her constant questioning would only draw a blank from me and I would let her know. Sara would say: "Why am I like this?" I would respond, "I don't know." She would press: "Why don't you answer me?" I would respond, "I am drawing a blank." She continued unrelentingly and experienced my lack of articulate responsiveness as cold and withholding. I would feel pressured and battered by her seeming helplessness. This dynamic, which persisted throughout the therapy, diminished upon interpretation of the pervasive object dimension of the transference. I said: "You experience me as your harsh and withholding mother, yet you pressure me the same way you described to me that she pressures you. It seems that Mother takes over in these moments." The room lightened up. Sara visibly relaxed. There was a sigh of relief. The heavy oppressive feeling in the air evaporated.

Diving Into the Abyss

However, this interpretation had inadvertently cut loose, for the moment, an anchor. A toxic anchor, but an anchor nonetheless. Sara described herself as floating or falling down into an abyss that seemed bottomless. I was tempted to break her fall—a reaction to my own anxiety (perhaps an identification with Mother's anxiety). Mother would not let Sara too far away from her, despite her seemingly paradoxical demand that Sara take care of herself. Realizing this mix of both real and induced anxiety, I maintained my stance and allowed her to fall. I simply let her be. Falling is fine if that is what is occurring. Why place a negative value on it? Reversals in perspective challenge the negative assumption. Sara could be plummeting into a psychic death or through a birth canal and into life. She might test the limits of tolerance of psychic death and deadening processes or give birth to a self. Both might occur in rapid oscillation at speeds too dizzying for accurate perception. Life and death intertwined. Simultaneous death of aspects and birth of others constitute essential movements of fluid psychic processes. For now Sara was floating in an abyss/birth canal. Acting on my need for security would deprive Sara of her experience. Where would she land? Would she land? Perhaps she could fall endlessly and disappear forever; like the incredible shrinking man, she could disappear into infinity or into the dark hole of herself or into the space where a self might have been. I became fascinated with her fall into infinity, almost envious, and asked her to share it with me. We began falling together. What appears as bottomless is also new, unknown, and holds the potential for something creative to evolve. Something was stirring up. Suddenly, she landed.

Sara broke the silence and said, "Suppose I went for a walk in the park during my break, read a book, went over to the museum?" She then queried, "That would not make me a terrible person, would it?" Something new was occurring, despite its inextricable intertwining with early transference manifestations and an associated anxiety. Perhaps the latter were aspects of an afterbirth and simply needed to be cleared away. Could room be made for this nascent self? Or would their weed-like proliferation once more ensnare and suffocate the possibilities of selfhood out of Sara? The pervasion of the object is insidious and unrelenting. I once again become a withholding and harsh rejecting mother while Sara begins to actively press into me in the same way she describes her mother's intrusions. For instance, an exclusive focus on Sara's sense of self, that she described as "not existing," began to dominate the discussion. Sara repeatedly complained of "not existing." This "not existing" self has become very solid. Self reified at a nihilistic extreme. This no-self fills up the room, swallows me up. She wants me to swallow her up. She wants to "crawl inside of me where it will be safe." Birth has become terrifying and dangerous. The womb feels safer, despite its paranoid/schizoid dynamics. She beats me up with her helplessness, neediness, and terror. I have lost sight of any situational dynamics and of myself. All of my responses exert no impact. She spits them out like unwanted food in the middle of the night. Like her mother, she rejects me out of hand. She demands my help and refuses it at the same time. Can she have an impact on me? Will it take an explosion? If so, who would be left to respond? Fragments fly everywhere, dissolving into the abyss of her dark bottomless center.

Sara cannot associate or tap into any fantasy. The prospect seems much too dangerous and only leads to nonverbal regression and dissociation. She has no recollection of her rage reactions, which she finds extremely disconcerting. Emerging transference and countertransference dynamics remain neglected or overlooked. Yet they are intense and vividly clear. Treatment boundaries are obliterated. She owes me too much money, calls me frequently on the telephone, has trouble leaving at the end of the sessions, and tries to intrude into the next patient's session. She has burned her way through the treatment container like hot coals in a paper cup. We have engendered and negotiated a difficult birth.

Sara relies on me for anchoring and containing. In my failure to provide this function, through inadvertently excessive gratification, in the form of returning telephone calls, allowing unpaid fees, and breaking the time frame, Sara is cast adrift on an ocean of chaos and despair. Meanwhile, I am feeling enraged, battered, and out of control. I find it difficult to tolerate anything about her. Her physical appearance becomes repulsive to me. Sara intrudes into my life, thoughts, dreams, and own analytic sessions. I am also feeling helpless. Any move on my part would, I imagine, feel like a sadistic retaliation, regardless of whether it really is or not. I am beginning to enjoy her pain. I remain silent and cut Sara off in the same way she described her mother would as an expression of her anger and displeasure: "She wouldn't talk to me for weeks at a time." Yet, I feel what Sara describes it is like to be so overwhelmed by Mother. I am speechless, helpless, like a piece of driftwood floating on a vast and turbulent ocean of Mother. Intense rage builds up. Rage, best managed in the treatment, spills out to various service providers. Sara almost gets arrested at one point. Not unlike my container, the security of her subsidized residency becomes jeopardized. Sara becomes filled with anxiety. She can vent her rage at these various service providers, but not at me. She will drown me and lose me in the process. She will drown.

Initially, Sara could not tolerate any conscious sense of identification with her mother. This first became apparent when Sara relayed a conversation that she had during a breakup with a man she had been dating. She mobilized enormous confidence and strength to deal with a man who was actively abusive toward her. Her strength and confidence were amazing to me. This also cast light on her need to present to me as helpless. However, my observation was so unsettling to Sara that she should possess any of her mother's good or useful qualities that any conscious aspects were actively and immediately split off. Now this identification with her mother was once again in the ascendance in relation to me. Once we began to actively address the identification in the here and now the situation changed. To summarize a series of sessions,

> No wonder you feel like you don't exist, Mom is all over the place and there is no room for you. You experience me like your cold, angry, cutting-off, withholding mother who doesn't take care of you. I don't return your calls, I cut back your sessions until you pay your bills, and I insist that you leave promptly at the end of the sessions. On the other hand, you treat me the very same way that you have consistently described that she treats you.

Within a few weeks the treatment stabilized. In retrospect, while my perception of feeling states and experiences were quite vivid, until the actual familial interaction patterns that had unfolded in the transference and countertransference, specifically the pervasive object transference, the treatment remained at an impasse. Sara's expectation was that I, like her father, would acquiesce to her demands. That if she, not unlike her mother, continued to exert pressure, I would wimp out like her father, siblings, and herself. However, underneath these relational dynamics lurked a deeper, more primitive perception, largely unconscious. I operated like a cold, harsh, withholding, demanding, perfection-seeking, pressuring mother. How frightening! How disappointing to watch her castle dissolve in the sand, becoming obliterated with the ebbing and rising of the emotional tides that we were navigating.

Actually, Sara expressed relief that I remained firm. She felt reassured and anchored. The growth-promoting function of the transference that had become derailed by my indulgences appeared to reinstate itself by my assertion of treatment parameters, by my interpretation that the parameters were experienced by Sara as another harsh, demanding mother, who gives nothing in return, and by the expression of my understanding of her reactions. She felt anchored and returned to the synagogue. She began to study again and passed an important final exam. This work paved the way for addressing issues around Sara's need to feel separate as reflected in her need for validating reassurance as she continued to pursue her education and her spiritual practice, which symbolically represent the birth and growth of a self.

Transference Versus Didactic

Gradually, Sara developed some capacity to rely on her practices and emerging inner resources as an alternative to flights into an illusion of self-sufficiency or attempted flights into merger with me. From this vantage point, that is, through the validation of her feelings related to her prayer practice as an expression of an emerging healthy self, a form of calming meditation is quietly reinforced through her participation in her own experience and religious tradition. For example, when she would bring it up I would respond by quite typically saying, "Your prayer practice seems very useful and helps you focus your day."

Sara's prayer practice seems to be gradually generalizing into her daily routines and seems to contribute to a diminution of her negative self-perceptions and dysfunctional behaviors described above. She also can, at times, access states of peace, well-being, ecstasy, and what she describes as her "place of oneness with life." This example demonstrates the efficacy of working through the transference/countertransference dynamic rather than through direct educational measures. In terms of the adaptive functions that spiritual practice served for Sara, any introduction of meditation in the form of direct instruction by me would have been invalidating, intrusive, and terrifying. While understanding the effectiveness of meditation techniques for learning disabled or anxious individuals (Cooper, 1983, 1984; Richard, 1972), an active educational intervention on my part would be experienced in the transference as the nonvalidating hypercritical mother, who dictates to Sara every step of the way. This would constitute a serious structural threat to the supportive function that her self-generated spiritual discipline served. Sara would interpret such an intervention as the critical mother who asserts: "You must be stupid, you don't know what you are doing, and you must do things my way and my way only." This is, among other aspects of the treatment situation, how she experienced my strict adherence to appointment times. However, to return to my original point concerning the ascertainment and perception of the interdependently arising transference/countertransference dynamic, while I was initially attuned to Sara's self-experience, I did not fully ascertain the transference repetitions based on our actual interactions. The overemphasis on her self states without much discussion or exploration of the impact of my interpretations left us at an impasse. They assume enough of a self to respond to and take in the feedings of interpretation in an emotionally meaningful way with impact. Further, they assume that it is Sara who is being responded to. Experience demonstrates otherwise. My initial understanding or misunderstanding led me to believe that Sara was empathically understood. However, any understanding that was engendered remained incomplete. I speculated that Sara felt safe enough to allow split-off feelings back into awareness and out in the open. However, over time, we obviously found ourselves caught in an impasse that required understanding and intervention.

Conclusions

In retrospect, I realized that all of my explanations centered on Sara's sense of self-experience from her own side. They did not take account of the subjective impact of the interpretations and behaviors that Sara experienced as harsh parental criticisms, withdrawals, and rejections. Simultaneously, Sara was responding to me in the same way as her mother responded to her—with rejection, criticism, and pressure. Such interpretations engendered a reliving of past self and object interaction patterns. The most predominant pattern constitutes a father who lacked the capacity for appropriate emotional involvement and who was disconnected to the point of delusion, coupled with a mother whose ambivalent and confusing overinvolvement is inappropriately mediated in terms of her own narcissism. She exerts control but not any caring.

Sara tends to wall herself off from her mother's narcissistic demands. However, this need precedes the development of a cohesive or viable sense of self. There is no self to experience or take in self-oriented interventions. What emerges is an "I don't exist self." However, this "I don't exist self" is very brittle and resistant to movement. School, housework, religion, myself—all become demanding mothers. Sara becomes walled off, depressed, inattentive, and bored. My own inattentiveness, boredom, and fatigue become multiply determined. On the one hand is the emerging need to maintain my own autonomy, identity, and separateness (Kohut, 1971). On the other hand, these states reflect a resonance with Sara's emotional states. Consistent attention to manifestations of the pervasive object gradually contributes to an attenuation of depressive symptoms through the clearing away of pervasive object elements, which then creates the space for the birth of a self.

References

Abe, M. (1985). *Zen and Western thought*. London: Macmillan.

Abe, M. (1990). Kenotic god and dynamic sunyata. In J. Cobb, Jr. & C. Ives (Eds.), *The emptying God: A Buddhist-Jewish-Christian conversation* (pp. 3–65). Eugene, OR: Wipf & Stock Publishers.

Abe, M. (1992). *A study of Dogen: His philosophy and religion* (S. Heine, Ed.). Albany: State University of New York Press.

Adams, B. (1995). Ulysses and I: A brief memoir of a long analysis. *Psychoanalytic Review, 82,* 727–740.

Aitken, R. (1991). *The gateless barrier: The Wu-Men Kuan (Mummonkan)*. New York: North Point Press.

Akhtar, S. (2007). *Listening to others: Developmental aspects of empathy and attunement*. Lanham, MD: Jason Aronson.

Alexander, F. (1931). Buddhistic training as an artificial catatonia. *Psychoanalytic Review, 18,* 129–145.

Almond, P. (1988). *The British discovery of Buddhism*. Cambridge, UK: Cambridge University Press.

Atwood, G., & Stolorow, R. (1984). *Structures of subjectivity: Explorations in psychoanalytic phenomenology*. Hillsdale, NJ: The Analytic Press.

Barratt, B. (1993). *Psychoanalysis and the postmodern impulse: Knowing and being since Freud's psychology*. Baltimore: Johns Hopkins University Press.

Bartolomy Saint-Hillaire, J. (1895). *The Buddha and his religion*. London: Routledge.

Beck, C. (2005). Foreword. In B. Magid, *Ordinary mind: Exploring the common ground of Zen and psychotherapy* (pp. ix–xi). Boston: Wisdom Publications.

Benson, H., & Klipper, M. (1976). *The relaxation response*. New York: Hearst Books.

Benson, H., & Procter, W. (1985). *Beyond the relaxation response*. New York: Penguin Group.

Berger, D. (1987). *Clinical empathy*. Northvale, NJ: Jason Aronson.

Bion, W. (1959). Attacks on linking. *International Journal of Psychoanalysis, 40,* 5–6.

Bion, W. (1962a). A theory of thinking. In *Second thoughts: Selected papers on psychoanalysis* (pp. 110–119). London: Heinemann.

Bion, W. (1962b). *Learning from experience*. London: Heinemann.

Bion, W. (1965). *Transformations*. London: H. Karnac (Books) Ltd.

Bion, W. (1967). Notes on memory and desire. In E. B. Spillius (Ed.), *Melanie Klein today: Developments in theory and practice: Mainly practice* (Vol. 2, pp. 17–21). London: Routledge.

Bion, W. (1970). *Attention and interpretation*. London: Karnac Books.

Bion, W. (1978). *Clinical seminars and four papers*. Abingdon, UK: Fleetwood Press.

Bion, W. (1980). *Bion in New York and São Paulo* (F. Bion, Ed.). Perthshire, SCT: Clunie Press.

Bion, W. (1990). *Brazilian lectures: 1973 São Paulo; 1974 Rio de Janeiro/Sao Paulo.* London: Karnac Books.

Bleandonu, G. (1994). *Wilfred Bion: His life and works 1897–1979.* New York: Guilford Press.

Blyth, R. H. (1942). *Zen in English literature and oriental classics.* Tokyo: Hokuseido Press.

Boykin, K., & May, G. (2003). *Zen for Christians: A beginner's guide.* New York: John Wiley & Sons.

Breuer, J., & Freud, S. (1895). Studies in hysteria. In J. Strachey (Ed. & Trans.), *The standard edition of the complete psychological works of Sigmund Freud* (Vol. II, pp. 1–321). London: The Hogarth Press.

Buswell, R. (1987). The short-cut approach to k'an-hua meditation: The evolution of a practical subitism in Chinese Ch'an Buddhism. In P. Gregory (Ed.), *Sudden and gradual approaches to enlightenment in Chinese thought* (pp. 321–377). Delhi, India: Motilal Bararasidass Publishers.

Casement, P. (2002). *Learning from our mistakes: Beyond dogma in psychoanalysis and psychotherapy.* New York: Guilford Press.

Chayat, R. (2008). *Eloquent silence.* Boston: Wisdom Publications.

Coltart, N. (1992). *Slouching towards Bethlehem.* New York: Guilford Press.

Coltart, N. (1996). *The baby and the bathwater.* London: Karnac Books.

Cooper, P. (1983). Yoga and learning disabilities: Traditional techniques—Modern applications. *Chalk Dust, 31,* 21–22.

Cooper, P. (1984). Yoga for the special child. *Yoga Journal, 36–37,* 51.

Cooper, P. (1997). The disavowal of the spirit: Integration and wholeness in Buddhism and psychoanalysis. In A. Molino (Ed.), *The couch and the tree: Dialogues in psychoanalysis and Buddhism* (pp. 231–246). New York: North Point Press.

Cooper, P. (1998). Sense and non-sense: Phenomenology, Buddhist and psychoanalytic. *Journal of Religion and Health, 37,* 357–370.

Cooper, P. (1999). Buddhist meditation and countertransference: A case study. *American Journal of Psychoanalysis, 59,* 71–85.

Cooper, P. (2000a). Unconscious process: Zen and psychoanalytic versions. *Journal of Religion and Health, 39,* 57–69.

Cooper, P. (2000b). Clouds into rain. *Journal of Religion and Health, 40,* 167–184.

Cooper, P. (2001). The gap between: Being and knowing in Zen Buddhism and psychoanalysis. *American Journal of Psychoanalysis, 61,* 341–362.

Cooper, P. (2002a). Between wonder and doubt: Psychoanalysis in the goal-free zone. *American Journal of Psychoanalysis, 62,* 95–118.

Cooper, P. (2002b). The pervasion of the object: Depression and unitive experience. *Psychoanalytic Review, 89,* 413–439.

Cooper, P. (2007). *Into the mountain stream: Psychotherapy and Buddhist experience.* Lanham, MD: Jason Aronson.

Cooper, P. (2008). *Three stones: Zen poetics.* New York: Three Stones.

Dickes, R. (1965). The defensive function of an altered state of consciousness. *Journal of the American Psychoanalytic Association, 13*, 356–403.

Doré, H. (1938). *Researches into Chinese superstitions* (M. Kennely, Trans.). Shanghai, China: T'usewei Press. (Original work published 1914)

duHalde, J. (1741). *The general history of China*. London: J. Watts.

Eigen, M. (1983). Dual union or undifferentiation? In A. Phillips (Ed.), *The electrified tightrope* (pp. 157–176). Northvale, NJ: Jason Aronson.

Eigen, M. (1985). Between catastrophe and faith. In A. Phillips (Ed.), *The electrified tightrope* (pp. 211–225). Northvale, NJ: Jason Aronson.

Eigen, M. (1986a). *The psychotic core*. Northvale, NJ: Jason Aronson.

Eigen, M. (1986b). Mindlessness-selflessness. In A. Phillips (Ed.), *The electrified tightrope* (pp. 237–242). Northvale, NJ: Jason Aronson.

Eigen, M. (1991). The area of faith in Winnicott, Lacan, and Bion. In A. Phillips (Ed.), *The electrified tightrope* (pp. 109–138). Northvale, NJ: Jason Aronson.

Eigen, M. (1992). *Coming through the whirlwind*. Wilmette, IL: Chiron Publications.

Eigen, M. (1995). Stones in a stream. *Psychoanalytic Review, 82*, 371–390.

Eigen, M. (1998). *The psychoanalytic mystic*. London: Free Associations Books.

Eigen, M. (1999). *Toxic nourishment*. London: Karnac Books.

Eigen, M. (2001). *Damaged bonds*. London: Karnac Books.

Eigen, M. (2004a). *The sensitive self*. Middletown, CT: Wesleyan University Press.

Eigen, M. (2004b). A little psyche-music. *Psychoanalytic Dialogues, 14*, 119–130.

Endo, S. (1969). *Silence* (W. Johnston, Trans.). New York: Taplinger Publishers.

Epstein, M. (1984). On the neglect of evenly suspended attention. *Journal of Transpersonal Psychology, 16*, 193–205.

Epstein, M. (1988). Attention and psychoanalysis. *Psychoanalysis and Contemporary Thought, 11*, 171–189.

Epstein, M. (1995). *Thoughts without a thinker: Psychotherapy from a Buddhist perspective*. New York: Basic Books.

Evans-Wentz, W. Y. (1954). *The Tibetan book of the great liberation*. London: Oxford University Press.

Faure, B. (1993). *Chan insights and oversights: An epistemological critique of the Chan tradition*. Princeton, NJ: Princeton University Press.

Faure, B. (1996). *Visions of power: Imagining medieval Japanese Buddhism* (P. Brooks, Trans.). Princeton, NJ: Princeton University Press.

Fauteux, K. (1995). Regression and reparation in religious experience and creativity. *Psychoanalysis and Contemporary Thought, 18*, 33–52.

Ferro, A. (2005). *Seeds of illness, seeds of recovery*. London: Routledge.

Fields, R. (1981). *How the swans came to the lake: A narrative history of Buddhism in America*. Boulder, CO: Shambhala.

Finn, M. (1992). Transitional space and Tibetan Buddhism: The object relations of meditation. In M. Finn & J. Gartner (Eds.), *Object relations theory and religion: Clinical applications* (pp. 109–118). Westport, CT: Praeger.

Frances, S. (1952). *The goat that went to school*. Chicago: Rand McNally & Co.

Freud, S. (1900). The interpretation of dreams. In J. Strachey (Ed. & Trans.), *The standard edition of the complete psychological works of Sigmund Freud* (Vol. IV, pp. ix–627). London: The Hogarth Press.

Freud, S. (1911). Two principles of mental functioning. In J. Strachey (Ed. & Trans.), *The standard edition of the complete psychological works of Sigmund Freud* (Vol. XII, pp. 218–260). London: The Hogarth Press.

Freud, S. (1912a). A note on the unconscious in psycho-analysis. In J. Strachey (Ed. & Trans.), *The standard edition of the complete psychological works of Sigmund Freud* (Vol. XII, pp. 260–266). London: The Hogarth Press.

Freud, S. (1912b). Recommendations to physicians practicing psycho-analysis. In J. Strachey (Ed. & Trans.), *The standard edition of the complete psychological works of Sigmund Freud* (Vol. XII, pp. 109–120). London: The Hogarth Press.

Freud, S. (1914). Remembering, repeating and working-through. In J. Strachey (Ed. & Trans.), *The standard edition of the complete psychological works of Sigmund Freud* (Vol. XII, pp. 145–156). London: The Hogarth Press.

Freud, S. (1915). The unconscious. In J. Strachey (Ed. & Trans.), *The standard edition of the complete psychological works of Sigmund Freud* (Vol. XIV, pp. 159–209). London: The Hogarth Press.

Freud, S. (1923). The ego and the id. In J. Strachey (Ed. & Trans.), *The standard edition of the complete psychological works of Sigmund Freud* (Vol. XIX, pp. 13–66). London: The Hogarth Press.

Freud, S. (1925). The resistances to psycho-analysis. In J. Strachey (Ed. & Trans.), *The standard edition of the complete psychological works of Sigmund Freud* (Vol. XIX, pp. 213–224). London: The Hogarth Press.

Freud, S. (1927). The future of an illusion. In J. Strachey (Ed. & Trans.), *The standard edition of the complete psychological works of Sigmund Freud* (Vol. XXI, pp. 218–226). London: The Hogarth Press.

Freud, S. (1930). Civilization and its discontents. In J. Strachey (Ed. & Trans.), *The standard edition of the complete psychological works of Sigmund Freud* (Vol. XXI, pp. 64–145). London: The Hogarth Press.

Freud, S. (1933). New introductory lectures on psycho-analysis. In J. Strachey (Ed. & Trans.), *The standard edition of the complete psychological works of Sigmund Freud* (Vol. XXII, pp. 1–182). London: The Hogarth Press.

Freud, S. (1938a). An outline of psycho-analysis. In J. Strachey (Ed. & Trans.), *The standard edition of the complete psychological works of Sigmund Freud* (Vol. XXIII, pp. 144–207). London: The Hogarth Press.

Freud, S. (1938b). Some elementary lessons in psycho-analysis. In J. Strachey (Ed. & Trans.), *The standard edition of the complete psychological works of Sigmund Freud* (Vol. XXIII, pp. 281–286). London: The Hogarth Press.

Fromm, E. (1950). *Psychoanalysis and religion*. New Haven, CT: Yale University Press.

Fromm, E. (1956). *The art of loving*. New York: HarperCollins Publishers.

Fromm, E. (1960). Psychoanalysis and Zen Buddhism. In: E. Fromm, D. T. Suzuki & R. DeMartino (Eds.) *Zen Buddhism and Psychoanalysis* (pp. 1–76). New York: Harper & Brothers.

Fromm, E., Suzuki, D. T., & DeMartino, R. (1960). *Zen Buddhism and psychoanalysis*. New York: Harper & Brothers.

Galatzer-Levy, R. (2002). Emergence. *Psychoanalytic Inquiry, 22,* 708–727.

Gallagher, L. (1942). *China in the sixteenth century: The journals of Matthew Ricci, 1583–1610.* New York: Random House.

Glass, N. R. (1995). Working Emptiness: Toward a third reading of emptiness in Buddhism and postmodern thought. Atlanta, GA: Scholar's Press.

Green, A. (2006). *Key ideas for a contemporary psychoanalysis: Misrecognition and recognition of the unconscious.* London: Routledge.

Gregory, P. (1987). *Sudden and gradual approaches to enlightenment in Chinese thought.* Delhi, India: Motilal Bararasidass Publishers.

Grotstein, J. (1981). *Do I dare disturb the universe?* London: Karnac Books.

Grotstein, J. (2007). *A beam of intense darkness: Wilfred Bion's legacy to psychoanalysis.* London: Karnac Books.

Gunn, R. (1999). Dualism, splitting, gender, and transformation. *Gender and Psychoanalysis, 4,* 413–431.

Gunn, R. (2000). *Journeys into emptiness: Dogen, Merton, Jung and the quest for transformation.* New York: Paulist Press.

Habito, R. (2004). Living Zen, loving God. Boston: Wisdom Publications.

Harrison, J. (1994). Dream as a metaphor of survival. *Psychoanalytic Review, 81,* 5–14.

Heiler, (1922). Die Buddhistische Versenkung. In F. Alexander (Trans.), Buddhistic training as an artificial catatonia. *Psychoanalytic Review, 18,* 129–145.

Heine, S. (1994). *Dogen and the koan tradition: A tale of two Shobogenzo texts.* Albany: State University of New York Press.

Heine, S. (1997). *The Zen poetry of Dogen: Verses from the mountain of eternal peace.* Boston: Charles E. Tuttle Company.

Heine, S. (2002). *Opening a mountain: Koans of the Zen masters.* Oxford: Oxford University Press.

Heine, S. (2008). *Zen skin, Zen marrow.* Oxford: Oxford University Press.

Heine, S., & Wright, D. (2000). *The Koan: Texts and contexts in Zen Buddhism.* Oxford: Oxford University Press.

Hopkins, J. (1983). *Meditation on emptiness.* London: Wisdom Publications.

Hopkins, J. (1987). *Emptiness yoga.* London: Wisdom Publications.

Hori, V. (2000). Koan and kensho in the Rinzai Zen curriculum. In S. Heine & D. Wright (Eds.), *The koan: Texts and contexts in Zen Buddhism* (pp. 280–315). Oxford: Oxford University Press.

Hori, V. (2003). *Zen sand: The book of capping phrases for Zen practice.* Honolulu: University of Hawaii Press.

Horney, K. (1945). *Our inner conflicts.* New York: Norton.

Johnston, W. (1976). *Silent music.* New York: Harper & Row, Publishers.

Joseph, B. (1975). The patient who is difficult to reach. In P. L. Giovacchini (Ed.), *Tactics and techniques in psychoanalytic therapy: Countertransference* (Vol. 2, pp. 205–210). New York: Jason Aronson.

Kapleau, P. (1966). *The three pillars of Zen*. New York: Harper & Row.

Kapleau, P. (1989). *Zen: Merging east and west*. New York: Anchor Books.

Kelman, H. (1960). Psychoanalytic thought and Eastern wisdom. In J. Ehrenwald (Ed.), *The history of psychotherapy*. New York: Jason Aronson.

Kennedy, R. (1996). *Zen spirit, Christian spirit: The place of Zen in Christian life*. New York: Continuum Publishing Group.

Kennedy, R. (2004). *Zen gifts to Christians*. New York: Continuum Publishing Group.

Klein, A. (1986). *Knowledge and liberation: Tibetan Buddhist epistemology in support of transformative religious experience*. Ithaca, NY: Snow Lion Publications.

Klein, M. (1935). A contribution to the psychogenesis of manic-depressive states. In *Love, guilt, reparation and other works, 1921–1945* (pp. 262–289). New York: Delacorte Press/Seymour Lawrence.

Knoblauch, S. (1995). The selfobject function of religious experience: The treatment of a dying patient. In A. Goldberg (Ed.), *The impact of new ideas: Progress in self psychology* (Vol. 11, pp. 207–220). Hillsdale, NJ: The Analytic Press.

Kohut, H. (1971). *The analysis of the self*. Madison, CT: International Universities Press.

Kohut, H. (1977). *The restoration of the self*. Madison, CT: International Universities Press.

Komito, D. (1987). *Nagarjuna's seventy stanzas: A Buddhist psychology of emptiness*. Ithaca, NY: Snow Lion Publications.

Kovel, J. (1990). Beyond the oceanic feeling: Further reflections on Freud and religion. *Psychoanalytic Review, 77*, 69–87.

Kurtz, S. (1989). *The art of unknowing: Dimensions of openness in analytic therapy*. Montvale, NJ: Jason Aronson.

Langan, R. (1997). On free-floating attention. *Psychoanalytic Dialogues, 7*, 819–839.

Langan, R. (2006). *Minding what matters: Psychotherapy and the Buddha within*. Boston: Wisdom Publications.

Leong, K. (2001). *The Zen teachings of Jesus*. New York: The Crossroads Publishing Company.

Lichtenberg, J. (1991). What is a selfobject? *Psychoanalytic Dialogues, 1*, 455–479.

Loori, J. (1994). *Two arrows meeting in mid-air: The Zen koan*. Boston: Charles E. Tuttle Company.

Loori, J. (Ed.). (1998). *Zen Mountain Monastery liturgy manual*. Mt. Tremper, NY: Dharma Communications.

Loori, J. (2009, Spring). What is a teacher? *Mountain Record*, 30–41.

Lopez-Corvo, R. (2005). *The dictionary of the work of W. R. Bion*. London: Karnac Books.

Lopez-Corvo, R. (2006). *Wild thoughts searching for a thinker: A clinical application of W. R. Bion's theories*. London: Karnac Books.

Luk, C. (1993). *Ch'an and Zen teaching*. York Beach, ME: Samuel Weiser.

Mac Isaac, D., & Rowe, C. (1991). *Empathic attunement: The technique of psychoanalytic self psychology*. Northvale, NJ: Jason Aronson.

Maezumi, T. (2001). *Appreciate your life: The essence of Zen practice*. Boston: Shambhala Publications.

Magid, B. (2000). The couch and the cushion: Integrating Zen and psychoanalysis. *Journal of the American Academy of Psychoanalysis, 28*, 513–526.

Magid, B. (2005). *Ordinary mind: Exploring the common ground of Zen and psychotherapy*. Boston: Wisdom Publications.

Matte-Blanco, I. (1975). *The unconscious as infinite sets*. London: Duckworth.

Matte-Blanco, I. (1988). *Thinking, feeling and being: Clinical reflections on the fundamental antinomy of human beings and the world*. London: Routledge.

McRae, J. (2000). Antecedents of encounter dialogue in Chinese Ch'an Buddhism. In S. Heine & D. Wright (Eds.), *The koan: Texts and contexts in Zen Buddhism* (pp. 46–74). Oxford: Oxford University Press.

Meltzer, D. (1992). *The Claustrum: An investigation of claustrophobic phenomena*. Perthshire, SCT: Clunie Press.

Merzel, D. (1991). *The eye that never sleeps: Striking to the heart of Zen*. Boston & London: Shambhala Publications.

Merzel, D. (1994). *Beyond sanity and madness: The way of Zen Master Dogen*. Rutland, VT: Tuttle.

Milner, M. (1987). *The suppressed madness of sane men*. London: Routledge.

Mitchell, S. (1998). Letting the paradox teach us. In J. Teicholz & D. Krieger (Eds.), *Trauma, repetition and affect regulation: The work of Paul Russell* (pp. 49–58). New York: Other Press.

Mitrani, J. (2001). *Ordinary people and extra-ordinary protections: A post-Kleinian approach to the treatment of primitive mental states*. Philadelphia: Brunner-Routledge.

Miura, I., & Sasaki, R. (1965). *The Zen koan*. New York: Harcourt Brace & Co.

Molino, A. (Ed.). (1998). *The couch and the tree: Dialogues in psychoanalysis and Buddhism*. New York: North Point Press.

Morris, K. (2008). Oedipal flowers: Through poetics to "O." *Psychoanalytic Review, 95*, 501–514.

Morvay, Z. (1999). Horney, Zen and the real self: Theoretical and historical connections. *American Journal of Psychoanalysis, 59*, 25–35.

Nagao, G. (1989). *The foundational standpoint of Madhyamika philosophy* (J. Keenan, Trans.). Albany: State University of New York Press.

Ogden, T. (2005). *This art of psychoanalysis: Dreaming undreamt dreams and interrupted cries*. London: Routledge.

O'Shaughnessy, E. (1988). W. R. Bion's theory of thinking and new techniques in child analysis. In E. Bott Spillius (Ed.), *Melanie Klein today: Developments in theory and practice: Mainly practice* (Vol. 2, pp. 177–190). London: Routledge.

Parsons, W. (1999). *The enigma of the oceanic feeling: Revisioning the psychoanalytic theory of mysticism.* Oxford: Oxford University Press.

Powell, W. (Trans.). (1986). *The record of Tung-shan.* Honolulu: University of Hawaii Press.

Quinn, S. (1987). *A mind of her own: The life of Karen Horney.* New York: Addison-Wesley Publishing Co.

Rayner, E. (1995). *Unconscious logic.* London: Routledge.

Rayner, E., & Tuckett, D. (1988). An introduction to Matte-Blanco's reformulation of the Freudian unconscious and his conceptualization of the internal world. In I. Matte-Blanco, (Ed.), *Thinking, feeling and being: Clinical reflections of the fundamental antinomy of being in the world* (pp. 3–42). London: Routledge.

Rhode, E. (1987). *On birth and madness.* London: Duckworth.

Rhode, E. (1994). *Psychotic metaphysics.* London: Clunie Press/Karnac Books.

Rhode, E. (1998). *On hallucination, intuition and the becoming of "O."* Binghamton, NY: Esf.

Richard, M. (1972). Attention training: A pilot program in the development of autonomic controls. *Contemporary Education, 43,* 157–160.

Ringstrom, P. (1998). Therapeutic impasses in contemporary psychoanalytic treatment: Revisiting the double bind hypothesis. *Psychoanalytic Dialogues, 8,* 297–315.

Roland, A. (1981). Induced emotional reactions and attitudes in the psychoanalyst as transference in actuality. *Psychoanalytic Review, 68,* 45–74.

Roland, A. (1987). The familial self, the individual self, and the transcendent self: Psychoanalytic reflections on India and America. *Psychoanalytic Review, 74,* 239–252.

Rosemont, H. (1970). The meaning is the use: Koan and mondo as linguistic tools of the Zen masters. *Philosophy East and West, 20,* 109–119.

Rosenbaum, R. (1998). *Zen and the heart of psychotherapy.* Philadelphia: Brunner/ Mazel.

Rosenfeld, H. (1965). *Psychotic states: A psychoanalytic approach.* New York: International Universities Press.

Rosenfeld, H. (1987). *Impasse and interpretation: Therapeutic and anti-therapeutic factors in the psychoanalytic treatment of psychotic, borderline and neurotic patients.* London: Routledge.

Ross, N. (1975). Affects as cognitions: With observations on the meanings of mystical states. *International Review of Psychoanalysis, 2,* 79–93.

Rubin, J. (1985). Meditation and psychoanalytic listening. *Psychoanalytic Review, 72,* 599–614.

Rubin, J. (1996). *Psychoanalysis and Buddhism: Toward an integration.* New York: Plenum Press.

Safran, J. (2003). *Psychoanalysis and Buddhism: An unfolding dialogue*. Boston: Wisdom Publications.

Sally, F. (1952). *The goat that went to school*. New York: Rand McNally.

Sanford, J. (1981). *Zen-Man Ikkyū*. Chico, CA: Scholar's Press.

Schlütter, M. (2000). Before the empty eon versus a dog has no Buddha nature: Kung-an use in the Ts'ao-tung tradition and Ta-hui's kung-an introspection Ch'an. In S. Heine & D. Wright (Eds.), *The koan: Texts and contexts in Zen Buddhism* (pp. 168–199). Oxford: Oxford University Press.

Sells, M. (1994). *Mystical languages of unsaying*. Chicago: University of Chicago Press.

Sharrin, R. (2002). An American koan: The sangha as an object of awareness. *Groundwater: The Journal of Buddhism and Psychotherapy, 1*, 1–10.

Shibayama, Z. (2000). *The gateless barrier: Zen comments on the Mumonkan* (S. Kudo, Trans.). New York: HarperCollins Publishers.

Smith, H. (1970). Preface. In S. Suzuki, *Zen mind, beginner's mind* (pp. 3–42). New York: Weatherhill.

Soeng, M. (1996). *Heart sutra: Ancient Buddhist wisdom in the light of quantum reality*. Cumberland, RI: Primary Point Press.

Sogen, Y. (2005). *Selected teishos on gateless gate*. New York: The Zen Studies Society Press.

Speeth, K. (1982). On psychotherapeutic attention. *Journal of Transpersonal Psychology, 14*, 141–160.

Spillius, E. (1988). General introduction. In E. Spillius (Ed), *Melanie Klein today: Developments in theory and practice: Mainly theory* (Vol. 1, pp. 1–7). London: Routledge.

Spillius, E. (2007). *Encounters with Melanie Klein: Selected papers of Elizabeth Spillius*. London: Routledge.

Stambaugh, J. (1999). *The formless self*. Albany: State University of New York Press.

Stern, D. (1983). Unformulated experience: From familiar chaos to creative disorder. *Contemporary Psychoanalysis, 19*, 71–99.

Stewart, J. (1926). *Chinese culture and Christianity: A review of China's religions and related systems from the Christian standpoint*. New York: Fleming H. Revell Co.

Stolorow, R., & Atwood, G. (1992). *Contexts of being: The intersubjective foundations of psychological life*. Hillsdale, NJ: The Analytic Press.

Stolorow, R., Brandchaft, B., & Atwood, G. (1987). *Psychoanalytic treatment: An intersubjective approach*. Hillsdale, NJ: The Analytic Press.

Stone, C. (2007). *Sand in the rice: Attention, attunement and hearing what is not said*. Unpublished manuscript.

Stryk, L., & Ikemoto, T. (1973). *Zen poems of China and Japan: The crane's bill*. New York: Grove Press.

Stryk, L., & Ikemoto, T. (1995). *Zen poetry: Let the spring breeze enter*. New York: Grove Press.

Suler, J. (1993). *Contemporary psychoanalysis and Eastern thought*. Albany: State University of New York Press.

Suzuki, D. T. (1949). *Essays in Zen Buddhism: First series*. London: Rider & Co.

Suzuki, D. T. (1960). *Introduction to Zen Buddhism*. London: Rider & Co.

Suzuki, D. T. (1972a). *The Zen doctrine of no mind*. York Beach, ME: Samuel Weiser.

Suzuki, D. T. (1972b). *Living by Zen*. York Beach, ME: Samuel Weiser.

Suzuki, D. T. (1994). *The Zen koan as a means to attaining enlightenment*. North Clarendon, VT: Tuttle Publications.

Suzuki, S. (1970). *Zen mind, beginner's mind*. New York: Weatherhill.

Suzuki, S. (1999). *Branching streams flow in darkness: Zen talks on the Sandokai*. Berkeley: University of California Press.

Symington, J., & Symington, N. (1996). *The clinical thinking of Wilfred Bion*. London: Routledge.

Taketomo, Y. (1989). An American-Japanese transcultural psychoanalysis and the issue of teacher transference. *Journal of the American Academy of Psychoanalysis and Dynamic Psychiatry, 17*, 427–450.

Thera, N. (1973). *The heart of Buddhist meditation*. York Beach, ME: Samuel Weiser.

Thurman, R. (1994). *The Tibetan book of the dead: Liberation through understanding in the between*. New York: Bantam Books.

Trungpa, C. (1967). *Meditation in action*. Boulder, CO: Shambala Publications.

Trungpa, C. (1976). *The myth of freedom*. Boulder, CO: Shambala Publications.

Watts, A. (1957). *The way of Zen*. New York: Pantheon.

Webb, R., & Sells, M. (1997). Lacan and Bion: Mystical languages of unsaying. *Journal of Melanie Klein and Object Relations, 15*, 243–264.

Weber, S. (2006). Doubt, arrogance and humility. *Contemporary Psychoanalysis, 42*, 213–223.

Welter, A. (2000). Mahakasyapa's smile: Silent transmission and the kug-an (koan) tradition. In S. Heine & D. Wright (Eds.), *The koan: Texts and contexts in Zen Buddhism* (pp. 75–109). Oxford: Oxford University Press.

Wenger, M. (1999). Introduction. In S. Suzuki, *Branching streams flow in darkness* (pp. 11–16). Berkeley: University of California Press.

Westkott, M. (1998). Horney, Zen and the real self. *American Journal of Psychoanalysis, 58*, 287–301.

Wieger, L. (1927). *A history of the religious beliefs and philosophical opinions in China from the beginning to the present time* (E. Chalmers Werner, Trans.). New York: Paragon Book Reprint Corp.

Wilkenson, R. (1994). *Symbol and magic in Egyptian art*. London: Thames & Hudson.

Winnicott, D. (1964). *The child, the family, and the outside world*. Baltimore: Pelican.

Wright, D. (2000). Koan history: Transformative language in Chinese Buddhist thought. In: S. Heine & D. Wright (Eds.) *The koan: Texts and contexts in Zen Buddhism* (pp. 200–212). Oxford: Oxford University Press.

Yamada, K. (1979). *Gateless gate*. Los Angeles: Center Press.

Yasutani, R. (1966). Commentary on the koan mu. In P. Kapleau (Ed.), *The three pillars of Zen* (pp. 63–82). New York: Harper & Row.

Index